PROMISCUITY

By the same author:

The Sexual Behaviour of Young People

Sociological Aspects of Homosexuality

Society and the Young School Leaver

Drugs and Civil Liberties

Social Research

The Strange Case of Pot

The Sexual Behaviour of Young Adults

PROMISCUITY

by

MICHAEL SCHOFIELD

LONDON
VICTOR GOLLANCZ LTD
1976

The extract from *The New Step* by Leonard Cohen appearing on pages 87 and 88, is taken from his *Collected Poems* and is reproduced here by kind permission of Jonathan Cape Limited.

MADE AND PRINTED IN GREAT BRITAIN BY
THE GARDEN CITY PRESS LIMITED
LETCHWORTH, HERTFORDSHIRE
SG6 1JS

My thanks to
Anthony and Bryn
who were even more
helpful than usual

CONTENTS

Part I

The Ramifications of Promiscuity

Part II

A Positive View of Sex

Part I

THE RAMIFICATIONS OF PROMISCUITY

CHAPTER I

OBJECTIVES

The Underlying Concern

Most books about sex are designed to warn people about it (i.e. sex education) or to tell them how to improve their performance (i.e. sex manuals). Presumably the inadequacy of the first creates the demand for the second. This book is neither a sex education textbook, nor a sex manual. It is an attempt to take a long hard look at promiscuity, sex without love, casual sex—all those occasions when two people have sexual intercourse together without committing themselves to loving each other for ever or living together for life.

There are good reasons for concern about promiscuity. Clearly it is not a rare activity indulged in by a few deviates. Tens of thousands of people are promiscuous—the actual number depends on how you define the word. But even more important than that, the fear of promiscuity holds back many attempts to remedy the worrying deficiencies in the extent of sex education, the distribution of contraceptives, the operation of the law on abortion and the campaign against VD. People are afraid that the temptations will be too great when attempts are made to reduce the risks of sexual intercourse; and there seems to be common agreement that the biggest temptation of all is the urge to be promiscuous.

Do we need to fear promiscuity? This book is an attempt to answer that question. There is a shortage of factual information because surprisingly little research has been done on the subject of promiscuity. It is disconcerting to find that so little is known about something that is a continued cause for concern. A study of medical and sociological reports shows that, with few exceptions, the phenomenon is dismissed in a few sentences as an unfortunate consequence of a number of avoidable factors. Many authorities regard it as sinful or degrading or both and even the more objective writers assume that it is impossible to be both promiscuous and healthy.

This is puzzling because ordinary observation and outward appearances seem to conflict with these assertions. Most people will be able to think of at least one individual who is promiscuous and yet appears to be leading a reasonably happy life. Nearly everyone will know people who have been very promiscuous at one stage of their lives and do not seem to regret it.

Possibly we are being misled by outward appearances. Perhaps promiscuity inevitably brings with it hidden problems. But it is not a rare condition, so it is surprising that we do not know more about it. Although few people are promiscuous throughout their lives, many people have been very promiscuous for a limited period. Surely it should not be too difficult to get more specific information about the disadvantages and, if there are any, the advantages as well.

This book is divided into two parts. The first part deals specifically with promiscuity. There were a number of promiscuous people in the groups that I had previously studied and this has given me the opportunity to compare them with other people (Chapter 4). But this tells us only a little about the total situation. Just as important are the attitudes we adopt towards promiscuity (Chapters 2 and 3), the effects—real and imagined (Chapters 5 and 6), the various meanings that we attach to the word and the possible solutions to the problem (Chapter 7). The second part looks at the whole sexual scene and tries to see where promiscuity fits into the changed situation, in particular the recognized need for better health and sex education (Chapters 8 and 9), a more sensible attitude towards VD (Chapter 10), the increased availability of contraception and legal abortion (Chapters 11 and 12), and the likely effects of a more positive attitude to sex (Chapter 13–15).

The Challenge to Convention

An enquiry into the significance of promiscuity is especially relevant now because we are in a period when attitudes are changing very rapidly, especially among the younger generations.

Today young people have more freedom and more opportunities; they are healthier, better looking and wear more provocative clothes; they tend to distrust adult values and they are not frightened to challenge conventional standards. It is sometimes said that this is nothing new and that youth has always been in revolt. While it is true that our society has developed with the help of youthful criticism and idealism, whether it be through the Spanish civil war, CND, student demonstrations or flower power, there are fundamental differences today.

It is well known that children mature at an earlier age than in the past. Nowadays most boys complete their growth at about seventeen years of age; this compares with twenty-three at the turn of the century. The average girl starts menstruation at the age of about thirteen; a hundred years ago it would have been nearer seventeen. But although young people are now taller, heavier and more developed in every way, we keep them at school longer. Thus in many secondary schools there are rows of almost fully-grown men and women sitting at children's desks, often bored by the curriculum, and longing for the day when they can leave. More than two-thirds of all children leave school at sixteen. Few of them have taken GCE and many of them leave with a feeling of rejection and resentment, and the conviction that any kind of learning or further education is not for them.

Young people have always tended to decry complacent materialism; a good job, a nice house and material possessions have only become desirable objectives after getting married and starting a family. The difference today is that the limitations of materialist ideals have become clearer to all and most people want more out of life than a routine job, a colour television and an automatic washing machine. Teenagers are absolutely sincere when they shudder at the thought of living the same kind of life as their parents.

The biggest change of all is the development of the youth cult. Just as an adolescent learns to behave towards his family or his teachers by noting their reactions to him, so by a similar social learning process he learns the role of the teenager. Encouraged by the press, the advertisers and the special teenage and pop magazines, one of the strongest influences on the behaviour of modern youth in any sphere is the desire to be like other young people. In the past a person was most influenced by the groups in close proximity, such as his family, his social class and the other people in his area. Now the strongest influence is the youth cult, which is nation-wide and even international. His aspirations must fit in with this image and young people who cannot measure up to this archetype begin to feel that they are missing something, or else something is missing in them.

Some adolescents, rejected by the exam-orientated educational system, find themselves in a world to which they feel they can never belong. They see themselves as thrown into a social set-up which demands conformity and they cannot see where or how they fit into it. At its most destructive this leads to despairing resentment interspersed with mindless self-indulgence. But there can also be a constructive side to this social defiance. Many of these young people have felt the need to challenge the old traditions and look for ways of improving the quality of life.

The contribution made by individuals who question our old moral laws and customs is probably more valuable today than ever before, because the pressures to conform are greater than ever before. This is an age when conformity is over-valued, so it is the other side of the coin that needs emphasis; as the power of politicians, civil servants, businessmen and media men becomes centralized and concentrated into the hands of fewer people, we need to know how to resist it more than ever. This applies just as much to the moral authorities. It would be surprising if this challenge was not having a profound effect on our attitudes to sex, one of our strongest drives.

When a group of people question traditional sexual attitudes and suggest that there may be other ways of looking at things, they become immoral lechers at first, then tolerated non-conformists, and finally, (much later) modish innovators. The new attitude to premarital sexual intercourse is a good example of this.

Of course attitudes are not the same thing as activities (as several chapters in this book will indicate). Hardly anyone under thirty regards premarital chastity as important but not everyone does in fact have sex before marriage, either from choice or from lack of opportunity. Many young people insist that no one has the moral right to restrict the sexual activities of others; this may be a strongly held point of view, but it is not a guide to their actual behaviour. In my research into sexual behaviour of young people carried out ten years ago, precautions had to be taken because some people had more sex than they were prepared to admit at first; a similar research today would have to guard against the people who have less sex than they say they have.

The so-called 'sexual revolution' has now reached its second stage, for many of the revolutionaries are approaching middle age, have become parents themselves, and are now passing on these sexual attitudes to their children who, in any case, are probably one step ahead of them. Attitudes are changing rapidly and what may seem tolerant and permissive to the parents may appear sedate and conventional to the children. The young teenage girls of today have sex on their minds almost as much as their elders.

Unfortunately many older adults resent these changes. There is sometimes an element of jealousy when an adult criticizes the sexual behaviour of the younger generations—"I did without all this sexual freedom, why shouldn't you?" But adults should remember that it is not just teenage sexual activity which has increased, but also teenage liability to become pregnant due to better nutrition and the earlier onset of menstruation. Consequently it is more than ever important that young people should receive good advice.

When young people find that adults are critical, they are disinclined to accept advice from parents, teachers or other adults. Although adolescents are ready to talk impersonally about sexual matters, they often feel that their own sexual behaviour is very much their own concern. The result is that there are sexual problems where sympathetic adults could give useful advice but are not allowed to help.

A familiar jibe from older adults is that nowadays it is difficult to tell the girls from the boys, but the young people themselves do not appear to find this a problem. Girls and boys like to be together and they will continue to find each other sexually attractive. It is disheartening that sex, which should be a wholly pleasurable activity, so often results in misfortune and unhappiness.

More than any other human activity, sexual behaviour provokes ambivalent attitudes. Some people perceive it as a necessary burden, while others regard it as the greatest joy. Most people adopt attitudes in between these extremes and sometimes their views change according to their moods and the circumstances.

Promiscuity is usually regarded as the antithesis of love, but it was impossible to write this book without considering in detail the traditions and expectations that surround our ideas of romantic love. Social policy and public opinion are influenced by myths and preconceptions as well as by actual facts. Cause and effect are shrouded in mystery and confused with one another. My objective is to clear up some of the misconceptions and to suggest ways in which the problem can be avoided or at least diminished.

CHAPTER 2

THE FEAR OF SUCCESS

Sex Education

Although the word means different things to different people, most people regard promiscuity as undesirable behaviour to be avoided if at all possible. Most books on sex education are quite forthright when they deal with the subject,* and even those who take a more permissive line imply that the promiscuous are unfortunate and to be pitied if not censured. It follows that anything that might encourage promiscuity is to be avoided at all costs.

Unfortunately this fear of promiscuity has impeded many attempts to increase understanding of sexual matters. This is particularly true of sex education. Most people are now in favour of this, provided it is limited to simple anatomical facts, but opinion polls show that about one-fifth of the population is still against giving any kind of sex education. The main fear, sometimes declared, but more often unspoken, is that sexual knowledge leads to sexual promiscuity.

But the majority now say they are 'in favour' of sex education. Many junior schools give information about childbirth and many secondary schools attempt to give some kind of sex education usually in the Biology or Religious Education periods under headings such as 'hygiene', 'human biology' or 'the family'. But one research (Harris, 1969) found that masturbation and homosexuality were hardly ever mentioned and 90 per cent of schools gave no information about methods of contraception. The Longford Committee on pornography complained that sex education was too explicit. For some reason it is acceptable to arouse curiosity, but not to give plain facts. Thus anatomical drawings are to be found in most books, but not photographs.

* Perry (1969) "The question is whether this is promiscuous sex, which is a sign of mental illness, or whether this is a genuine anticipation of marriage...."

Dallas (1972) notes that: "Sex educators are often those who have had further eduction in Biology, if not medical or para-medical training and are used to the visual symbolism of the anatomical textbook.... Unfortunately many of the children receiving sex education do not possess these skills, and many have not perhaps reached the necessary level of mental development to enable these skills to develop. A large picture of a sperm revolted one class, as it looked more like a snake or a worm than anything which one would like to have in one's insides.... Others have had to be convinced that their Fallopian tubes were not purple and did not have white tacking stitches running down them. Relating the size of the uterus to reality and demonstrating its position in the body have also created difficulties, as the uterus in one much-used loop film looks as though it had been given wings (the fimbriated ends of the Fallopian tubes) and is about to take off in flight."

There has been a vast amount of material for the teacher produced by educational publishers, including special kits from national and local curriculum reform projects. Considering how great a demand there is for sex education and how often teachers complain that they cannot find relevant material, it is surprising how little use is made of all this help. This is partly because many teachers are unaware of what is obtainable and frequently ask for material that already exists. Also, many teachers who are embarrassed by the idea of taking classes in sex education find the active learning situations encouraged by the new curriculum pro-jects much too demanding.

Dorothy Dallas's book (1972) is one of the latest to review the present situation and she writes: "One cannot assume that a child changing school at eleven has had any sex education at all." Although 11,000 schools use the BBC/TV *Merry-go-Round* programmes, 77 per cent decided not to take the three pro-grammes on sex education (Rogers, 1974). There are nearly always some teachers in the staffroom who will be against the idea because they personally would find it too difficult. But the most usual reason for not introducing more than a minimum amount of sex education is that many heads feel they will pre-judice their careers if they get complaints from parents or em-barrass the local educational committee. They feel there will be fewer unfortunate consequences if they fall back on the old argument that parents are the best people to do it.

The latest trend seems to be for sex education to split into two subjects which appear to have practically nothing to do with each other. One might be termed the plumbing side of sex with emphasis on tubes and canals. Rather less emphasis is placed on how the penis becomes erect and so some girls cannot imagine how the whole thing can possibly work. But now the new idea is that the biological side is not enough and so talk about personal relationships and love are introduced. Of course this is much more difficult to teach. Often there is strong emphasis put on the importance of love, but as the word is apt to mean one thing to a teenager and something quite different to a teacher, the result is often an unworldly blandness, if not complete confusion.

In all this a central fact gets buried in cant and misunderstandings : that sex is great fun but there are certain traps into which the unwary may fall. Understandably many teachers are reluctant to be too explicit about these traps and the methods of springing them because they know that this will soon arouse the hostility of parents. Consequently little or nothing is said about contraception and information about VD is used as a warning or a threat.

The Longford Report on pornography asked for a change of the law to enable the children of worried parents to opt out of sex education lessons. So far the Minister of Education has rejected the suggestion that parents should have the right to prevent their children from learning about sex or contraception. It should not be forgotten that young girls get pregnant without their parents consent.

In practice most schools use some method to inform parents about the content of sex education courses, particularly when they are first introduced. In some cases the parents are invited to meet and discuss the situation. A few parents are indignant that anyone should suggest that they are incapable of instructing their own children, but the majority are only too grateful for the school to undertake something that they themselves feel unable to do.

But there are usually a few who object and they can sway a parent's meeting if they are outspoken or insistent. Dallas (1972) reports a group of middle class parents in Surrey in 1970 who refused to sanction the showing of a film on birth, although the same film had been acceptable and successful in many similar schools. Another group of quite different parents in East London rejected the BBC Radiovision programmes which they felt were 'dirty pictures'. The difficulty for some parents is that they try to conceal from their children that they have any sex life themselves and so questions arising from sex education at school are likely to cause acute embarrassment at home. A further difficulty is that some parents will protest if their own moral views do not wholly prevail and there are even some parents who press the headmaster to impose on their children standards of behaviour that they themselves do not adhere to.

My research into the sexual behaviour of young adults (Schofield, 1973) canvassed the views of the clients instead of the parents. In this representative group of twenty-five-year-old men and women, those who received sex education were just as dissatisfied as those who did not. Among those who had received no sex education, 80 per cent felt they should have been given some help about sexual problems when they were at school; among those who received sex education, 81 per cent were dissatisfied with the help they received at school. There were many complaints, but the most frequent cause of dissatisfaction was that the sex education was too limited and too late.

The subject has been discussed endlessly and numerous courses have been reported in the educational press. Most of the pupils and a majority of the parents want it, yet most of the sex education in our schools is more likely to be too slow than too fast, and more likely to be too timid than too frank.

The one pervasive reason for this slowness and timidity is the fear of promiscuity. Since modern education encourages the discovery method of learning, the dread is that once the children have heard about sex, they will want to put these theories into practice. The fears about sex education are sometimes expressed in the phrase: "It might put ideas into their heads." So it might, for that, after all, is the object of education. But no pains are spared to see that only the conventional moralities are propounded. Every course, book and visual aid emphasizes the virtues of a loving stable relationship and condemns promiscuity. Some of them still insist that the choice is only between chastity and promiscuity until they are married; others are equivocal about premarital sexual intercourse, but all of them are united in denigrating promiscuity. Despite all this persuasion and propaganda, the main impediment to progress is this fear of promiscuity.

But there is no research evidence to suggest that sex education encourages promiscuity. Those who maintain there is a connection should produce the evidence. It would not be difficult to set up a longitudinal research to find out if there is any relationship between effective sex education and promiscuous behaviour. The only difficulty would be to find enough schools who give good sex education, so that the sexual development of their pupils can be compared with the pupils who come from schools where there is little or no sex education.

My own research provided no evidence that people who received sex education were more likely to be promiscuous. In one way it could be said that this is surprising because most of the sex education concentrated largely on the biological aspects with the result that many of the pupils were left with a vague notion that sex was simply doing what comes naturally.

It is also significant to note that the rise in the number of illegitimate children, the VD rate, the divorce rate—all said to be indications of increased promiscuity—started before there was much sex education in the schools. Furthermore there has been a marked increase in illegitimacy, abortion and VD rates in those countries where there is still little or no sex education. On the other hand there is no association between the rise in VD, abortion and illegitimacy rates and the introduction of sex education in Sweden where it has been a compulsory subject in the schools for over twenty years.

Contraception

Despite some uncertainty, the Government has decided that the provision of contraceptives should become part of the National Health Service. When he was the Secretary for Social Services, Sir Keith Joseph was concerned that supplying contraceptives on the NHS should not become an inducement to 'promiscuous living', although he did eventually agree to supplies on prescription. It is estimated that the present scheme will prevent 150,000 unwanted births each year which would save the country about £300 million during the childhood of those unintended children. This is a very convincing economic argument for a free birth control service and does not even take into account the other results of the prevention of unwanted pregnancies, such as the increased welfare of individual families and the abolition of a large amount of human misery.

But any move by the Government or local authorities to make contraceptives more readily available brings forth opposition and the accusation that those in authority are condoning promiscuity and loose living. Although the medical profession now tends to think that the supply of contraceptives is their exclusive prerogative, for very many years doctors refused to have anything to do with birth control. As far back as 1868 the British Medical Journal objected to the idea "of assigning to medical men the intimated function of teaching females how to indulge their passions and limit their families". Less than ten years ago the Assistant Secretary of the British Medical Association declared : "As a doctor I can tell you that extra and premarital intercourse is medically dangerous, morally degrading and nationally destructive." In a book published in 1971, Dr Morton, a consultant based in Sheffield, wrote that the contraceptive pill was the cause of more long-term misery than anything precipitated by thalidomide.

Alex Comfort (1963) suggests that the real objection to contraception is, "the argument that illegitimacy is a valuable safeguard against vice, and should be fostered for the public benefit". The idea that the pill is a cause, and teenage sex an effect, is one that appeals to many people. One of the sponsors of the Responsible Society, until recently the advisor on venereology to the Department of Health has stated : "The existence of the (family planning) clinics leads to sex outside marriage." In an address to the Royal Society of Arts, Sir Brian Windeyer, Chancellor of London University, said : "In our increasingly permissive society, the pill has taken away an important constraint, and has contributed to a greater laxity in sexual morals and to greater promiscuity."

The feeling seems to be that birth control is in order as long as it is not too easy to get; that would be encouraging promiscuity. It is also felt that it should not be free so that some small sacrifice should be made for the pleasures it will bring. One woman was living on social security in one room with her four-year-old child. She had tried the pill and found it did not suit her and had two abortions over quite a short period, so she had the coil fitted by her doctor. She sent the doctor's bill of £5.25 to the social security department. After a lapse of a month she was informed that it was not the policy of the department to pay for contraceptives because women living apart from their husbands should not require birth control facilities. Apart from the unwarranted assumption that a mature woman without a husband does not have a sex life, it is also unrealistic because if this woman has a child, it will cost the state far more than the £5 which they refused to pay.

From time to time all the clinics, whether Family Planning Association, Brook Centre, local health authorities or others, issue statements to say that nearly all their unmarried clients are either engaged to be married or are responsible girls having mature and lasting relationships with one boy. It is true that this is the sort of girl who will take the trouble to find out about contraceptives and will use them, and it is easy to understand why the clinics try to appease their critics by emphasizing this. They do not want to be accused of encouraging promiscuity. Unfortunately this means that the imprudent girls, who need help just as much as anyone else, are not finding their way to the clinics. From the point of view of the community it is much more important to prevent the unplanned pregnancy of a feckless girl who either cannot or does not want to bring up a child, than of a girl engaged to be married.

It is the least promiscuous who use the pill. Woodward's (1970) study of the clients who came to the Birmingham Brook Advisory Centre suggests that contraceptive advice has a stabilizing influence on already existing relationships. "Going on the pill" is often a preliminary to marriage, a decision arrived at as a result of a discussion with the boy-friend. Ashdown-Sharp (1972) even found that in over half the cases the boy-friend was sharing the cost and 12 per cent of them were paying the full price of their girl's pill.

In a survey of 2,995 women who had unwanted pregnancies, Lambert (1971) found that the more promiscuous they were, the less likely they were to use contraceptives, and hardly any of the very promiscuous used birth-control at all.

But attempts to make contraceptives more readily available always meet the accusation that an improved service will encourage promiscuity and lower moral standards. A slightly more sophisticated objection is that more contraception means more promiscuity and therefore more illegitimate children. But it is doubtful if an increase in the number of sexual episodes using contraceptives will produce more unwanted pregnancies than a smaller number of sexual episodes without the use of contraceptives.

When a reliable method of birth control becomes more readily available, unmarried people will have sexual intercourse more often, but will not necessarily be more promiscuous. It is important to note again that the increase in VD and illegitimacy rates pre-date by a long time the introduction of the contraceptive pill; in fact the increase in illegitimate births during the five years 1962–7 (i.e. up to the Abortion Act) was less than in the previous quinquennium.

There is a large number of unmarried girls who are neither promiscuous, nor on the pill. Many of them have sexual intercourse infrequently and so do not feel it is necessary to use contraceptives. Unfortunately many of them become pregnant. It has often been noted that it is the 'quiet' girl who gets into trouble. Morton Williams and Hindell (1972) noted that for many in their group: "The pregnancy arose from beginners' ignorance and naïveté rather than from frequent intercourse or promiscuity."

In my research into the sexual behaviour of young adults, I suggested that one of the most frequent causes of unwanted pregnancies was the gap between first intercourse and the first use of contraceptives. What stops these girls from using birth control? Undoubtedly many of them associated the pill with promiscuity. They felt that it was the promiscuous girls who used contraceptives. Somehow they felt that taking the pill would expose them to moral dangers.

As I have shown, the opposite is the truth. It is the girl with the stable relationship who goes to the clinic. So where could these other girls have got the idea that the pill was only for the promiscuous? Undoubtedly they got it from people in authority declaring that the pill leads to immorality. Thus the fear of promiscuity not only impedes the ready supply of contraceptives, but makes it more difficult for girls to go to a clinic and ask for them. The finger-wagging moralists are an indirect cause of one of the situations they are anxious to avoid.

Abortion
The opposition to abortion is much more complex, compounded by strong religious beliefs and, in particular, by the argument about when life begins. In addition to this controversy, the

opponents of abortion use other arguments based upon the idea that you must reap what you sow. Even some of those who support the present Abortion Act feel there must be a complicated procedure so as to prevent what is generally called abortion on demand. It is a strange expression. People do not talk about any other operation on demand, or seeing a doctor on demand, or even getting social security or going to a shop and buying a book on demand.

Even in the medical profession there is a feeling that the new abortion laws have made it too easy for the promiscuous and the immoral. Cartwright (1970) quotes a doctor who said: "If they are going to have their fun they should pay for it. There's too much spoon-feeding today." The Abortion Law Reform Association received a request for help from a social worker on behalf of a young girl who had attempted suicide the previous year and was threatening to do so again; her parents were separated and the mother was receiving psychiatric treatment; there was no family support; the GP, in explaining that it would be good for the girl to have the baby, said it would make her "face up to her responsibilities and develop a more mature attitude to life". There are still some people who act as if the Bible said: "The wages of sin is birth."

Some people are ready to help "the nice girl who has slipped up", but will not lend a hand to "the bad girl who has got no more than she deserves". But from the point of view of the community and especially for the sake of the poor unwanted child, it is the so-called bad girl who most needs our help. There are indications from my research* that she is not likely to get it. Only 3 per cent of those with regular partners had more than one premarital pregnancy, but 13 per cent of those without a regular partner had two or more premarital pregnancies. These figures are surprising because my findings also showed that those who have one partner usually have intercourse more often than those who have several partners.

This suggests that those who are promiscuous find it much more difficult to get advice and help, and consequently they are less likely to avoid a second premarital pregnancy. Indeed it is fair to assert that it is almost always a sign of medical and social negligence when an unmarried girl has to have a second abortion.

* Page 138 of *The Sexual Behaviour of Young Adults*.

Those who oppose the present law because they think it will make things too easy for the promiscuous should remember that over half of all abortions are performed on married women. Many of these women already have large families and they feel they cannot cope with the extra burden of another child.

Nevertheless the need of the unmarried promiscuous girl is just as pressing. Many married couples who find they have another addition to the family are able to accept the situation even though the pregnancy was unwanted in the first place. A couple who intend to marry may have to bring forward the wedding day as a result of an unplanned pregnancy. But the girl who does not want to marry the man who is the putative father, perhaps knows very little about him except that she finds him sexually attractive, should certainly be given the choice of avoiding a premarital pregnancy.

In practice the promiscuous girl does not find it easy to get an abortion. Only 4 per cent of the unmarried women with unwanted pregnancies in the group studied by Lambert (1971) were promiscuous, and in the whole group of 2,995, 6 per cent were classified as promiscuous.

There are many women who are turned down but persist in their request for an abortion; if they are successful at a second or later attempt, the delay means that the operation has become more difficult and more risky. Pare and Raven (1970) reported that forty-three of 120 who were refused an abortion, obtained it elsewhere. Similarly Todd (1971) found that eleven of thirty-three cases who were initially refused managed to obtain a termination.

This suggests that many women are so desperate that they will go to very considerable trouble and expense in order to avoid an unwanted pregnancy. No doubt it can be argued that there will be more who will choose to have an abortion if legal and social controls offer this option. But it is hard to believe that the provision of these extra facilities will have much influence on the extent of promiscuous behaviour.

Nevertheless authoritative people continue to use the fear of promiscuity as a reason for limiting these facilities. Sir John Peel, surgeon-gynaecologist to the Queen, former President of the British Medical Association, says: "It is a vicious circle. The more easy it is to get an abortion, the more people take chances and don't use contraceptives. There should be more control of abortion in my view."* Incredibly Sir John Peel was also the current President of the Family Planning Association at the time he made these remarks. It is an extraordinary suggestion that a promiscuous girl should be so thoughtless as to tell herself that it did not matter if she slept around a bit because if anything went wrong she could always get an abortion. Such an idea would certainly not occur to anyone who is aware of the tedious business of getting an abortion under our so-called liberal Act: the anxious waiting between appointments when every day makes the operation more difficult and dangerous; the possible cost because in some areas it is very difficult to get it done on the NHS; the inquisitorial questions and the censorious attitudes of some of the doctors and nurses; and, of course, it would be even more worrying and costly to have an illegal operation. It is most unlikely that even the most capricious think of the existing abortion act as an opportunity for promiscuity.

Although premarital sexual intercourse is now more acceptable and although more unmarried couples are now using birth control, there is often a long gap between the first experience of sexual intercourse and the regular use of contraceptives.† Or, as the clinics say with unjustifiable pride, "All the girls coming here are already sexually experienced". If this situation continues, the demand for abortions is going to increase. Unless you are prepared to encourage girls to use contraceptives before they start to have intercourse, there will always be a need for abortions.

Time and money is now being spent in persuading more people to use more effective contraceptives. Once the idea is accepted that families can be planned, that it is better to have a space of a few years between each child, that large families are an economic burden to the parents and to the whole community, then people are going to begin to demand facilities for abortions when contraceptives have failed to prevent an unwanted pregnancy.

We are still a long way from persuading all women of child-bearing age of the advantages of using contraceptives and it will require a big educational campaign to convince them of the benefits. Even though the family planning services are now free and on the NHS, there will still be some eventualities in which

* *Daily Express*, 5 March 1973.
† Page 123 of *The Sexual Behaviour of Young Adults*.

abortion is necessary. Current research (Todd, 1971; Pare and Raven, 1970) seems to suggest that even after the provision of information and the availability of birth control services, some will fail to practise contraception, including some women for whom a baby would be a disaster.

It is wrong and medically unethical to use the fear of increased promiscuity to prevent women from obtaining an abortion, and in particular to delay the introduction of new methods which are simpler and safer. Furthermore the facts indicate that there is no clear connection between the abortion rate and the extent of promiscuous behaviour.

Venereal Diseases

The increase in the incidence of VD has been very rapid and this has caused alarm in some quarters, including pronouncements about the moral state of the nation. In fact more could be done to control this disease than is being done at present, but there is again that outstanding difficulty which I have called the fear of success. Many people, including members of the medical profession, have the feeling that the elimination of the venereal diseases would cause more harm than good, because it would encourage promiscuity. In his book, *The Anxiety Makers*, Dr Comfort (1967) gives many quotations from the medical press which support the notion that efforts to stop the spread of venereal disease were unjustified because VD was regarded as a proper punishment for sexual irregularities. After I had written an article on "VD and the Young" for *New Society*, I received many letters from readers asking why we should waste time on this nasty subject, often quoting Romans 6.23: "Sin pays a wages."

Many commentators have concluded that the high incidence of VD is the price that society must be prepared to pay for sexual freedom. The feeling is that promiscuity would be boundless were it not for the restricting influence imposed by the fear of VD. But the task of containing these infectious diseases is complicated as much by ignorance and anxiety as it is by the new permissive attitude to sex. Unfortunately the authorative pronouncements have persuaded most people to associate VD with promiscuity. So for many people, especially women, to admit you have gonorrhoea is to admit that you are promiscuous. These are the people who will go on infecting others and will refuse to believe that they are the source of infection.

What makes the rise in the VD rate so hard to comprehend is that both syphilis and gonorrhoea can be cured relatively easily. In spite of the availability, cheapness and widespread use of nearly perfect methods of treatment, sexually transmitted diseases become more and more common in every country of the world.

It is, however, possible to read too much into the rise in the incidence of VD. In the same period that the VD figures increased by 47 per cent, hospital admissions for all types of illnesses went up 34 per cent; some may say that society is much sicker, but a more feasible explanation is that both rises are due to changes in medical practices. It is certain that more people who have contracted a venereal disease now go to a clinic whereas in the past many of them went to a family doctor, who may not have reported the disease.

The reasons for the rise in the VD rate are varied and complex. Those who think the VD statistics are a sign of the moral decline of the British should note that it is a world-wide problem and many countries have a higher rate than Great Britain.

One of the important causes of the rise is the increased mobility of people of all ages and social classes. The available evidence suggests that people are more likely to contract VD away from their home town. This means that any outbreak in one area can soon be spread throughout the country, while the increased amount of foreign travel means that the infection may be brought in from other countries where the disease may be more common. The Chief Medical Officer of Health in his annual report notes that 15 per cent of all new cases of syphilis and 3.4 per cent of all new cases of gonorrhoea were contracted abroad.

There is an unknown number of women with gonorrhoea who are a continuing source of infection because they do not know they are infected and so do not seek treatment. Cauthery (1971) estimates that about half of all infected women have no symptoms. In such cases a woman does not know she has got gonorrhoea until the man she has infected notices the symptoms. The time between the original infection and the moment when the woman attends the clinic is unlikely to be less than a week and it is possible that she may infect other people during this period.

Unfortunately there are some cases when the infected woman with no symptoms does not go to the clinic; either because her partner does not know her name or is reluctant to tell her that she has gonorrhoea because he is embarrassed or irresponsible; or she may be unwilling to go for treatment, even after she has been informed; this may be stupid of her but if there are no symptoms and if she hardly knows the man who has told her she is infected, it may not be difficult for a woman to convince herself that there must be some mistake.

Another explanation is the increase of NSU (non-specific urethritis) which is similar to gonorrhoea but which appears to be more difficult to cure completely. It is also said sometimes that the rise in the VD statistics is due to the increasing resistance of the germs to penicillin, but this possibility has been exaggerated by those who want to frighten people into becoming sexually chaste. There is no killer germ being imported from some distant country that can defy the best efforts of our venereologists. It is not unusual for germs to develop a tolerance to a particular drug after it has been used for a long period and this is a problem medical men meet and combat with many different kinds of diseases. At present nearly all cases of gonorrhoea can be treated successfully by increasing the dosage or by using other antibiotics. Dr Catterall, one of the leading venereologists in Great Britain reports: "There is no report of a completely penicillin-resistant strain."

Despite the fact that there are many causes for the rise in the VD statistics, it is obvious that promiscuity must be one of the fundamental reasons for the increase. It is of course true that if a man and a woman have sexual relations only with each other and have no outside contacts, then they cannot catch VD. It follows that if no one ever had sexual intercourse outside marriage, the venereal diseases would soon be brought under control. But it is neither sensible nor realistic to attempt to ban all sex before marriage.

In an attempt to corroborate the association between VD and promiscuity, some commentators have suggested that those who get venereal diseases have personality defects. Burton (1965) suggests that "the youngsters most at risk are already emotionally damaged goods", and Ekstrom's study (1966) noted that "young persons infected with gonorrhoea do not come from a good social milieu. . . ." But these surveys were to some extent distorted by the limitations of the control groups. Holmes, Nicol and Stubbs (1968) were able to make a better comparison and they report: "There is no evidence that they come from the lower stratum of society and little evidence that they come from broken homes. Many showed responsible attitudes towards their partners and the possibility of an illegitimate child. Some 26 per cent had had only one sexual partner. . . ."

It is important to emphasize that one catches VD, not by having sex with a large number of people, but by having sex with one person who is infected. Of course it is also true that the more sexual partners you have, the more likely you are to catch a venereal disease, just as the more miles you drive a car, the more likely you are to have an accident, for the same reason in both cases: it does not wholly depend upon your own care and conduct, but also upon the care and conduct of others and this is outside your control. It is, in any case, bad medical ethics to blame the patient rather than the disease.

It is not true that those who get VD are always promiscuous. In my research promiscuity was a factor in only about half the cases. Many of those who were infected when young are now married and faithful. There were cases of people who had only ever had sexual intercourse with one person but were, nevertheless, infected by their partners. Although it can be shown that the more promiscuous are more likely to get VD, it does not follow from this that the less chance there is of getting VD, the more promiscuous people will be.

More people would go to a VD clinic without hesitation if there were less stigma attached to these diseases. Unfortunately it is still true that visiting some of the older VD clinics can make a person feel like a social outcast. There is room for improvement in the physical surroundings and in the attitude of the staff. "Some just add a touch of punishment as part of their free service," says Nicholas Saunders in his handbook, *Alternative London*. It is unfortunate that some health authorities do not welcome any action which would reduce the shame of catching VD because they feel this would be condoning promiscuity.

CHAPTER 3

PREVALENCE AND FUTURE TRENDS

In the Past

I have suggested that the fear of promiscuity is hindering progress in important areas where people need help. I have further argued that this fear is unjustified in most cases. Better sex education, readily available free contraceptives and a more liberal approach to abortion are unlikely to increase the amount of promiscuity; obviously VD and promiscuity are linked in some way, but there are worthwhile counter-benefits to be gained if we emphasize that VD is a curable disease. In this chapter I examine the small amount of information on the prevalence of promiscuity and try to estimate future trends.

Certainly promiscuity is not a new phenomenon; it is as old as the oldest profession. In three instructive volumes, Henriques (1962, 1963, 1964) has written a historical and analytical study of prostitution. He finds the institution has existed from the most primitive times in all countries. In many societies dominant roles have been played by temple prostitutes, licensed whores, courtesans, coquettes, street-walkers and call-girls; brothels have been run by municipalities and for hundreds of years the English theatre has been intimately associated with strumpets. He also discusses the curious interplay between vice, the liquor trade and the licensing laws in nineteenth-century England.

But prostitution was not the only form of promiscuous behaviour. Wife exchange, various types of sexual hospitality, intercourse with gods or priests, and religious promiscuity have all met with social approval in different communities.

The Roman Saturnalia was the occasion for indiscriminate sexual intercourse between men and women. The early Christian Church, following the lead of St Paul, was obsessed with the sinfulness all around them. The penitential books of the Middle Ages were preoccupied with sex as sin.

In the Dark Ages a woman was often given as a reward for

the services of a knight, but the gift was temporary—it was not supposed to lead to marriage. The thirteenth-century troubadours were not singing about married love, but adultery which was the ideal kind of romantic love. Histories of the medieval period would agree with Traill (1893) that "the first thought of every knight on finding a lady unprotected and alone was to do her violence".

Although sexual offences ceased to be the concern of ecclesiastical courts after the Renaissance, the Church still condemned variations in positions during sexual intercourse because this might enhance pleasure when the only function of sex was procreation. The Reformation was an era of freedom and licentiousness which the puritanism of Cromwell's Protectorate stifled but did not eliminate; as Samuel Pepys noted in his Diary, some people found a way round the restrictions. The manner of the Restoration comedies indicates that there was considerable sexual freedom after 1660, which continued through to the reign of George III and the Regency. It was said that there were 2,000 brothels and 50,000 whores in England, but not all the girls demanded money; James Boswell found that "village love" could be had for a drink or a meal. Casanova remarked : "There is no need for harlots in this fortunate age. So many decent women are as obliging as one could wish."

Meanwhile adventurers and explorers were bringing back stories from other lands. Among the Banyoro of Uganda, according to Roscoe (1923) : "The relationship between members of the same clan was of such a character than any man's wife was common to him and the other members of the clan. It was perfectly legitimate for a man to have relations with the wives of the men he called brothers, that is, his clan fellows, and such action was not looked upon as adultery." Among the Masai in East Africa, Hollis (1908) reported : "At marriage all individuals in an age grade can demand intercourse with the bride."

Henriques (1968) noted "the extraordinary willingness with which many savage peoples offered their women-folk to the first Europeans they encountered. There are accounts from all over the world : these are generally couched in terms deploring the sexual depravity and lasciviousness of the 'natives'." Spanish and French explorers were less indignant than the British, and their reports detail extensive fraternisation.

The sexual hospitality of the Eskimoes is well known; on

certain occasions the host is bound to lend his wife to a visitor as commanded by a religious law (Boas, 1888). In Siberia the tribe of Koryak carry this hospitality to extravagant lengths. Apparently they used to pester Tsarist officials, especially postmen, to sleep with their wives and "overwhelmed him on his return with presents because a son had been born from the transient alliance". (Erman, 1848).

The Abbé Dubois found a form of religious promiscuity as recently as the eighteenth century in India at Tirupati "to which women flock in crowds to obtain children from the God Venkateswara". They were advised by the priests to pass the night in the temple, and "the great Venkateswara, touched by their devotion, will perhaps visit them in the spirit and accomplish that which until then has been denied to them through human power. I must draw a curtain over the sequel of this deceitful suggestion. The reader already guesses at it. The following morning these destestable hypocrites, pretending complete ignorance of what has passed, make due enquiries into all the details; and after having congratulated the women upon the reception they met with from the gods, receive the gifts. . . ."

Bowdich (1819) wrote about the yam festivals in Ghana. "The Yam custom is like Saturnalia; the grossest liberty prevails, and each sex abandons itself to its passions. . . ." In the well-known account of life in New Guinea, Malinowski reports: "The dancing which takes place with increased intensity during the few days of the feast, seems to be associated with opportunities for short-lived intrigues, and occasionally there even seem to be features of licentiousness, groups absconding together. . . ."

Modern festivals are said to exhibit some of the same tendencies, if stories about the Fasching in Europe and the carnivals of South America are to be believed. In some festivals the sexual roles are reversed; in Tenerife, for example, the men wear masks and dress up as girls. Even some of the recent music festivals have gained reputations for sexual licence. As far as I am aware, no festival in Britain is particularly well-known for this aspect, but VD statistics and other evidence suggests that many British people are much more sexually permissive on their foreign holidays than they are during the rest of the year at home.

But this country is as sexually free as most. Even the well known prudery of the Victorian era was almost entirely a middle class morality. It was accepted as inevitable that those lower in the social scale, which meant the majority, could not aspire to those gentlemanly standards of conduct. In the nineteenth-century child prostitutes were still a prominent feature of the sexual landscape. Mayhew (1862) found that one in 14.8 births was illegitimate in 1848 compared to a figure of about one in every 12.1 today—not so very different.

After the Great War, popular songs of the twenties indicated that promiscuous love could be sung about quite openly:

> Rings on your fingers and heartaches inside,
> You're the lonesomest gal in town.
> Everyone's body but nobody's bride,
> You're the lonesomest gal in town

A popular song of 1938 referred to "a pounce in the clover, then when it's over, so long, and what's your name"? And a short-lived affair could be dismissed as "a trip to the moon on gossamer wings, just one of those things". Although prostitution has declined considerably over the last thirty years, the double standard of morality, which some people still uphold, demanded a minority of promiscuous and disrespected girls with whom a boy was supposed to get his early sexual experience before marrying a virgin.

The most important trend on the sexual scene today has been the success of the movement for the emancipation of women, in particular the realization that women's need for sexual fulfilment is as great as men's. Women are no longer regarded solely as the target for seduction or merely as producers of children, but as people who are entitled to choose their own mode of sexual activity. It would be extremely optimistic to assert that this new view of the status and social significance of women is accepted without argument. But it does mean that there is now a group of women, significantly larger than in the past, who are promiscuous by choice.

The Situation Today

People often say we are living in the middle of a sexual revolution, but a study of recent sexual behaviour suggests that changes are more likely to follow a gradual trend. The famous Kinsey reports showed that changes in sexual behaviour varied only slightly over the years. John Gagnon (1965) who was at the Kinsey Institute for Sex Research before becoming Professor of

Sociology at Stonybrook, believes that there have been very few basic changes in sexual behaviour over the last fifty years. In his paper on *Sexuality and Sexual Learning*, he writes: "The long predicted change in American sexual patterns has not, in fact, occurred, despite the advent of the automobile and other artifacts of a changing technology.... Given our difficulties in changing the behaviour of schizophrenics, drug addicts, or juvenile delinquents, or even of changing the political party affiliation of others, there seems to be a curious contradiction in the belief that sexual behaviour is immediately amenable to change from the slightest external impulse."

Attitudes, of course, change faster than actual behaviour. It is much easier to express an opinion than to put it into practice. One of the more recent changes in attitudes is that in some sections of society, outspokenness about sex is not only fashionable, but lack of sexual success is something to be ashamed of. This would encourage some people to exaggerate their sexual adventures. It is possible that promiscuous behaviour may not really be quite as prevalent as some people seem to expect and fear.

Self-administered questionnaires circulated among students sometimes produce quite misleading results. A certain amount of promiscuity is to be expected in a tolerant community and where facilities are available; but it is a different matter in a small town or village, where everyone knows what everyone is doing and where it is difficult to obtain much privacy.

It is also possible to be misled by plays, novels, films and all kinds of fiction where it is assumed that physical attraction creates an irresistible urge for two people to go to bed together. It is not as easy as all that when you are married, or committed in some way, or living in crowded conditions, or short of money; and consequently it does not happen as often as in the fictional stories.

In my own research into the sexual behaviour of young people, only 12 per cent of the boys and 2 per cent of the girls aged fifteen to nineteen had experienced sexual intercourse with more than one partner. This was ten years ago and there have certainly been changes since then. But the original percentages are very small and it is probably still true to say as I did then*

* Page 253 of *The Sexual Behaviour of Young People* (Longmans edition).

that "promiscuity, although it exists, is not a prominent feature of teenage sexual behaviour".

Table 1 gives the number of sexual partners in the previous year among 376 twenty-five-year-old men and women. A total of sixty-three (17 per cent) said they had intercourse with more than one person. In the whole group thirty-six (9 per cent) did not have sexual intercourse at all in the last year, so that leaves 277 (74 per cent) who had only one sexual partner.

This table shows that most of the promiscuous were unmarried, but not all of them. In fact, 7 per cent of this group had been unfaithful to their spouses in the last year. This is quite a large figure when consideration is given to the age of these men and women; most of them had only been married a few years and none of them for more than seven. This percentage does not include those who were divorced or separated.

Among the unmarried, 32 per cent had not had intercourse in the previous year, 29 per cent had one sexual partner only and 39 per cent had sex with more than one person. It is no surprise that the unmarried had more sexual partners, and even a quarter of those who said they had regular partners admitted to being promiscuous; but it is also worth noting that 61 per cent of the unmarried had only one partner or no sexual intercourse at all.

TABLE 1*

Those who have had more than one sexual partner in the previous year

Marital situation

Number of partners	Married	Divorce or sep	Living together	Steady partner	No steady	Tota No.	%
Only one partner	240	5	3	23	6	277	74
One other, once	2	0	0	1	0	3	1
One other, many times	2	3	0	2	0	7	2
Several, once each	1	0	0	3	3	7	2
Several people, many times	12	1	2	14	17	46	12
No sexual intercourse	0	1	0	9	26	36	9
Total	257	10	5	52	52	376	100

* From page 179 of *The Sexual Behaviour of Young Adults*.

For those who would prefer a less strict definition of promiscuity, the table shows that 14 per cent had several different sexual partners in the course of the year; this applied to 5 per cent of the married and 36 per cent of the unmarried.

These results come from a group of young adults of about the same age, still at the height of their sexual powers, living in a world where commercial enterprise emphasizes sexual success. It is possible that there is more promiscuity among the older age groups, but I doubt if there is much difference. In his group of nearly 2,000 married informants of all ages, Gorer (1971) found that 8 per cent "had made love to somebody beside their spouse since marriage; 5 per cent said they had gone 'all the way', 3 per cent that they had not". Of those who had gone 'all the way', 3 per cent had had two or more partners, and so qualify for our less strict definition of promiscuity.

It would be a mistake to attribute any degree of accuracy to these figures. A certain amount of under-reporting must be expected on a subject as delicate as this and, even in the most friendly interview, there must be some who do not feel inclined to admit to infidelity or other socially disapproved acts. It is impossible to estimate the extent of this under-reporting but it is reasonable to regard all these percentages as the minimum amount of promiscuity to be found in representative samples of the married population. Obviously it is not a rare or isolated event. Nor is it so prevalent that it can be regarded as typical behaviour.

Gagnon and Simon (1970) estimated that "about half of all married men and a quarter of all married women will have intercourse outside of marriage at one time or another". Whatever may be the precise figure—and it is not terribly important to get the exact figure—it is certain that there are over 4 million people in this country who are promiscuous by our definition. No matter what moral judgements one may care to make about promiscuity, there are a lot of people who choose to behave in this way. It is unrealistic as well as unhelpful to dismiss such people as moral degenerates.

Changing Attitudes
The connection between changes in attitudes and how they are translated into overt behaviour is still obscure. Obviously they are associated in some way, but the time span between a varia-

tion in attitude and a change of behaviour appears to be difficult to predict. However, attitudes do indicate the likely direction of a behavioural change, and recent attitude changes make it seem probable that more and more people are going to be promiscuous. A good illustration of the way people have changed their attitudes to premarital sexual intercourse is shown dramatically in the group I saw first when they were teenagers, and then as young adults seven years later. At the first interview, 45 per cent of the men were in favour of sex before marriage; when we met seven years later, 83 per cent were in favour. Even more of the girls changed their minds; 24 per cent of the teenagers approved of premarital sex; now 88 per cent are in favour.

They are still young adults, but opinion polls, self-administered questionnaires (Kind, 1969) and other researches (Gorer, 1971) have shown that premarital sexual intercourse is now thought to be acceptable behaviour by most people of all ages and in all social classes. This is a remarkable change in opinion, especially among church leaders, youth workers, local government officials and others in authority who were implacably opposed to all sex before marriage until quite recently.

In particular the Churches have tried to present a united front over the necessity of chastity prior to marriage. Although not reluctant to make use of the threat of venereal disease or illegitimacy, the basic argument against premarital sexual relations is that they are contrary to God's purpose. When the British Council of Churches published a report in 1966 in which a minority of the committee members expressed the view that "we should leave the individual parties free to decide whether a personal relationship has achieved the intimacy and tenderness of which sexual intercourse is the appropriate expression", the Archbishop of York, with the Bishops of Coventry, Blackburn and Liverpool among other clerics, issued a statement: "We believe that the Christian Church should say plainly that sexual intercourse outside marriage is less than the best kind of loving and therefore wrong." It was not just the higher echelons of the Church that rejected premarital sex. Dr Sherwin Bailey, who holds liberal views on the Christian attitude to homosexuality, contends that coition outside marriage can never be justified. Similar views are held by churchmen like Bishop Huddleston,

Bishop Montefiore* and Lord Soper who are well known for liberal views on other matters. Indeed Lord Soper's views are quite extreme: "To accept the pleasures of sexual attitudes and practices without relating them to the purposes for which these pleasures were intended is a form of perversion and must be condemned as delinquent.... A boy who takes sex because he wants it will tend to take somebody else's goods for precisely the same reason. The girl who is encouraged to see nothing wrong in pleasing herself with somebody else's body will be unlikely to see any objection in pleasing herself with somebody else's money."†

Most sex education books discredit premarital sex. Lakeman (1958) thinks that boys should only marry "a pure sweet girl who has always behaved herself in the presence of men", and "all decent maidens wish to marry men who have similarly behaved in the presence of women". Such men will be hard to find. Hutchin (1969) implies that premarital sex is practised only by people who are not in love: "Two people who are in love ... will realise that sexual intercourse is something that should be saved for the future."

Today the attitude towards premarital intercourse may be less prohibitory, but there is still the strong feeling, among older generations especially, that it is only permissible between two people who intend to get married. Indeed there may be occasions when this is an indirect cause of promiscuous behaviour; if a young man or woman has overt sexual intercourse with just one person, he may find there is parental and social pressure to regard this as a prelude to marriage, but not all young people want to make so firm a commitment before they have their first sexual experience. Consequently they may find it easier to be covertly promiscuous when perhaps they would prefer to have an overt affair with one person, but without definite commitment.

In order to find out more about their ideas on promiscuous behaviour, we asked our group of twenty-five-year-old inform-

* Hugh Montefiore, Bishop of Kingston, writes: "But although the case of an engaged couple is quite different from a passing fancy, it does not follow that the church smiles on their living together."

† From a chapter by Lord Soper in *Does Pornography Matter?* edited by C. H. Rolph.

ants more questions on their attitudes towards premarital sexual intercourse. We asked them : "Do you think it is all right for two people to have sex before marriage when they are really in love?" It is remarkable that only 4 per cent disapproved; 88 per cent found the idea acceptable. So premarital sexual intercourse between couples who are in love is now sanctioned by the vast majority of this age group, and it is the few that think it is wrong or sinful who are the exception.

The informants were then asked if they approved of premarital intercourse between two people who were not in love. A third (36 per cent) disapproved of this and another 6 per cent were doubtful. But 58 per cent said they did not object to premarital sex between couples, even if they were not in love.

This is a significant finding. All these people have been brought up to believe that sex without love is to be deplored. The conventional morality decrees that sexual activities must be linked with love if they are to command respect. The major part of modern fiction assumes that two people go to bed solely because they are in love with each other and infidelity is explained in most plays, films and novels by the irresistible power of love. Despite these and many other social pressures, repeated almost without opposition, over half the young adults in this group do not accept this moral principle. Instead they accept the evidence of their eyes and their senses. They are aware that hundreds of people separate love from sex and enjoy sexual activities without pretending that it is part of a loving relationship.

There was one other question about sex and love. Everyone was asked : "Is it all right to have sex with one person when you are in love with someone else?" Unlike the other attitude questions, this question was intentionally phrased in a personal way and, not surprisingly, produced a much larger negative response, particularly among the married. More than two out of three people (69 per cent) said they did not approve of this. A small proportion (11 per cent) did not know what to think about it, but a fifth of the group (20 per cent) said they might have sex with one person, even though they were in love with another. So a considerable minority seem to feel that it is possible to take part in sexual activities without prejudicing the continuation of another, more important, loving relationship.

Of course people are usually more tolerant in their attitudes than in their behaviour. But there are other factors which may have some influence on their sexual activities. A far larger proportion of the population now undergo some form of further or higher education and this often means they live away from home and parental influence, mixing with a permissive peer group at the height of their sexual powers. They may have a room of their own for the first time in their lives in many cases. Furthermore, young people have much more mobility. More of them are car owners; for many years the Americans have recognized the car as an important adjunct to premarital sex and the same thing is now happening in this country. More young people go on holiday together and enjoy a greater amount of freedom than in the past. Children reach physical maturity at a younger age but marriage often has to be delayed due to lack of housing and for economic reasons. Altogether there is less parental supervision than there used to be and the increased availability of contraceptives has made the fear of pregnancy less acute for some people at least.

But perhaps the most important change of all has been the sexual emancipation of the new generation of women. Many commentators have suggested that it is the changed attitude of women that will be most influential in the immediate future. This change in attitudes is illustrated in a rather over-simplified way in Figure 1.

In the past the boy's goal was sexual satisfaction, whereas the girl's goal was romance, love and marriage. After they had been courting for a time, the boy would modify his attitude and start to think in terms of the language of romantic love and marriage,

FIGURE 1

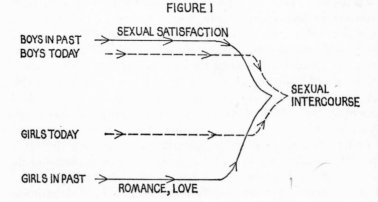

BOYS IN PAST
BOYS TODAY
SEXUAL SATISFACTION

SEXUAL INTERCOURSE

GIRLS TODAY

GIRLS IN PAST
ROMANCE, LOVE

and the girl would modify her attitude and become sexually aroused. As the two lines are drawn together, sexual intercourse is more likely to occur. But the broken lines in Figure 1 suggest that both boys and girls now start from different positions. The boys' attitude to love has softened, albeit only slightly; it is no longer considered to be so unmanly to express tenderness and affection. Meanwhile the girls' attitude to sexual satisfaction has changed considerably, so the two lines are closer than before and therefore it is easier for the two attitudes to be modified sufficiently to allow intercourse to take place.

The simplified diagram tends to make the process simpler than it is. Boys committed to sexuality and girls committed to romantic love often misunderstand each other's intentions; ironically, it sometimes happens that the boy lessens his attempts to seduce the girl as he becomes more emotionally involved, and at the same time the girl comes to feel that sexual intercourse is permissible because the boy's affection is so genuine. But as a generalization, it is fair to say that the two attitudes start closer together than in the past because of the increased sexuality of women.

There are no reliable figures to show that promiscuous behaviour is on the increase. It would be difficult enough to get reliable figures today and it is now impossible to get information from the past with any degree of accuracy. My own impression is that there is not as much promiscuity as some people appear to believe. Moral denunciations of modern youth seem to imply that it is an undisciplined sex-obsessed generation. My own researches and others suggest that promiscuity is still infrequent even among young people. But the future is a different matter.

The group of twenty-five-year-old men and women that I studied were not particularly sophisticated or permissive, but a considerable number of them now make a distinction between sex and love. We know that attitudes to sex have undergone a considerable change in the last few years. Although this may not be immediately reflected in changes of behaviour, all the indications are that there will be an increase in the amount of promiscuous behaviour in the not very distant future.

Will this bring about the moral collapse of the nation? It is important that we find out. In Chapter 5 we will study the effects of promiscuity, but first we should try to get more information about the sort of people who are promiscuous.

CHAPTER 4

CHARACTER AND PERSONALITY

Where Are They?

After hearing the laments of the traditionalists as they deplore the rapid slide down the slippery slope towards immorality, it might be assumed that it would not be difficult to locate a group of promiscuous people to study for research purposes. But they are not easy to find by any of the ordinary methods of social research.

Of course much depends upon the definition of the word. If one defines promiscuity as sexual intercourse outside the bounds of marriage at any time in their lives, then 54 per cent of the group in my research would qualify, although they are only twenty-five. But clearly this is a very strict definition. Some of those who would be labelled under this definition had isolated sexual experiences several years ago, but were now happily married with every intention of remaining faithful. At the other extreme, if one were to describe as promiscuous only those people who have several partners every month of the year, then only 2 per cent of my sample would come under the definition of promiscuity.

At one time I considered adding to the number under study, by seeking out girls whom one might suppose were likely to be promiscuous. Accordingly a group of unmarried mothers, and girls in Holloway prison, were all interviewed. This proved to be quite an expensive failure as far as learning anything about promiscuity was concerned. The large majority of the unmarried mothers were not at all promiscuous. Even among the prisoners the promiscuous were a minority. But there were a very few girls who were utterly indiscriminate in the selection of their sexual partners.

Complete indiscrimination is undoubtedly very rare in sexual relations as it is in all kinds of human activities. Such behaviour is nearly always symptomatic of some severe disturbance unrelated to sexuality. Psychiatrists and criminologists meet such people and their patients' fruitless quests from stranger to stranger for love and tenderness has often been described in medical textbooks.

It has been pointed out that whereas disturbed boys express their discontent and frustration through delinquency and aggression, disturbed girls express these feelings through flaunting their sexuality and by drifting from man to man. Many of them have run away from a home where there was little love or hope. These girls find their sexual favours provide for their immediate needs, such as shelter, clothing and food. The psychiatrists describe their behaviour as attention-seeking and a cry for help.

Very little research has been done but it is quite possible that these impressions are correct. But they apply to only a very small proportion of the population. It would be a mistake to make general statements about promiscuity based on a study of these disadvantaged girls. For many years nearly all the information about homosexuality was obtained from studies on homosexuals under treatment or in prison. In an earlier research (Schofield, 1965) I was able to show that homosexuals under treatment or in prison were more like heterosexuals under treatment or in prison than like homosexuals who were not in trouble. A similar situation now exists with regard to promiscuity. Many writers make unwise and incorrect statements based only on studies made on disturbed and deprived girls who have so many problems that it is impossible to separate their promiscuous behaviour from their other personality problems.

It is important to realize that even when studying a very selective group such as those who have committed offences, sexual depravity is not a common factor; indeed indiscriminate promiscuity is quite rare even in these disadvantaged groups. This is supported by Carter (1969) who studied a group of fifty girls in an approved school and then compared her results with my research which was based on a representative sample (Schofield, 1968). She writes: "It is commonly believed that juvenile delinquency and early sexual sophistication go hand in hand, but the great similarity between the sample of approved school girls and Schofield's general population sample suggests that this is not the case."

I have suggested that making the definition too wide or too narrow makes the numbers so large or so small that sociological

investigation becomes impossible. Indeed I found the search for
special groups that seemed likely to contain a higher proportion
of promiscuous girls proved to be unrewarding, partly because
the proportion was not very much higher, and especially because
it brought in many extraneous factors, which only confused the
picture. Accordingly I must be content with the midway definition which I used for my previous research. The results are given
in the following sections of this chapter.

Who Are They?

In my group of 376 young adults, there were sixty (forty-seven
men, thirteen women) who had intercourse with more than one
person in the twelve months before they were interviewed. This
excludes three people who had one isolated experience apart from
their regular partner. Strictly speaking these three had been
unfaithful but it is too rigorous to classify them as promiscuous.

The other sixty were studied in some detail. The number is
too small to allow an elaborate statistical analysis, but the results
obtained from specially selected groups (i.e. unmarried mothers
and female offenders) were so distorted by other factors, that I
decided that smaller numbers obtained from a general sample of
the population would give a more valid picture of the real situation than larger numbers from groups with an in-built bias, such
as promiscuous girls drawn from the prison population.

As there was usually little difference between men and women
the percentages given in the following paragraphs are combined,
except in a few cases where a difference is noted. In the analysis
that follows these sixty people are called the promiscuous group,
but it is important to remember that there is a disparity within
the group. Some are married but have one or more partners as
well as their spouses; some have had a series of one-night stands;
some have had short-lived but passionate affairs lasting a few
months; some unmarried men have had intercourse only a few
times in the past year. The remaining 316 people in our sample
had either had only one partner or no sexual intercourse in the
last twelve months and they will be referred to as the *other*
group for purposes of comparison.

In the promiscuous group 25 per cent were married; 7 per
cent were divorced or separated; 35 per cent said they had a
steady relationship with one partner and 33 per cent did not
have a regular partner. So only a quarter could be said to be

unfaithful in the strictest sense of the word, although it is possible that the sexual adventures of those no longer living with
their spouses may have been the direct cause of the breakdown
of the marriage.

The sixty people in the promiscuous group were better educated than the other 316 people; 23 per cent of the promiscuous
were still at school or college at the age of eighteen compared
with 13 per cent of the others; 70 per cent of the promiscuous
left school at the age of sixteen or older compared with 46 per
cent of the others.

They stayed at school longer and were academically more
successful. In fact almost a half (49 per cent) of the promiscuous
group got one or more GCE 'O' levels (over a third got more
than five) compared with 38 per cent of the others (among
whom a quarter got more than five 'O' levels). Fewer (39 per
cent) of the promiscuous left school without passing any kind
of exam compared with nearly half (48 per cent) of the others.

Table 2 shows their social class rated according to their present
occupation. The promiscuous were more likely to be middle
class, and those who were working class were more likely to be

TABLE 2

The social class of those who were promiscuous
compared with the others

Social class	Promiscuous %	Others %
Middle class	26	19
Non-manual	45	36
Manual	26	41
Not known	3	4
No. (100%)	60	316

in non-manual occupations, whereas the others were more likely
to be manual workers. The promiscuous were also better paid;
over a third (35 per cent) came into the top income bracket
compared with less than a quarter (24 per cent) of the others.

The salient finding is that the promiscuous are better educated,
better paid and come higher on a socio-economic scale. It has

been suggested that women's liberation has something to do with this; emancipation and sexual freedom has been more readily adopted by the better educated women. But in fact the tendency for the promiscuous to be better educated is more pronounced among the men than the women. A possible explanation, put forward with some hesitation, is that education encourages the individual to question traditional sexual customs and this in turn may lead to increased tolerance and fewer inhibitions. A more pragmatic explanation is that middle class girls find it easier to obtain contraceptives, as shown in my earlier report on this group (Schofield, 1973).

Table 3 shows that there is not much difference between the two groups among those who never go to church. But a far smaller proportion of weekly attenders at church are to be found in the promiscuous group; perhaps it is surprising that as many as 7 per cent of the promiscuous go to church every week.

When they were asked about their religious denomination, no clear differences emerged, except that many more of the promiscuous said they had no allegiance to any denomination (47 per cent compared with 11 per cent and many of those in the other group said they were Church of England (61 per cent compared

TABLE 3

The church attendance of the promiscuous group
compared with the others

Church attendance	Promiscuous %	Others %
Every week	7	13
Less than once a week	23	18
Never	70	69
No. (100%)	60	316

with 26 per cent in the promiscuous group). Many people who do not go to church are quite likely to say they are Church of England, but this is less true of those who were in the promiscuous group. More often they said that they did not belong to any denomination. This reinforces the idea that the promiscuous are more likely to question traditional beliefs and are less likely to pay lip-service to old customs.

Interviewers were required to rate all informants on a five-point scale for verbal fluency and for appearance. Of course this is a subjective rating but the interviewers' bias would apply to both groups under consideration. The promiscuous were found to be far more talkative; 42 per cent were rated as being loquacious compared with 24 per cent of the others; 16 per cent were rated as reserved compared with 25 per cent of the others. This is one of the several signs that the promiscuous tend to be more extrovert.

The idea that the pretty girl will more often receive propositions and so will be more promiscuous does not get any support from these results. Nor does this apply to the handsome man, who may have more opportunities. In the promiscuous group, 14 per cent received the highest rating (very good looking) compared with 18 per cent of the others. On the other hand only 12 per cent of the promiscuous were given a low rating compared with 21 per cent of the others. So it may be more difficult for the ill-favoured to be promiscuous.

All the informants were asked how many jobs they had had since leaving school and Table 4 summarizes the results. The

TABLE 4

The number of jobs since they left school : the promiscuous group compared with the others

Number of jobs	Promiscuous %	Others %
1	21	24
2–3	40	38
4–6	30	23
7–20	9	10
20+	0	2
Not known	0	3
No. (100%)	60	316

differences between the two groups are not large, but the promiscuous do seem to move from one job to another more frequently. It is hard to say whether this is a sign of ambition or discontent. However those who have had a very large number of jobs, a sure sign of occupational maladjustment, were less likely to be in the promiscuous group.

Several other non-sexual comparisons were made between the groups. Hardly any striking differences were found between those who were promiscuous and those who were not. A strange finding, which is hard to explain, is the cigarette smoking habits of the two groups. Only a quarter (26 per cent) of the promiscuous group were non-smokers but almost half the other group did not smoke. Nearly one in four of the promiscuous (23 per cent) smoked more than twenty cigarettes a day compared with 14 per cent of the others. Almost all (85 per cent) the promiscuous girls smoked at least one cigarette a day; 23 per cent were heavy smokers compared with only 6 per cent of the other girls in the sample. The reader is reminded that the number of girls in the promiscuous group is very small and it would be a mistake to draw definite conclusions. But it is clear that this association between cigarette smoking and sexual behaviour requires further investigation. In an earlier research* which was based on a large sample of 464 teenage girls, all of those who smoked more than twenty cigarettes a day had early sexual experiences.

The drinking habits of the two groups were also studied and perhaps it is no surprise to find that the promiscuous visited public bars far more often than the others. Table 5 shows that three out of four in the promiscuous group could be described as regular drinkers compared with about half of the other group. At the other end of the scale the infrequent drinkers were far less likely to be in the promiscuous group.

In addition they were all asked: "Have you ever been a bit drunk?" Each informant was left to interpret in his own way what he meant by being drunk. Most of them were prepared to admit that this had happened at least once or twice; only 12 per cent of the promiscuous and 18 per cent of the others said it had never happened. It was a more frequent occurrence for the promiscuous; 30 per cent said they had been drunk more than ten times (compared with 17 per cent of the others); 14 per

* Page 178 of the *Sexual Behaviour of Young People* (Longmans edition).

cent said they had been drunk more than fifty times (compared with 4 per cent of the others).

The drinking and smoking habits of the promiscuous, together with the tendency to be more talkative, and to change jobs more frequently, strongly suggests that they are likely to be more extrovert and outgoing than the others. Eysenck's (1972) results agree with this suggestion. He questioned students about their sexual attitudes. According to his own well-known theory of personality, he would expect extroverts to have intercourse earlier than introverts, and to have it more frequently and with more

TABLE 5

The number of times the promiscuous group visited public bars compared with the others

Frequency of visits	Promiscuous %	Others %
Within 24 hours	49	24
2–7 days ago	30	28
8–28 days ago	5	12
Over a month ago	7	21
Rarely or never	9	15
No. (100%)	60	316

partners. As usual these predictions were borne out by his results. The extroverts were characterized by lack of nervousness and were satisfied in their sexual relationships. They were easily excited sexually, and tended to favour promiscuity. The introverts tended to hold more traditional sexual attitudes and attached more value to fidelity.

These findings are supported in an interesting way by the answers to questions about getting into trouble with the law and the police. One of these questions was about the number of times they had been brought before a court. Table 6 shows that a large proportion of the promiscuous and an even larger proportion of the others had never appeared before a court. But the promiscuous were far more likely to have made only one appearance; for two or three appearances the differences between the two groups is narrowed considerably; and for those who made more frequent court appearances, the situation has changed and there are now more in the non-promiscuous group. The other questions about delinquency also seem to suggest that the promiscuous were more likely to get into trouble, but less likely to get into frequent or serious trouble; 25 per cent of the promiscuous admitted to some trouble with the police which was not serious enough to come to court, compared with 11 per cent of the others. But when the others did get into trouble it tended to be more serious and was more likely to end up in court.

A comparison between the two groups shows that the promiscuous were not more likely to come from a broken home, an

TABLE 6

The number of times the promiscuous appeared before a court compared with the others

Number of court appearances	Promiscuous %	Others %
Never	76	86
One	16	6
2–3	5	3
3+	3	5
No. (100%)	60	316

unhappy home, or a less religious home. A study of the background and early environment fails to bring out any situation where the promiscuous were deprived or disadvantaged in any way. On the contrary, they seem to have come from homes where further education was encouraged. At the time when they were interviewed the promiscuous were better educated, better paid, more extrovert and more inclined to question traditional values.

In the next section I consider the sexual acts and attitudes of those who had more than one partner in the last twelve months.

What Are They?

All the informants were asked how they found out about conception. School friends were most often mentioned as the source of information, followed by books. Only a few said their parents had told them how babies are born and the teacher was hardly ever given as the source of information. The results show that there is practically no difference between the promiscuous group and the others. Most people, whatever their later sexual attitudes or acts may be, start off by picking up a kind of sexual folklore which is misleading and inadequate.

Most of the men and women felt they should have been told more about sex at school, but the promiscuous felt this need less often than the others. A majority also felt their parents could have been more helpful, although the promiscuous were less likely to be dissatisfied with the part their parents played in their sexual education. The percentages given in Table 7 suggest that,

TABLE 7

The demand for more information about sex at school
and from parents: the promiscuous group
compared with the others

Wanted more help	Promiscuous %	Others %
At school		
Yes	68	82
Don't know	2	3
No	30	15
From parents		
Yes	51	62
Don't know	2	3
No	47	35
No. (100%)	60	316

while many of the promiscuous were disappointed, they were less likely than the others to express discontent, possibly because they felt they had now achieved effective sexual adjustment, at least to their own satisfaction, even if their parents and teachers would not have approved.

But the promiscuous were not so confident about their sexual knowledge. As many as 47 per cent of the promiscuous felt that they did not know all they needed to know about sex, compared with 34 per cent of the others. This is an interesting finding. We tend to suppose that the promiscuous are sexually sophisticated. Perhaps they are, but half of them are prepared to admit that they do not know all about it, unlike the others, most of whom feel that there is nothing more to be learnt.

When it comes to a consideration of the sexual behaviour of the young, most people suppose that the promiscuous are early starters, but the association between the age of first intercourse and later promiscuity is not absolutely straightforward and this supposition needs to be qualified. The proportion who had sexual intercourse before the age of eighteen is only slightly larger among the promiscuous (28 per cent compared with 23 per cent of the others) and the percentage who had already had more than one partner by that age was not significantly different (14 per cent compared with 12 per cent). On the other hand, there is a big difference between the two groups when one compares those who had only a small amount of sexual experience before the age of eighteen; 26 per cent of the promiscuous had fairly limited experience compared with 40 per cent of the others.

The discrepancy is accounted for by those who had inceptive experience, defined as extensive sexual intimacies which fall short of intercourse*; 46 per cent of the promiscuous had inceptive experience compared with 37 per cent of the others. So the promiscuous seemed to be more active sexually as teenagers, but were not much more likely to have sexual intercourse. This finding is consistent with the results reported in the previous section. When they were young the promiscuous were found to be more active and out-going in other (non-sexual) ways.

The informants were also asked about their present sexual activities. Not everyone found it easy to answer such a personal question and 6 per cent in each group either declined to answer or said they could not estimate the frequency. Apart from these, all of the promiscuous informants said they had had sexual intercourse at least once during the previous twelve months, but this was not the case with 10 per cent of the others. But aside from those who did not have sexual experience in the last year (and 8 per cent of the others had never had intercourse), the frequencies of the promiscuous are lower, not higher, than the others, as shown in Table 8.

* Inceptive activities are defined in more detail on pages 41 and 55 of *The Sexual Behaviour of Young People* (Longmans edition).

High frequencies (more than once a week) are twice as likely to occur in the non-promiscuous group. One reason for this is that more people in this group are married (76 per cent as against 25 per cent in the promiscuous group). My earlier research

TABLE 8

The frequency of sexual intercourse in the last
year among the promiscuous and the others

Frequency last year	Promiscuous %	Others %
0	0	10
1–12	20	4
13–50	42	15
50+	32	65
Don't know or not known	6	6
No. (100%)	60	316

(Schofield, 1973) showed that the married had far higher frequencies than the single men and women; 79 per cent of the married had intercourse more than once a week compared with 18 per cent of the unmarried. But this only partly accounts for the difference between the promiscuous group and the others.

It is occasionally assumed that the promiscuous are licentious and lascivious with sexual demands so insatiable that they cannot possibly be satisfied by one partner. But sometimes it is the sexually unsuccessful who are promiscuous. Some are so inept that no one wants to have intercourse with them more than once; others profess to be so little interested in sex that they only seek out a partner two or three times a year; others are unable to find willing partners or a private place for frequent sexual adventures. A few promiscuous people are very active, but most of them have less sex than the married couples who remain faithful to each other.

The promiscuous tend to have less sex, but they would like to have more. This is shown in the answers to the question: "Would you say you were having enough, too much or too little?" Besides those who were not getting enough and the few who said they were having too much, a further division of the mid-way position became necessary. Some gave ebullient replies which revealed that things were *just right*, while others made less enthusiastic remarks but agreed that they were getting *enough*.

None of the promiscuous said they were having too much and only a few (3 per cent) of the others gave this reply. But over a third (35 per cent) of the promiscuous, compared with less than a quarter (21 per cent) of the others, said they were getting too little. The promiscuous appeared to be less contented about the amount of sex they were getting; 53 per cent of the promiscuous said they were getting enough, compared with 57 per cent of the others; and only 9 per cent of the promiscuous felt their sexual life was just right compared with 17 per cent of the others. There was hardly any difference at all between the promiscuous men and women, but the women in the other group were more likely to say they were very content with the situation.

Both groups were also asked: "Do you think your friends have more or less sex than you?" This was intended to follow up the idea put forward in the earlier research* that commercial exploitation has left many people with the impression that everyone else's sex life is far more exciting than their own. Some support is given to this notion because twice as many people (in both groups) thought their friends were having more rather than less sex. But many said, quite reasonably, that they could not answer this question because they did not know about the sexual activities of their friends and some added that they did not believe it was any of their concern. The promiscuous were more likely than the others to say that it was impossible to give a sensible reply to this question.

The promiscuous are less likely to be regular users of birth control. The first two columns of Table 9 shows the difference between the two groups in the usual way. The third column shows the percentages in the others groups when those who have had no sexual experience are discounted. This further calculation emphasizes that the others are more likely to be regular users (65 per cent compared with 49 per cent in the promiscuous group). But it also shows that those who have never used contraceptives are less likely to be in the promiscuous group (18 per cent compared with 26 per cent in the other group).

It is disturbing to find that more than half the promiscuous group do not always use contraceptives. Table 9 suggests that

* Page 175 of *The Sexual Behaviour of Young Adults*.

they are likely to use them occasionally but not regularly; 33 per cent of the promiscuous use contraceptives sometimes but not always, compared with 9 per cent of the others.

Promiscuous sex is more likely to be unexpected, hurried or furtive. It often takes place in unfamiliar surroundings and in circumstances in which neither partner has immediate access to contraceptives. It is possible that the partners do not know each other well enough to ask if either of them are using any birth control method; or they may feel that such a discussion would spoil the romantic passion of the moment.

There is also another factor which should not be forgotten: it is more difficult for the promiscuous to get contraceptives. The research into the sexual behaviour of young adults showed quite clearly that the single woman, especially the unmarried girl without a boy-friend, was sometimes afraid that it would be embarrassing to visit a family planning clinic. More often than not this fear is unfounded, but unfortunately it is true that some

TABLE 9

The extent to which contraceptives are used in the promiscuous group, and in the other group including and excluding those who have never had sexual intercourse

How often do you use contraceptives?	Promiscuous %	Others %	Others* %
Always	49	59	65
Sometimes	26	8	8
Rarely	7	1	1
Never	18	24	26
Not applicable	0	8	—
No. (100%)	60	316	290

*Excluding twenty-six people with no experience of sexual intercourse.

clinics ask too many personal questions and inadvertently give the impression that they do not willingly provide a service for the unattached female. In 1973 I reported: "In some areas the idea has spread (with some justification it is sad to report) that it will be much easier to get a supply of pills if you say you are engaged and just about to get married. It would be quite beyond the nerve of most girls to go to a clinic and tell the inquisitor that she had not got a regular chap but feels it would be a sensible precaution to take the pill as she does occasionally have intercourse. . . . It is easy to understand that clinics try to appease their critics by emphasizing that most of the unmarried girls who come for contraceptives are, if not actually engaged to be married, at least involved in a mature and lasting relationship with one partner. From the client's point of view, if she says she is in love, there are smiles all round and much less embarrassment."

Things have got better since then, but there is still room for improvement. From the community point of view, it is particularly important that the result of a casual sexual encounter should not be an unplanned pregnancy. It is some small consolation to observe in Table 9 that the minority who refuse to use any kind of birth control method are rarer in the promiscuous group (18 per cent) than in the other group (26 per cent).

The figures on birth control are reflected in Table 10 which shows that the promiscuous are more likely to be involved in a premarital pregnancy.* The reasons why the promiscuous are less likely to use contraceptives all apply here. As birth control becomes more accepted and accessible, things will get better. But before that happens, this situation will be the indirect cause of an increase in the number of abortions. Promiscuous encounters result in more unplanned pregnancies which in turn will lead to more requests for abortions.

It was noted in Chapter 2 that the fear of promiscuity is often given as the reason for limiting the distribution of contraceptives. The effect is to make the consequences of promiscuity more serious than they need be. It is true that there are a few fanatics who say that a promiscuous girl should reap what she sows, but most of the good people who believe that casual sexual adventures are immoral would not regard a forced marriage, an illegitimate birth or an abortion as appropriate requital. It is

* Table 10 gives the percentages for men and women totalled together. Of course, in the men's cases, it refers to premarital pregnancies experienced by the girl-friends of the men. As it happens there is hardly any difference between the sexes; 31 per cent of the girls and 30 per cent of the girl-friends of the men had premarital pregnancies.

TABLE 10

The number of premarital pregnancies among the
promiscuous group and the others excluding those
who have never had sexual intercourse

Premarital pregnancies	Promiscuous %	Others* %
None	70	83
1	21	14
2 +	9	3
No. (100%)	60	290

* Excluding twenty-six people with no experience of sexual intercourse.

particularly depressing to see that 9 per cent of the promiscuous group had more than one premarital pregnancy. It is a serious criticism of the advice and help given by the medical and social services that this situation should occur more than once in so short a time.

It is always assumed that one of the consequences of promiscuity is venereal disease and therefore we would expect to find that those in the promiscuous group are more likely to be infected. It is difficult to confirm or deny this assumption because the proportion who get a sexually transmitted disease is very small, despite loose talk of a VD epidemic. Over the whole population the chances of getting VD are about 800 to 1. Even in this group of young adults at an age when they are sexually very active, only nineteen (5 per cent) out of 376 had gonorrhoea or syphilis and a further thirteen (3 per cent) probably had some other sexually transmitted disease, while another eighteen (5 per cent) thought they might have had VD but were not sure. As the numbers are small, numerals as well as percentages are as given in Table 11.

It was surprisingly difficult to find out how many in each group had really been infected. There was some confusion and vagueness about what kind of disease they had contracted and what they had done about it. This is partly because some of them had not sought medical advice and partly because the difference between gonorrhoea and other forms of urethritis is not clear to the general public. Another reason why these results lack precision is that there is still a stigma attached to these diseases. In view of the uncertainty about the disease they may have contracted, those who suspected that they might have had VD are put into one of three categories in Table 11.

The table shows that the proportion who were sure they had gonorrhoea or syphilis was equivalent in both groups. Other sexually transmitted diseases (urethritis, crab lice, etc.) appeared to be more common in the promiscuous group. Those who were unsure whether they had been infected or not were slightly less

TABLE 11

Those in the promiscuous group who suspected that they had been infected by a sexually transmitted disease compared with the others

Type of infection	Promiscuous		Others*	
	No.	%	No.	%
Certainly VD	3	5.0	16	5.5
Other diseases	3	5.0	10	3.4
Unconfirmed	2	3.3	16	5.5
Not suspected	52	86.7	248	85.5
Totals	60	100.0	290	99.9

* Excluding twenty-six people with no experience of sexual intercourse.

likely to be promiscuous. But the conclusion to be derived from this table is that the differences are slight. There is some doubt whether a larger sample would show greater differences. A larger sample would probably confirm that the promiscuous are slightly more likely to catch one of the sexually transmitted diseases, but the chances of becoming infected may not be as high as some people are apt to assume. Larger numbers would also probably confirm the indication, suggested in Table 11, that the promiscuous are less confused and are more likely to know when they have got a sexually transmitted disease.

The answers to another question about VD shows that the

promiscuous tended to be better informed about these diseases. Table 12 shows that only a minority in both groups gave a description of the symptoms of gonorrhoea and syphilis which could be rated as completely correct. The informants who had received sex education were more aware of the dangers of VD, but they were no better at recognizing the symptoms. Campaigns against the veneral diseases seem to have made most people aware of its existence, but have not provided them with the necessary information to enable them to recognize it and seek medical treatment.

A third (33 per cent) of the promiscuous group were unable to give a correct description of the symptoms; this compared with more than half (55 per cent) of the others. In this promiscuous group, 21 per cent gave a description of the symptoms which was quite correct, compared with only 3 per cent of the others. In an oblique way this is propitious and a reversal of the usual situation to be found in health education where those who are least likely to seek help are often those who most need

TABLE 12

The symptoms of the venereal diseases as described by the promiscuous group and the others

Rating of the description	Promiscuous %	Others %
Completely correct	21	3
Fairly correct	46	43
Incorrect	18	19
Don't know or no answer	15	36
No. (100%)	60	316

it. Table 12 implies that the promiscuous are more likely to find out about VD. This should be an encouragement to medical and social workers because it suggests that the sexual adventurers, although by no means well informed, do appear to be more likely to heed sensible advice about the venereal diseases. Unfortunately the signs are that the advice they are given is not particularly useful or helpful.

Finally we asked everyone if they always enjoyed sex. In the earlier report it was found that the married were more likely to say they enjoyed sex* and I expected this to be reflected in these figures. But Table 13 shows that there are only slight differences between the two groups and that in general the promiscuous got more pleasure out of their sex lives than the others. In the promiscuous group 56 per cent said they always enjoyed sex compared with 50 per cent of the others; only 2 per cent (one girl) said they rarely or never enjoyed sex compared with 5 per cent (sixteen people) of the others.

Moralists have often claimed that sexual intercourse is only pleasurable when it takes place within marriage, or at the very least, when it is between a man and woman who are in love. These results do not support this claim. Indeed these findings

TABLE 13

The extent of sexual enjoyment in the promiscuous
group compared with the others .

Sexual enjoyment	Promiscuous %	Others* %
Always	56	50
Not always	42	45
Rarely or never	2	5
No. (100%)	60	290

* Excluding twenty-six people with no experience of sexual intercourse.

suggest that over half the group derive a great deal of satisfaction from their promiscuous sex. Such a finding seems to be more in accord with ordinary day-to-day observation; most people must know of occasions in which two people who are not married have obtained intense enjoyment from their sexual relationships, often in the face of censure from family and friends.

* Only 2 per cent of the married found sex unenjoyable compared with 10 per cent of those with steady partners and 15 per cent of those with no regular partners—page 172 of *The Sexual Behaviour of Young Adults*.

Why Are They?

Three questions about the promiscuous have been asked in this chapter. When we asked where they were to be found, it was noted that they were in all sections of society. Although there are undoubtedly some oppressed and disadvantaged people who are promiscuous because they are unable to sustain a permanent relationship, there were others who had maintained an enduring loving relationship in addition to their promiscuous activities. There were some, especially girls, who were socially alienated and felt the need to draw attention to their plight; just as aggression among boys is often attention-seeking, so among girls casual sex may be a disguised plea for help. But although these promiscuously-inclined groups exist, they by no means account for all the promiscuous. Many very promiscuous people never come into contact with police, psychiatrists or social workers.

When we asked who the promiscuous were, we found that their home background was not very different from anyone else's. Only a very few of those in the promiscuous group came from deprived homes or were brought up in damaging circumstances. Many of them were well-educated and holding down good jobs.

In a third section we asked what sort of people the promiscuous were. We found that in general they were quite similar to the other group, although there were some differences. They seemed to be more curious and were more likely to start experimenting at an earlier age. Although they did not have their first experience of intercourse much before the others, they were more likely to have had inceptive experience and to be less naive as teenagers. Paradoxically, their sex lives at the time of the interview were less active, although this is partly accounted for by the larger proportion of married people in the non-promiscuous group. Among the promiscuous, one in three said they wanted more sex, but even in the other group, one in five wanted more, and this is as true of the non-promiscuous women as it is of the men.

The promiscuous were less likely to be regular users of contraceptives, not because they were against birth control in principle, but because conditions and circumstances sometimes made it difficult to have contraceptives available. In addition it was harder for the promiscuous girl to obtain the pill. An inevitable consequence is that the promiscuous are more likely to have an unwanted pregnancy. This is most unfortunate because an unplanned pregnancy is much more serious for a girl without a husband or boy-friend to stand by her.

Not surprisingly there are also signs that the promiscuous were more likely to get VD, although this association is not as obvious as many people assume. But the promiscuous were better informed about the venereal diseases, were more likely to recognize the symptoms and were more likely to go for treatment. Indeed they seemed to be better informed about most sexual matters, but many of them still said they did not know all they needed to know. This is in contrast to the others, who were inclined to think they knew all about sex. Unfortunately several questions at the interview revealed that this confidence was often misplaced.

It is interesting to find that the promiscuous were more reticent when they were asked about the sex lives of their friends. They did not imply either that they were much more successful than their friends, nor that they mixed in a group where everyone was equally promiscuous. They seemed to enjoy their sex lives as much as the others, despite the fact that they must have read many times that little satisfaction is to be derived from promiscuous sex.

In general their answers suggest that they are more gregarious and extrovert than the others. They also appeared to possess a more critical attitude towards the traditional moralities, but it is impossible to say whether this is the cause, or the result, of their promiscuity.

So after where, who and what, we are left with the question why. This is altogether much more difficult. Of course there are some people who will find it easy to supply an answer to this question. Throughout the medical literature it is possible to find quotations which declare that promiscuity is caused by a defect of the personality. For example, Wittkower and Cowan (1944) state that "promiscuity is seldom the result of positive mature sexual interest, but is mainly the result of attempts to relieve acute psychological stress" and conclude that it is a "disorder of emotional development". Watts and Wilson (1945) state that promiscuous men "are immature in attitude and behaviour". In an address to the London Medical Group in 1969, Dr Morton opposed the supply of contraceptive advice to single people: "Such licencing of premarital sexual intercourse seems likely to precipitate emotional complications in the formative years and in the long term the institution of marriage and the family will be threatened."*

But these doctors are making general statements based on observations of a group of mentally disturbed patients who are not typical of all promiscuous people. They are writing about people who have been deprived of love at home and are now desperately looking for affection but find they are unable to respond to it when they find it. Indeed some of them feel compelled to destroy love when it is offered. Medical men, especially psychiatrists, are inclined to make the quite unwarranted assumption that all promiscuous people are like this.

Some doctors see promiscuity as just one symptom of a neurotic condition. There is no doubt that some promiscuous men and women are neurotic and in need of psychiatric help. But this does not justify the inference that all promiscuous people are sick and should be regarded primarily as medical problems.

Reference has been made to the time when it was assumed that homosexuality was solely a medical problem. Homosexuals who seek psychiatric help are of three types : (1) those who have some mental illness, (2) those who have broken down under the strain of the social pressures directed against homosexuality, (3) those who have got into trouble with the law. Psychiatrists do not see typical homosexuals, but only homosexuals in trouble. A comparison between a group of heterosexual psychiatric patients and homosexual psychiatric patients revealed as many similarities as differences, and in the same research (Schofield, 1965) there were many important differences between the group of homosexual patients and a group of homosexuals who had never had psychiatric treatment. Similarly it was once assumed that those who smoked cannabis were sick, but it can be shown (Schofield, 1971) that fundamentally the social aspects are more important than the medical problems.

Promiscuity is usually derided as sinful and immoral, but there are some humane people who suggest that the promiscuous should be treated as sick people rather than criminals. The reclassification of a certain type of behaviour as a disease instead of a sin or a crime may be the sign of a more enlightened approach, like the change of attitude towards madness, once regarded as possession by an evil spirit, or alcoholism, a matter solely for the police until recently. But to describe promiscuity

* *Evening Standard*, 31 January 1969.

as a sickness is to use the term to disguise moral disapproval. It is part of the unfortunate tendency to regard a man as sick because he does not conform.

Those who think of promiscuity as an illness will look for some predisposing psychological cause that will explain why anyone should want more than one sexual partner. An essential component of the medical approach to promiscuity is that it is undesirable and that the patient is cured only when he stops being promiscuous. But the motives are so varied and the circumstances so multifarious that it is difficult to believe that any single cause can provide a satisfactory explanation. The medical profession neither know the cause of promiscuity, nor do they know how to 'cure' it. Most promiscuous people do not feel sick, do not seek treatment, and have never met a psychiatrist. But the idea persists that no one would be promiscuous if there were not something wrong with him.

For research purposes it has been necessary to compare two groups, the promiscuous (i.e. those who have had two or more partners in the last year) and the others (i.e. those who have had one sexual partner in the last year). But both of these groups are heterogeneous. In the promiscuous group there are people who have had only a small amount of sexual experience. The other group contains people who have been very promiscuous in the past but are now married and remain faithful to their spouses. There are all sorts of variations within the two groups and, as we have noted, there are also many similarities. Promiscuous people come from a wide range of backgrounds, classes and circumstances, their activities and opinions vary. It is impossible to say why they are promiscuous. It is inconceivable that one explanation can account for the various people in this group.

Psychiatrists have recognized character defects in some promiscuous people and I have noted certain personality traits in some, but not all, people in this promiscuous group. But there may be other less basic and less complex reasons why a person behaves promiscuously. It may be simply a question of opportunity.

It is no surprise to find that single men and women living away from home are more promiscuous than those who are married or those who are living with their parents. Not only do they have a room where they can take their sexual partners to bed, but they do not have to invent excuses for their spouses or parents to explain away their absences from home. Someone who lives in a large town can carry on his sexual adventures without attracting much attention, but a person living in a small community can soon get a reputation for 'sleeping around'.

It may be stressing the obvious to point out that the more promiscuous are those who have the time to look for willing partners and a place to go to when they find one. But the results of this research indicate that many people are promiscuous during this period when they have this relative freedom, but later on are not unfaithful when they are married. Opportunity is a more convincing explanation in such cases than the notion that the promiscuous suffer from some basic personality defect.

Lack of preparation and inadequate sex education may be another reason why some people are promiscuous. When sex education concentrates on the biological aspects, many people are left with the impression that it is best to leave it all to nature. Romantic stories and chats with friends reinforce the idea that sex is doing what comes naturally and then they find themselves in situations in which sexual intercourse just seems to happen.

Others can easily convince themselves that they are not going to let it happen, and then when it does, they tell themselves that it will not happen again. Much of what young people are told about sexual morality is based on the assumption that they will not have sex before marriage. But all the evidence suggests that most of them will; in my research 71 per cent had premarital sexual intercourse. The result is that the strength of the sexual drive takes many of them by surprise.

Many of the girls and some of the boys suppose that real sexual desire will only arise when they have fallen in love. Consequently they are quite unprepared when they suddenly become aware of their own intense sexual response in an intimate situation which they thought they could control. A typical remark (from a girl in the report by Morton Williams and Hindell, 1972) is: "They never told us how much we would want to do it." When these young people find they have given in to sexual desire, they look upon themselves as irredeemably promiscuous.

In the old days the young blade went to a prostitute because he was not allowed to have sex with his girl-friend. Today premarital sex has become more acceptable, but for most people it is only sanctioned as a prelude to marriage. Some boys and girls do not want to give such a firm undertaking when they are still young and thus feel less committed if they distribute their sexual favours more widely.

My own view is that the search for the cause of promiscuity is likely to prove unrewarding because this kind of behaviour appears to appeal to so many different types of people. It is probably more sensible to think of it as a preferred activity— some men and women want more sexual partners than others. As with any preferred activity, anyone is entitled to ask if this kind of behaviour is harmful. This question will be asked and answered in Chapter 5. It would be better to concentrate on alleviating the distress caused by the cases when it is harmful, than to continue the search for a single all-embracing cause.

One thing is certain: it has been going on for a long time and it is not likely than anyone or anything can put a stop to it overnight. At one time there were restrictions against fornication and adultery for good economic reasons (described in Chapter 5). Now the economic situation has changed and the restrictions are not so essential, but there are still strong moral objections to promiscuity.

The widespread use of the pill and other female methods of contraception has brought about important changes in the sexual relationships between man and woman. The traditional attitude used to picture man as the hunter and provider, while woman was the mate and the child bearer. But now there are signs that woman is becoming the huntress. She is no longer content to wait like the blushing heroine of romantic novels.

Among couples who are regularly having intercourse (whether they are married or not), sometimes it is the woman who takes the initiative and there are men who cannot stand the pace. Over a third of my research group said there were occasions when they had intended to have intercourse but were unable to get sexually aroused. This had happened to more men (39 per cent) than women (32 per cent). Furthermore it need not be emphasized that the consequences are rather more serious if this happens to a man because a woman can often feign arousal. Such a failure is also more deflating to the man's image of himself. A doctor in a university medical unit has said recently that he now sees hundreds of men who complain that they cannot cope with the demands of their girl-friends.

The modern generation of young women are not content to be sex objects whose role is to provide satisfaction for the men merely as a favour. They are much more aware of the possibilties of female sexual arousal. In my research group 10 per cent of the women said they felt sexually frustrated. In earlier times it might have been considered unladylike for a woman to say that she was entitled to enjoy sex, but the notion that strong sexual impulses are an exclusively male prerogative no longer stands up to scientific examination.

As these traditional attitudes change, it is inevitable that the old idea that promiscuity is permissible for men but not women is steadily dwindling. Women ask: if a man goes out for a bit on the side, why shouldn't a girl look for a handsome young man to have some fun with? Furthermore, girls now demand a higher standard of sexual performance from their sexual partners.

This enquiry into the character and personality of those who have had two or more partners in the last year reveals that there is no such thing as a promiscuous type. It is more useful to regard promiscuity as an activity which thousands of quite different people take part in at some period of their lives. The number who are found to be promiscuous at any one time is a fairly small proportion of any sample obtained for research purposes. But this should not disguise the fact that this proportion, small though it may be, amounts to many people scattered over the whole population—probably more than 4 million. (The proportion in my sample was 16 per cent. A very low estimate of the sexually active population in this country would be about 25 million. This suggests that at least 4 million people have been promiscuous during the last year, and many more have been promiscuous at some time in their lives.) When such large numbers are involved, it is not really surprising that it is impossible to give a psychiatric diagnosis, nor is it helpful to attempt a description of the typical characteristics to be expected in a promiscuous person.

CHAPTER 5

THE EFFECTS

Social Consequences
Do we have to fear promiscuity? If, as seems likely, there is
going to be more of it, we should try to assess the consequences,
first to society, and second to the individual. This is not an easy
task for we have all been brought up to regard promiscuity as
undesirable and there has been hardly any research into its
effects.

Although promiscuity is now regarded as primarily a moral
problem, the original objections to it were more social and
economic. Illegitimacy in the past was a personal tragedy for
the mother and an economic disaster in poor village and rural
communities. If the father of the child was not the husband, all
sorts of problems of succession were created and the bastard
child was not entitled to any of the family's land, a very serious
drawback in a subsistence economy. If the mother was not
married, this placed a heavy burden on the relatives who had
to look after her and her child.

The only stable institution for providing care for children
was the family; this is true for most of the poor communities in
the developing countries and indeed for the majority of the
earth's inhabitants. All sex outside the monogamous marriage
was a threat to the family, and thus to the stability of the community. Therefore it was essential to maintain strict control over
all matters to do with sex. There had to be harsh laws against
sexual intercourse with anyone before marriage and with no one
except the husband after marriage. There were very severe
punishments, including the death penalty in some societies,
against infidelity.

This strict discipline was reinforced by making all human
sexuality taboo. Its existence was kept secret from children and
the subject was never mentioned in polite adult society. Silence
and punishment created a fear of sex, which was thought to be

beneficial to the community because it helped to restrain young people from indulging in any kind of sexual activity.

The only sex relations that could be permitted were within marriage and there was no need to discuss it, husband and wife could find out about that in private. Thus privacy became another support for the strict disciplinary code and all public demonstrations of sexual feelings or actions were deemed to be immodest. Some religions, notably the Roman Catholic faith, took the next logical step and taught that sexual intercourse could only be justified if the intention was to produce children.

What was originally an economic necessity and a way of preventing social and personal catastrophies became a complex ethical system of pre-emptions, prohibitions, intolerance and taboos. The contribution of the Church was to give divine sanction to this strict regulatory system. The taboo on sex was declared to be holy and eternal; any infraction against this moral code was a grave sin.

In the past the Church and the law were closely interlinked, so the sexual code was bolstered by strong legal sanctions. Anything that threatened the monogamous marriage was forbidden. Adultery has been a crime in the legal history of most of the countries of Western civilization. There were laws against fornication, divorce, birth control, abortion, homosexuality and, of course, promiscuity. Sex was a disruptive influence and had to be kept within strict bounds.

These moral, religious, psychological and legal prohibitions had two further developments of some importance. The first was the creation of the double standard of morality. The second was the evolution of romantic love.

Sexual abstinence has always been particularly important to the woman; she is the one who will produce the illegitimate child when things go wrong. If some of the men occasionally went to prostitutes or loose women, that could be overlooked because it was not such a threat to the stability of the family. So gradually there developed this double standard and promiscuity became a male indulgence. No wonder it is the women who are against promiscuity in every opinion poll and attitude survey. For hundreds of years promiscuity has been forbidden to women. Until quite recently it was exclusively a male prerogative; the nymphomaniac was a very rare animal indeed; even the courtesans had sex for another purpose, not because they enjoyed it.

Unfortunately this double standard still exists today. You still hear young men talking about 'pulling birds' and thinking about girls, not as companions, but as scalps to be collected. In the old days a woman's virginity used to be described as a castle to be stormed. More recently it has been thought of as one in a series, like a photograph or a badge; the more the male could collect, the more he could boast about it. It was these same men who insisted that the girl they married should be a virgin and, curiously, many women agreed with these attitudes.

In the opinion of most men there were two kinds of women; girls for sex and girls for marriage. There are welcome signs that this double standard of sexual morality is on the decline, partly because of the improvement in contraceptives for the female, and particularly because women have now become powerful enough to protest about these inequalities. Or to put it another way, there is no reason why promiscuity should continue to be exclusively a male prerogative.

The other development was the glorification of romantic love, which first appeared at the end of the eleventh century and did not become a social force until the sixteenth century. Although both Chaucer and Shakespeare regarded it as a mixed blessing, today it is regarded with religious fervour. Not only is it the solution to all problems (love conquers all) but the desire to be in love (falling in love with love) becomes more important than the personality of the beloved. Not only does love make the world go round, but is approved by the authorities and blessed by religious leaders because it preserves and sustains the stability of the family.

The evolution of this very specialized sort of love deserves a section to itself later in this chapter. The relevant point to note here is that it is an important part of the concept that romantic love is pure, but sex is unclean. Sexual desire can sully the aura of romance. This perpetuates the idea that women are not supposed to have sexual feelings, and they are certainly not meant to enjoy sexual intercourse. This may sound like an exaggeration, but many of the girls in my research did not expect to enjoy the sexual side of their marriage but looked upon it as a way of giving pleasure to their husbands. Older women can still be heard discussing their husbands in these terms : "He's very good, really. He doesn't trouble me more than once a fortnight." Most girls were brought up to expect nothing of sex and some even came to fear it.

It follows that if sex was not to be enjoyed, there was no point in promiscuity. Furthermore it became the antithesis of romantic love which was the most desirable goal of all. So promiscuity is regarded not only as anti-social and anti-family, but also as anti-woman and anti-love.

The moral opposition to promiscuity was based on economic reasoning, right and sensible for those times and in those circumstances. Sexual freedom would have exposed the women to the disgrace of illegitimacy. To a certain extent women are still exposed to this danger, but illegitimacy is no longer thought to be such a disaster. The state is now prepared to give economic aid to the unmarried mother (albeit, not much in case it would seem to be condoning promiscuity) and a woman can now choose to bring up her child in a fatherless family.

Originally it was the grandparents who had to look after the illegitimate child. A later solution was to force the mother to marry if the father could be identified. So the custom of forced marriage grew up "to give the child a name" and "to make an honest woman" of the mother, whether or not the couple were suited to each other.

The pressures from parents to opt for this unfortunate solution are still strong even today. Over a third of teenage marriages take place when the bride is pregnant. Even in the new drug-orientated communes in America, there seems to be an understanding between the couples that should pregnancy occur marriage should follow (Speck, 1972). But people are beginning to realize that these forced marriages often end in the divorce courts. A study of parish registers from 1540 to 1820 suggests that "roughly one fifth of all brides in the earlier centuries (i.e. 1540–1700) and two fifths of all brides in the later centuries were pregnant". (Hair, 1970). Today it is 8 per cent and the percentage is going down each decade.

The historical arguments against premarital promiscuity are not convincing any more, and the moral arguments depend upon earlier circumstances which no longer apply. Extramarital promiscuity can still be thought of as a threat to family life and this is now considered in the next section.

The Threat to the Family

Sex before marriage is accepted in many quarters where only a few years ago it was thought to be evil; but sex by married men or women with partners other than their spouses is still quite unacceptable to most people. One reason for this is that premarital sex may help to cement a loving relationship, but extramarital sex is likely to lead to the break-up of a relationship. This is still true today and adultery is usually thought of as a sufficient reason for ending a marriage. Ironically until the divorce laws were changed one partner of the marriage often had to pretend to commit adultery by arranging to be caught in a compromising situation in order to put an end to a marriage that had broken down for non-sexual reasons.

In the past the husband used to prohibit sexual relations outside marriage because this was the best guarantee that he was the father of her children. But modern contraceptives make this less necessary and in any case the integrity of the family cannot be preserved solely by sexual prohibitions.

Nowadays the biggest fear is that the husband or wife will discover more sexual satisfaction outside the home and this will lead to the break-up of the marriage. Often there are other reasons apart from sexual satisfaction that persuades one partner to end the marriage and sex is merely the symbolic reason. When there are other weighty reasons besides sex, it is possible that the end of the marriage is the only workable solution, but it is worth asking whether sexual infidelity by itself need lead to the breakdown of a marriage.

Even in the recent past most people would not hesitate to affirm that adultery was sufficient reason for divorce. The logic of this is not altogether clear. There must be few marriages where more than 2 per cent of the time is spent in having sexual intercourse. If the marriage is satisfactory in every other way, it is open to doubt if an extramarital adventure is a good reason to end it.

We tend to assume that sexual compatibility is an essential part of marriage, but this may not be true. The reason for this assumption is the evidence derived from investigations on broken marriages or marriages in trouble. But we do not know much about the sexual component in marriages that remain intact. We do know that the frequency of sexual intercourse declines steadily after the first few years of marriage (Kinsey, 1953) and this decline can only be partly attributed to the male's decline in biological capacity. We also know that as sexual passion cools, sex declines in importance and other forms of gratification become more important in a marriage. "Most of the time sex is really a relatively docile beast," say Simon and Gagnon (1970). Perhaps we are exaggerating the part that sex plays in a happy marriage. If so, we must be careful not to allow a casual sexual encounter to break up an otherwise satisfactory relationship.

Sometimes extramarital affairs are very highly charged and all the romantic passionate years are experienced again in these illicit affairs. The partner's wife or husband rediscovers sexual attractiveness and seems to become younger in mind and body. This rejuvenation might be a welcome stimulus, bringing a new impetus into the life of the individual, but in nearly all cases it is regarded as a threat by the spouse because the expected outcome is to split up the home and family.

Logically a promiscuous married partner is less of a risk to the family than one who is having an affair with one other person. The man or woman who occasionally has extramarital sex may need the stability of his home. But the married partner who is having an affair often asks the spouse for a divorce in order to be 'free' to make love with another. In a sense this is a defence against the stigma of promiscuity.

In fact all the evidence suggests that there is a very large number of people who find it difficult to maintain a high level of sexual performance with a single partner over a long period of time. This may not matter for some of them because sexual fulfilment may be relatively unimportant and other areas of life give greater satisfaction. But this is not the case for everyone. It has been said that about half of all married males and a quarter of all married females will engage in extramarital sexual activity at one time or another (Gagnon, 1974). It can be argued that the ability of a married couple to tolerate an extramarital sexual relationship is a demonstration of confidence in the marriage and of the futility of possessiveness. Some even maintain that wife swapping and other non-secret extramarital experiences help to strengthen the marriage, although it must be said there is little real evidence to support these views.

In any case the whole attitude to family life has changed radically in the last few years. It is no longer accepted without question that family life is the only satisfactory way to bring up children. Most people would argue that it is the best way, especially in the extended family where the child grows up among several adults of varying ages, as they did in the past and still do in some communities, for example in many Jewish and Mormon families. There are fewer advantages in the smaller family of two parents and children isolated from other people in little houses in crowded urban conditions. Dr Ross Speck, an American psychiatrist who has specialised in family therapy, thinks that "the family as a functioning, nurturing, joy-producing, sensation seeking, sexually fulfilling, God-experiencing phenomenon is hopelessly outdated".

Not everyone would go that far, but as new psychological knowledge makes us more aware of how important aspects of our personalities are shaped during our early childhood in the home, at the same time we are beginning to realize that the typical urban family of Western civilization is by no means the ideal foundation for rearing children. It is often too restricted and too narrow; and much research has shown that family history repeats itself—mothers who are illegitimate are more likely to have illegitimate children (Krellin *et al.*, 1971), men and women who were abused by their parents are more likely to harm their own children (SSMAC, 1971*), parents from very large families are likely to have large families themselves (Thompson and Illsley, 1969), criminal families produce delinquents (West, 1967).

In the Ciba symposium on *The Family and its Future* (1970), Robin Fox remarks: "The failures are probably simply those families which refuse to ignore the natural conflicts inherent in the situation, while the successes are the families with the greatest capacity for collective self-delusion." Even a supporter of family life like Morton (1971) writes: "The prospects for the family do not appear inviting ... already there is talk that the nuclear family constricts the development of children and as such is an anachronism." Dissatisfaction with the restrictions of the modern family has led to new experiments based on the old idea of communal living, like the kibbutzim in Israel and the youth communes that have started here and in America, where a small number of people of similar age and outlook live together and share their experiences with each other. Many commentators

* *The Battered Child*, a report by a working group of the Scottish Standing Medical Advisory Committee, 1971.

lament the decline of the family as they knew it when they were children, but there is no reason to suppose that marriage and family life are institutions that are perfect and will never change.

Kanowitz (1969) has pointed out that our idea of a family as a group is only recent history. "Originating in the fifteenth and sixteenth centuries (depending on the economic development of the region), it reached its full expression no earlier than the seventeenth century, and all the hoary traditions we surround it with can't be much more than three or four hundred years old, if that." O'Neil (1967) suggests that "the Puritans were among the first to adopt the conjugal family system. It was their rejection of society in favour of the family that helped make them so unpopular in England". Similar criticisms are made today about Indian and Pakistani immigrant groups.

The idealized version of the contemporary family as pictured by politicians, churchmen, advertisers and others who mould public opinion, is little more than a fantasy in which children show reverential respect for the parents, accepting their authority, while all parents are seen as stern but wise. Any discrepancy is compared invidiously with this ideal family which has almost ceased to exist in the face of new ideas about child rearing and the emergence of a powerful youth culture.

One has only to think of the wife's position now and a hundred years ago to realize that marriage is not a changeless institution. The Christian marriage of the nineteenth century in which the wife and children were hardly more than chattels would be considered quite un-Christian today. There is nothing in the Christian religion that supports the idea of marriage as an eternal state. St Paul approved marriage only because it was better than fornication. "But if they cannot contain, let them marry : for it is better to marry than to burn." (I Corinthians 7 :9). Indeed our attitude towards family life cannot be supported by anything that Jesus said in the Bible. On the contrary He seems to urge the abandonment of close family ties in favour of a far broader concept of communal living.

At present the idea of several families living and sharing one house does not appeal to many people. Most would prefer the nuclear family—mother and father bringing up their children away from others. Most psychologists would prefer the extended family where the children are reared in a close relationship with several adults—grandmothers, grandfathers, uncles, aunts, nephews and nieces. Neither of these methods need necessarily last a lifetime and sexual fidelity need not be an essential part of the arrangement as it had to be in the past.

Despite frequent statements to the contrary, it is perfectly possible for two people to be good parents and provide a loving home for their children without having to keep the marriage vows of love, honour and obey till death do us part. Child rearing has nothing to do with sexual morality. Kathrin Perutz (1972) writes: "I have married friends who are both homosexual, though each is of a different sex. . . . Both have had affairs with people of their own sex, and each now has one particular lover. They are more fond of each other than most couples I've seen, and their teenage daughter loves them happily and admires them. . . . She enjoys their friends and is closely attached to their lovers, who are part of the family. She's a secure and happy child."

Some people are unsuitable for marriage. Almost everyone can probably think of at least one person who should be positively discouraged from marrying. The idea that love will solve all marital problems has been the cause of many misalliances. The happiest marriages are those which imitate the conditions of friendship rather than those of passion. But this does not mean that those who are unsuitable for marriage must lead a life without sex.

Some people may be suitable for marriage but not for monogamy. For some a permanent monogamous relationship is the only one that is comfortable for their emotional stability. For others this would be quite unsatisfactory and it would be very difficult to convince them that it is natural to be committed to one partner for life. It may unnecessarily warp some people's personalities to force them into a strict monogamous state.

Some of these people will want and expect variety before marriage, but will settle down to some rather more prolonged relationship during the child rearing years, then later will move on to new lovers and friends. This is probably a sensible solution, but it cannot be proved that sexual infidelity even during the years when the children are growing up will necessarily have a bad effect on their development. What is more likely to be deleterious is the break-up of the family home because one or other of the parents wants to feel free to have sex with someone else.

In present circumstances possessiveness and jealousy are still an almost inevitable part of extramarital sex. Perhaps we are putting too high a price on fidelity. It may still hurt and offend if one's married partner is promiscuous from time to time, but it is not a sufficient reason to abandon wife, husband, children, home, comfort, or even the possibility of a loving and placid life later on when the erring spouse tires of sexual variety.

The Consequences for the Individual

The historical background to promiscuity still has a powerful effect on our attitudes. Promiscuous activities are deviant, using this word in the sociological sense, meaning they arouse social hostility. Consequently promiscuous acts tend to be secret and furtive.

In addition there are other more personal consequences, the most obvious of which is the possibility of catching one of the venereal diseases. There are many reasons for the rise in the VD statistics and promiscuity is only one of them. But it is true that the more promiscuous are more likely to be infected and this is something that should be brought to the notice of young people. Even so it is more sensible to blame the disease than the activity. Much more could be done to decrease the VD rate, both in the area of health education and in medical research. The amount of time and money spent on research in venereology compares unfavourably with the investment put into finding cures for less prevalent but more respectable diseases.

Another possible physical risk is cancer of the cervix (considered in detail in Chapter 6). Some of the evidence does suggest that early and frequent sexual activities (but not specifically promiscuous sex) does increase the risk. Now that routine tests for cancer of the cervix, including a follow-up check three to five years later, are part of the National Health Service for women over thirty-five with three or more children, it should not be difficult to start to produce research results so that factual information about the extent of this risk can be obtained without delay.

From time to time it is reported in the press that promiscuity may be the cause of other physical ill-effects, but there is very little evidence to support these allegations. As Dr Comfort showed in his book, *The Anxiety Makers*, it has long been the custom of doctors to find spurious medical dangers in immoral activities, such as the harmfulness of masturbation or the debilitating effects of fornication.

Of course it is always possible to find isolated examples of individuals who suffer because they are inordinately promiscuous. Too much of almost anything is likely to be harmful, whether it is excessive alcohol, hash, food or exercise. The same may be true of an immoderate amount of sexual activity, although this is unlikely to happen to a man because he will become incapable before impairment. The abuse of sex, like the abuse of anything else, can bring about adverse consequences. But paradoxically the risk of physical damage is small because the abuse leads to a diminution of the sex drive, and ultimately to weariness and boredom.

The relationship between promiscuity and psychopathology must be viewed with great caution. The term *sexual psychopath* became fashionable in psychiatric circles a decade ago and even became enshrined in some state laws in America, but it is a very inexact term. As a clinical entity it does not exist and it is really a term to denote moral and legal disapproval. Many psychiatrists regard promiscuity as a sign of psychopathology, so it is not surprising that they find that one is the cause of the other.

Although most psychiatric illnesses seem to be associated with a reduction in sexual activity, some people with personality disturbances are very promiscuous. This may be because they are fearful of any kind of human relationship or because they have a destructive urge to reject any demonstration of kindness. For such people promiscuity may be the only kind of sexual activity they are capable of and the alternative would be to deprive them of any sexual outlet. But it does not follow from this that because promiscuous behaviour is the only outlet for some, that all promiscuity is pathological. There are many cases where promiscuity appears to be compatible with full mental health.

The medical approach is that the patient is ill as long as he continues to be promiscuous. Therefore the doctor looks for some psychological trait to explain why these sick men and women behave in this way. But it would be very hard to find a common personality factor among all the people who are and have been promiscuous. Sheer numbers make it very unlikely that any general personality type could be identified. If promiscuity is a pathological condition, then it must be one of the most common psychological disorders known. It would be an illness from which many millions of men and women were suffering and would constitute a far greater health problem than schizophrenia.

Some people are lonely, or sexually sick, or unable to support a close emotional relationship. These people need help, not condemnation. If they are depraved, it is because they have been deprived. Promiscuity may be a symptom of their unhappy state, but it is not the cause.

Stress is the cause of some mental breakdowns and it can often be the result of strong feelings of guilt. Some doctors have said that promiscuity may not be a serious psychiatric illness in the strictest sense, but it is the cause of much suffering because of these guilt feelings. It is still true that many people, especially girls, will go to a great deal of trouble to avoid being labelled as promiscuous. It is not unusual for a girl to agree to have intercourse with a boy providing he promises not to tell anyone. This is partly because she is ashamed of having given in to sexual desire, which she is taught is unladylike, but also because such a reputation would prejudice her chances of getting married; there are still men who want to marry a virgin, even when their own sexual activities make it more and more difficult to find one.

As promiscuous behaviour often involves evasions, lies and deceit, it is liable to bring regrets and guilt feelings in its train. But it is clear that it is the attitude of society that is the cause of these guilt feelings, not the activity itself. The same thing used to be said about women who had an abortion. The medical establishment always insisted that a woman who had undergone an abortion was very likely to suffer from serious guilt feelings. Now that social disapproval and legal condemnation have decreased, the whole theory that it has a bad psychological effect on the woman is open to doubt.

If public attitudes to the promiscuous individual were to change, then regrets and feelings of guilt would diminish. Such a change would not, of course, take place with the blessing of religious leaders and other moral authorities. They rely upon social disapproval to keep promiscuity in check, and it certainly does have this effect overtly, if not always covertly. Whatever may happen behind closed doors, the vast majority publicly voice their strong disapproval of promiscuous behaviour. This is a perfectly sensible method of social control, and in these circumstances much to be preferred to legal control. But it is also a fact that social disapproval of a fairly common activity does lead to a large amount of guilt, distress and mental conflict. In the final section of this chapter we ask whether this kind of social hostility might be doing more harm than good.

Those who claim that promiscuous activities result in guilt feelings and distress, often use a contradictory argument against the same activities. It is said that promiscuity is habit-forming. It is not suggested that it is addictive, like heroin or tobacco, but it is alleged that it is possible to set up some kind of psychological dependence. It is difficult to know what people mean when they talk about psychological dependence. Usually the term is used in the sense that individuals are upset if they are deprived of something they like very much, such as tea, television or dancing—anything that gives them pleasure. To suggest that people develop a psychological dependence on promiscuity is similar to the argument sometimes used against homosexuality— that homosexual behaviour will inhibit the development of heterosexuality; this seems to assume that people will not have sexual intercourse because homosexual activities are so much more exciting—an assumption that most people would wish to dispute.

An extension of this argument is that people who are promiscuous get so used to it that they become incapable of being faithful when they fall in love. Is it expecting too much of a person to make an untroubled shift from sex-as-fun to sex as a demonstration of love in marriage, when the same bodily responses are activated at one time to express simple pleasure, and at another to express an altogether much more profound emotional bond? The argument carries some weight, but most of us are used to making a similar tactile gesture mean different things in different circumstances; for example, the kiss on greeting friends, the kiss among members of the same family, and the erotic kiss between lovers. Indeed romantic writers have often proclaimed that one of the mysteries of being in love is how ordinary acts are transformed into sensuous delights.

In fact there is no evidence that people who are promiscuous for a period of their lives will continue to act in this way. In the follow-up of my research on the sexual behaviour of young people, the promiscuous boys and girls aged eighteen were seen again at the age of twenty-five; those who were promiscuous when they were teenagers were just as likely as the others to have got married, and they were neither less nor more faithful as young adults.

There are many who argue that promiscuous activities should be condemned because they are so much less satisfactory than sexual intercourse within marriage with a beloved partner. As one of them writes in the Longford Report on Pornography : "Sex only works properly if the person you are having it with is someone you care so deeply about that you will stay around to raise the children who may come. Anyone who doesn't know that doesn't know about sex." Despite these strong words, there are people who seem to prefer promiscuous sex to fidelity, as everyone knows. Even more confusing, there are numerous examples of people who are positively and sincerely in love with one person and have sexual intercourse with others.

It is a strange philosophy to maintain that promiscuous sex is less than the best and therefore wrong. If those activities which do not measure up to the highest standards were forbidden, there would be many things that we would have to do without. In fact we go through life accepting without complaint things that are less than the best because to do so is quicker, cheaper or more economically viable. No one should be discouraged from seeking out the best, but it is merely idealism to suggest that all sexual stimulation should be forbidden unless it is between two people who are really in love. If promiscuous sex were as inferior as the moralists would have us believe, the problem would not arise because no one would want to bother with it.

Another very insistent group maintain that promiscuity has a dehumanizing effect. David Holbrook writes : "This exploitation of 'sex' should surely be seen, like all other indecencies of hate, as belonging to a tendency towards dehumanization that threatens those values by which alone we can hope to survive and find a new sense of the meaning of being human." In a sex education book, a tutor at a college of education writes : "Sexual intercourse without true love is cold, callous and cruel. It is abusing another person to use her body. It is exploiting another human being for your own gratification. It is taking God's most precious gift of love and trampling it in the dust." It is difficult to comprehend that this is a description of two people who find each other sexually attractive. But this is what it is, because apart from prostitution and rape, promiscuous sex is a mutual sharing of excitement and pleasure.

When people write about 'using' another person just to gratify a physical urge, it is hard to see if the words are intended to be anything more than abusive. Sex is usually more enjoyable when it is done with someone else. The same is true of most leisure activities. If you want a game of tennis, you have to find someone to play with. You are not 'using' your opponent just to provide you with physical sensations. You hope you will both derive mutual enjoyment from the game, just as you do when you have sexual intercourse. Promiscuity is a social activity involving two people in a close relationship, even if there is no commitment.

Puritanical traditions assume that sexual desire is egotistical and must be tamed or controlled. But experience suggests that sexual pleasure is often mutually satisfying. In intimate sexual activities the distinction between giving and receiving is blurred or obliterated. Wilheim Reich believed that an individual could not experience full orgasm until he had learnt how to give himself as an act of unconscious selflessness.

Some people go further and say that sex is a great way of getting to know people. In bed a close intimate relationship may be established which, if not abused, may lead to friendship and, in some cases, even to love. This argument will be rejected by many people, but the idea of sex leading eventually to love is no more absurd than the opposite theory of love at first sight. If the word is to mean anything at all, love must be more than outward appearances, which is all one can judge at first sight. The individual is much more likely to reveal his real personality during the intimacies of a sexual relationship.

It is true, of course, that more often than not casual sexual encounters lead to nothing resembling love, and may result in disappointment, especially if one partner is more emotionally involved than the other. But even in this situation the disappointment is unlikely to be traumatic. On the level of personal relationships, a broken engagement or the end of a close friendship must be a far more serious trauma than the regrets experienced when a casual affair collapses.

Of course there are people who are selfish in bed without consideration for their sexual partner, but this is just as likely to happen in the marriage bed. People can be tricked or forced into having sexual intercourse but this is not promiscuity; it is deception or violence, either of which are to be deplored in sexual activities, as in any other type of activity.

It is reasonable to assume that in most promiscuous encounters, both people find each other sexually attractive. Far from using another person's body for self-gratification, both are experiencing the joy of giving pleasure as well as receiving it.

In the nature of things, promiscuity is nearly always a two-way activity, if only because it is not much fun when it is not. It is strange that the moralists fail to notice that their dire predictions do not seem to come true. Most promiscuous people do not regret it; on the contrary they thoroughly enjoy it. The claim that sexual pleasure is only obtainable when accompanied by love is manifestly untrue as anyone who has his eyes open must know.

Of course things can go wrong and there are risks to be taken, as there are in all intense physical or emotional activities. More time should be spent trying to eliminate these risks, than in trying to deny people the right to choose their own particular form of sexual satisfaction.

Romantic Love

Of course love is a word which is used for many different states of mind. The Christian idea of love, of giving and sharing, need not be restricted to one person or limited to one's marriage partner. There is also love for parents and family, love for dear friends including those of one's own sex, a devotion to dogs, cats and other pets, and some saintly people seem to radiate a spiritual love for mankind. The kind of love described in this section is like none of these.

Everyone knows about romantic love. It is projected by the media with all possible persuasiveness. It may sometimes be embellished with rosebuds, satin and lace, but it is a dedicatedly selfish attitude of mind based upon sexual passion.

Although there is never a lack of lavish praise and even the authorities smile benevolently upon romantic love, in reality it is the cause of quite as much misery as happiness. Some of the most difficult problems encountered early in marriage are caused by the rosy idea that love solves everything. Some of the most stupid acts are done in the name of love. Some of the most pitiless cruelties are the result of vanished love.

The myth of romantic love is to be found in the make-believe world of women's magazines and popular romantic novels. Although often a subject for jokes, romantic fiction should be taken seriously. "Twenty-five million new romantic novels a year are sold in this country" and "a recent survey showed that people who buy romances themselves lend them to five or six friends to read". (Anderson, 1974). All this in addition to library readership and the mass circulation women's magazines. So romantic fiction is still an important influence on the thoughts of millions of women. This is where they get some of their ideas about what to expect from and contribute to a loving sexual relationship.

These stories are more than escapist fantasies. They are a substitute for sex. No real man or woman can live up to this dreamy fantasy in which sexual passion would interrupt the romantic idyll. The romantic fiction is backed up by the advertisements in magazines and elsewhere. These promise that a girl only has to wear these corsets to be desired, only has to put on the latest lipstick to be kissed, only has to use luxurious bath salts to get a date with Prince Charming. It is often said that the advertising agents use sex to sell, but it is usually fantasy sex.

Sex is quite at variance with this romantic notion of love. To feel sexual desire would be shameful. Girls who have sexual desires are lustful, and will end up sleeping around with anyone. No wonder this romantic myth is fostered by the establishment. It strongly supports the only morally acceptable sequence; romantic bliss, followed by marriage (or at least commitment), and then sexual intercourse.

So most girls and many boys wait and hope for the once-only blinding revelation that heralds the dawn of true love bliss. If it does not come the young person feels deprived; in the words of the song, "You're Nobody Till Somebody Loves You". When it does happen, the romantic image cannot be sustained for long. It soon becomes obvious that the fantasy merchants in the advertising world do not inhabit the same world as the ordinary working girl.

The origins of romantic love do not go back very far. Before the eleventh century sexual passion was an affliction; the bane of love was a subject for mirth. "Don't visit your mistress on her birthday," Ovid advised. "It will cost you too much." Then in the twelfth century the idea of courtly love appeared in French poetry; these poems celebrate a specialized sort of love expressed as courtesy, adultery and the religion of love.

It is important to note that this kind of love was first associated with adultery. Marriage in a feudal society had very little to do with love and the wife was nothing much more than a piece of her husband's property. In a society where marriage was utilitarian, the idealization of love had to be about adultery. But by the end of the eighteenth century romance had gained the approval of the church and the establishment so that it became respectable and sanctified as a prelude to marriage.

With the rise of the novel the course of true love was shown to run untrue, but it nearly always triumphed in the end. For one man there must be one woman, but as Jane Austen and her successors in the nineteenth century have shown, there would be complications if the practicalities of class and property were flouted. Even if every story did not end with the lovers living happily ever after, there grew up a formula for the novel, which included the assumption that romantic love must lead to marriage, or tragedy.

The romantic myth encourages the belief that love swoops upon powerless men and women and consumes them. When people say they have 'fallen hopelessly in love', they indicate that they have abdicated responsibility. They had no choice. They were transported into a romantic state by processes over which they exerted only a very limited amount of control. This in no way makes the love less true or less romantic. Furthermore this irrational and inconsequential behaviour gives rise to warm social approval—all the world loves a lover. Indeed many people frown upon a marriage of convenience because it is thought to be too closely calculated and too unromantic.

The power of romantic love is also used as an excuse for falling out of love, as well as into it. The expression *to fall in love* is closely analogous to the phrase *to fall sick*. A person may even be *love-sick*. There is this implicit assumption that he is not to be blamed for his feelings, nor indeed for his choice of beloved. The point is neatly made in this conversation piece by Leonard Cohen.

Diane : *It's not his fault.*
Mary : *Not his fault?*
Diane : *He fell in love.*
Mary : *Fell in LOVE?*
Diane : *Yes.*
Mary : *With someone else?*
Diane : *Yes.*
Mary : *He fell out of love with you?*

Diane : *I suppose so.*
Mary : *That's terrible.*
Diane : *He said he couldn't help it.*
Mary : *Not if it's love.*
Diane : *He said it was.*
Mary : *Then he couldn't help it.*

Luckily, romantic love does not last for long in most cases. If the popular songs and stories are to be believed, lovers think of nothing else; their judgement is impaired and they have no time to think about work or any of the ordinary things in life. If everybody was to fall madly in love, civilization would collapse. Romantic love, as pictured in songs and stories, is ridiculous, unrealistic, egocentric, and certainly not an emotion upon which to base a serious relationship with far-reaching commitments.

Of course it is not denied that romantic love may lead on to a more satisfying and enduring kind of love. Often it does. Many people have successfully transformed an intense romantic passion into a mature lasting sexual relationship, an investment in another person from which the return is fulfilment, security and satisfaction.

Perhaps the reason it so often does not work is that romantic love seems to imply ownership—I love you therefore you are all mine. This is likely to lead to sexual jealousy or possessiveness. So either the roof caves in on the affair and it ends in tears, or the partners patch up a compromise with their own disappointments and tacitly agree to work it out together. When sexual passion dies, it can give way to something more permanent— boredom.

Sex educators never fail to point out the dangers of promiscuity and VD, but only rarely are the pupils warned about the drawbacks of romantic love. As well as disillusion and heartbreak, nastier pitfalls can follow, such as possession, domination, passivity, slavery, coercion, or something closely akin to statutory rape.

Such warnings would not be believed and would sound like profanity because romantic love has become a religion, so people worship love and the idea of being in love. In fact there are definite restrictions to romanticism. It is only acceptable to the church and establishment if it leads to marriage. False starts and trial runs are not sanctioned. There are also recognized age limits. Girls and boys now come to sexual maturation in the early teens, but love is not supposed to occur until later. Love between a young man and an older woman who "might be his mother" is frowned upon, but love between a young woman and a man who is her father's age seems to be more acceptable.

The ideal combination is thought to be when the man is a few years older than the woman. But this is not a good solution for the community. As women live longer than men, it implies that there will be many widows. This combination also conflicts with the finding (Kinsey, 1948, 1953) that men are at the height of their sexual powers around the age of twenty, but women's sexual desires are at their strongest ten to twenty years later. But this is to apply logic to a situation where rational thinking is notably absent.

Indeed romantic love is essentially ritualistic. The man has certain things he is supposed to do in a certain order, and the woman likewise. There is very little room for individual initiative. Actions and reactions are prescribed in advance according to the rituals of meetings between the sexes—the first date, courting, petting and 'how far to go'. There are hundreds of special manuals that actually describe, step by step, the actions that boys and girls are supposed to perform when going out together, and when one or other of the partners does not live up to expectations, there are 'aunties' in the teenage magazines to offer advice. A person from another culture might be dismayed by the jocular insults of a boy 'chatting up a bird', but in fact it is the ritualized language she expects and the ceremony is as formulistic as the mating of a peacock and peahen

For the energetic young there is only one way of satisfying their sexual drive that is socially approved. That is why romantic love is so popular with the participants. If an unmarried girl goes to a family planning clinic and says she wants the pill because she has fallen in love, everyone will be pleased to help; if she goes there and says she wants the pill because she enjoys sex and wants to have more of it, she would not be so welcome. Even churchmen and others who have rigorously opposed pre-marital sex seem to soften when it is explained that the couple are really in love.

The editor of the *Peking Workers Daily* is not so easily softened : "Love between man and woman is a psychosomatic activity which consumes energy and wastes time. On the other hand, love of the party and of the chairman, Mao Tse-tung, takes no time at all, and is in itself a powerful tonic."

The term *love* has been used to describe many different relationships, some of which are wholly beneficial and rewarding. But there is much confusion and sometimes this seems to be deliberate. It seems to be in the interests of those who support the status quo to make 'true love' mean different things at different times. Romantic love is tolerated by moralists because, in effect, it is an attempt to desexualize the passions of the young. If premarital sex cannot be prevented, then at least it must be restricted to one man with one woman.

In the past the concept of romantic love was useful, either to control premarital sexual activities, or to expiate guilt when these controls broke down. But this is no longer necessary. Human sexual passion, one of the most exciting aspects of our civilization, can now be enjoyed without it necessarily being harmful. When it is harmful, it is caused by public attitudes and these can be changed. It is possible, although at present difficult, to disassociate sexual passion from romantic love.

The romantic myth is not part of 'human nature', whatever that is. It is something we have invented. It is also something we can change, if that is what we want. The romantic myth described in this chapter is a perversion of love. Occasionally it is the cause of euphoric sensuousness, but just as often it gives rise to unreal expectations and hampers the individual in his search for sexual happiness.

Social Hostility

It may seem that the disadvantages of promiscuity have been understated in this chapter. In fact the physical drawbacks have been considered and found to be limited; VD is a curable disease; the association with cancer of the cervix is uncertain; the chances of an unwanted pregnancy can now be reduced considerably. But there are other drawbacks besides the physical aspects, and these are often the most practical and relevant disadvantages.

Sometimes a man has been taught to have little respect for a girl who allows herself to be easily seduced and so treats her with disdain after he has satisfied his sexual urge. If her activities become known, a girl might get a reputation that would seriously hinder her chances of getting married, for many men still have the idea that the girl they will marry should be chaste, or in-experienced at the very least, before they take her to bed. If it is known that a girl has slept with more than one sexual partner, she will get propositions from other men and any attempt on her part to be selective will be met with indignation and rudeness.

A girl may decide to sleep with a steady succession of boy-friends until one eventually becomes her husband; although this would seem to be a sensible and logical preparation for marriage, such a procedure would arouse much criticism and hostility. Older people do not hesitate to show their disapproval of some-one who is known to be promiscuous and there is still confusion in some people's minds between promiscuity and prostitution.

It is less difficult for men who wish to gain some sexual experi-ence before they get married, but extramarital affairs usually have to be secret and furtive. This often leads to intrigue and deception which in turn can be the direct cause of the break-down of a marriage. Because people are so afraid of getting a reputation for promiscuity, the actual sex may be unsatisfactory because it is hurried, uncomfortable and sordid. All these are realistic disadvantages to promiscuity and may well be the reason why many men and women think it is better to resist these temptations. But it is important to note that these practical draw-backs are caused, not by the activity itself, but by the public reaction to promiscuous behaviour.

Public attitudes to promiscuity take two forms : the moral view which sees it as evil ("indulging lusts" and "the morals of the farmyard" to quote two recent letters to *The Times*); or the more compassionate view which sees the promiscuous as people who are sick ("the minds of the young are being poisoned" or "a blighted search for affection").

Some Christians still support the idea that earthly enjoyment is unimportant and real joy comes when we put aside the pursuit of pleasure to follow Christ. Consequently Christians tend to be unimpressed by the arguments that promiscuity is a relatively harmless activity or that sexual attraction is a good reason for two people to make love. Christian morality has always insisted that sexual activities should be rigorously restrained, but this was not emphasized in Christ's own teaching. As Professor Carstairs (1963) said in his famous Reith Lectures over ten years ago : "For Him, the cardinal virtue was *charity*, that is, consideration of and concern for other people. It was His intemperate disciple, Paul, an authoritarian character, who introduced the concept of celibacy as an essential part of Christian teaching, and centuries later it was the reformed libertine St Augustine who placed such exaggerated emphasis upon the sinfulness of sex. It has always been those whose own sexual impulses have been precariously repressed who have raised the loudest cries of alarm over other people's immorality."

In order to maintain moral standards, the authorities tend to overstate the consequences of disobedience; in religious circles the threat is hell fire; in the secular state it is spurious medical and psychological afflictions. It is interesting that the strongest advocates of moral orders usually hold chauvinistic views. Their genuine concern is that moral infractions will lead to the decline of the British way of life. In fact research evidence shows that signs of increased promiscuity are to be found in all the developed nations. The irony is that most of the social disadvantages that arise from promiscuity are self-inflicted in the sense that they are the direct result of the hostility aroused within the community.

Society tends to relieve its sense of guilt by using sexual immorality as a scapegoat. This provides us with the flattering illusion that we are superior to the scapegoat. There might be something to be said for this if it worked; if we were all that much better off after we had sacrificed the goat, not many people would defend the poor animal; if we were that much better off as a result of our hostility towards promiscuity, this behaviour could be justified, but in fact we have found that this concern about promiscuity impedes progress in sex education, the use of contraceptives, the campaign against VD, and in other ways.

Tolerant thinkers prefer to think of promiscuity as a sickness. This is the approach which regards non-conformity and mental illness as synonymous. In fact secret promiscuous behaviour seems to have only minor effects on the personality, but the attitudes of other people when they find out about a person's promiscuity sometimes creates a stress situation which can lead to guilt feelings and social isolation. On the other hand there are many promiscuous people who are able to disregard this hostility and are well integrated with the community.

Nearly everyone takes part in some behaviour which would be considered deviant by other members of the same society. Exceeding the speed limit, getting drunk, wearing unusual clothes are all examples of minor deviations. Some people think that anything but the 'missionary position' is a sexual deviation. Sexual behaviour is always the subject of strong convictions, and yet the norms of sexual behaviour are not the same throughout one community and vary considerably from one society to the next. For example, some forms of precoital sex play are esteemed among middle class couples but are vilified by working class married men and women.

An added complication is that there are often two systems of morality coexisting together in one individual. There is the private morality which has certain definite rules, but is not usually so strict as the public morality which is the one that is openly expressed. This is not just a description of a few hypocrites. A great many people have these two levels of morality and it is a reasonably effective way of controlling strong sexual urges without repressing them.

Men in public life are denied this privilege. In Great Britain they are expected to keep to the tenets of public morality and if it becomes known that their private life falls below this level, the penalties are severe. It is notable that the reason for this severe punishment is that the public man who strays from this strict morality is said to be endangering the security of the state. There is usually only a little justification for this argument, but there are historical reasons for these fears. When the state was smaller, non-conformity was a real threat to its security. Some of the rulers in developing countries still think that short skirts and long hair put their people in jeopardy. But a democratic state should be able to tolerate many different shades of opinion and permit pluralistic views on morality. People need not be concerned with the sexual acts of well-known men and women unless it is thought that their private behaviour affects their public work.

Nevertheless promiscuous behaviour repudiates the standards people value and threatens the validity of their moral code. To demonstrate to an individual that what he has believed all his life is false, must be one of the quickest ways of provoking moral indignation. To point out that he himself does not always adhere strictly to his own moral code may be warranted, but it is unlikely to prolong a friendship.

Despite these difficulties, attitudes to sexual morality do change and circumstances sometimes make changes necessary. A moral code that is inviolate is unworkable. The sexual history of mankind is full of examples where an activity is degraded in one situation and then becomes socially approved behaviour in another. One extreme example was when brothels were established officially for soldiers, separate ones for officers, during the First World War; according to Morton (1971), "After intercourse men were obliged, as a drill, to urinate, wash, douche and apply a freely provided ointment". The rapidly changing attitude to premarital sexual intercourse is a modern example of the same phenomenon. Oral-genital sex was cited as evidence of obscenity in a recent trial, but is now recommended in a book published by the British Medical Association.

One way in which our moral ideas are changing is that codes of conduct are becoming less prescribed. As man develops, the independence of the individual becomes more important. Any strict moral code with narrow limits as to what is correct behaviour is bound to put many people beyond the pale because they are not prepared to confine their private behaviour in this way. Conformity is not a virtue of itself. The only reason for conforming to a particular standard is because it can be shown to be for the general good at that particular stage in history. But change and variety are the essence of progress and this applies to modes of sexual behaviour as to anything else.

One fundamental change in our thinking is that nearly everyone agrees that sexual intercourse is not only for procreation. Most moral and religious leaders now accept that sexual intercourse is permissible even if the objective is not to produce a child, but they have not gone on to answer the question that follows logically from this premise. If sexual intercourse is not always for procreation, what is it for? There are several possible answers. It is for satisfying sexual desire; for showing affection; for getting to know one another better; for gaining experience; and, most important of all, for enjoyment. None of these realistic answers imply that sexual intercourse must necessarily be with only one partner, even though many people would prefer this.

The effects of promiscuity upon society, the family and the individual are not as calamitous as they used to be because circumstances have changed. Improved contraceptives and a growing awareness of women's rights have removed the necessity to censure promiscuity in order to protect the family and maintain the security of the state. It is certain that society will continue to vilify promiscuous behaviour for some time to come, but we should realize that this is for historical and emotional reasons, not because of the positive harm it is alleged to do.

CHAPTER 6

ADVANTAGES AND DISADVANTAGES

Learning from Experience
It has been suggested that many fears about promiscuity have
been exaggerated and some of them, but not all, are groundless.
But this does not mean that most people will want to be promiscuous. We have a strong cultural conditioning against such
behaviour and a high regard for the selfless dedication that
fidelity requires. Although not everyone would wish to subscribe
to Christian values which require a man to put aside the
pursuit of pleasure to follow Jesus, most of us gain more satisfaction from a commitment which incorporates an element of
sacrifice, and to love and honour only one person is a challenging
undertaking.

With these considerations in mind, it may not be so contentious as it may first appear to suggest that the problem in the
future may not be promiscuity, but the lack of it. For it
is possible to argue that there are some positive advantages in
this kind of behaviour, now that sex for reproduction can be
separate from sex for pleasure.

One advantage is that promiscuity facilitates sexual learning.
In ordinary circumstances the least effective way of learning a
skill is to be told how to do it without the chance of putting
this new information into practice. A much more effective
method is to find out how to do it for yourself with help and
instruction from an experienced teacher. Hence modern education puts the emphasis on the discovery method—learning by
doing. Clearly any headmaster who advocates this method for
sex education is asking for trouble.

It is inevitable that a large part of sex education must be at
second hand. There will be a very long gap between learning
and doing, with the consequence that some of the learning will
have been forgotten and some of it has, in all probability, never
been properly understood because the pupil was not able to

practice the skill he was being taught. Eventually the day comes when the student has the chance to put this learning into practice. The first experience is unlikely to be a success if he has not been well taught. It is likely that he or she will fare better if the partner has been better taught or is more experienced.

Sexual information can be obtained in three ways. At second hand, as in sex education, manuals of sex techniques and other media methods, and from gossip between friends and workmates. Or it can be learnt slowly by trial and error with one partner. Or it can be obtained directly from experiences with other people, learning how they react to various sexual situations, accepting or rejecting their ideas and solutions. Two people learning from each other in harmony makes an appealing picture, but learning by trial and error implies that many mistakes will be made before the couple hit upon satisfactory solutions, and of course it is possible that many avenues of possible pleasure remain unexplored. If an individual has sex with different people, he draws on all their experiences and incidentally passes on this learning to his next partner. In this way a person develops his sexual techniques and learns how to give pleasure to others, including his spouse when he decides to marry.

Put in a rather more dramatic way, seduction is a private lesson in an advanced course of sex education. Perhaps the seducer's intentions are not entirely pedogogic, but a good way for a novice to learn is through apprenticeship with someone more experienced. Furthermore many people would prefer to make their embarrassing mistakes with strangers.

Others go further than this and insist that promiscuity is more than a learning situation; it allows emotionally backward adolescents to learn how to cope with their sexuality without getting involved in commitments they are not ready to make. Perhaps it is too much to ask people to look upon promiscuity as a 'cure' for the emotionally deprived, but it is possible to argue that the convention of only one sexual partner may hinder sexual understanding and development.

An important by-product is that the individual will develop tolerance for other peoples' sexual proclivities even if they do not suit him. It is also possible that sexual experience will destroy some of the lingering myths, for example, that there is only one proper position for sexual intercourse, that women do not have orgasms, that penetration is essential for sexual satisfaction, that oral sex is a perversion, or that a big penis gives more pleasure to a woman.

The social disapproval of premarital intercourse has decreased in the last few years, but attention has already been drawn to the strong feeling, especially among older people, that it is only acceptable between two people who intend to get married. Many family planning clinics are now prepared to help un-married girls, but their own statistics show that nearly all of them are engaged or at least have regular boy-friends. It is still quite difficult for a promiscuous girl to obtain contraceptives.

When the parents know that two young people are sleeping together, even stronger pressures are put upon them to regularize the situation by getting married. The result is that many couples drift into marriage, even though they are not certain they will be happy together, because everyone expects it and the decision not to marry somehow turns their previously acceptable behavi-our into a rather sordid affair. The premarital sex was accept-able as a prelude to marriage, but when the engagement has been broken, they feel ashamed of it. Unfortunately the easiest way to rid themselves of these guilt feelings is to go through with the marriage and to tell themselves that it will probably work out all right in the end. Perhaps it will, but generally speaking, this is not a good basis for a happy marriage.

> Next at our altar stood a luckless pair,
> Brought by strong passions and a warrant there.*

Young people have a strong inclination to try themselves out sexually, as in many other ways. All the talk, all the jokes and all the warnings excite their curiosity and, understandably, they want to find out for themselves what it is all about. But we are forcing teenagers into premature obligations which curtail further experience and growth. Not all young people want to make such a firm commitment before they have their first experience of sexual intercourse. Although there is no evidence that promiscuous boys and girls make bad husbands and wives, there is plenty of evidence that there is a high divorce rate among those who marry young. It is possible that we do not allow young people to scan a wide enough range from which to select a suitable mate; and the increasing acceptance of premarital intercourse seems to be restricting the choice instead of widening

* George Crabbe in *The Parish Register*, 1807.

it. Young people should be encouraged to meet a large number of other people before being required to make such important decisions and give long-standing undertakings. There is no reason to suppose that the less one searches, the more likely one is to find the perfect marriage partner.

Headmistresses sometimes say, incredulously, that it is often the quiet girl, the less glamorous pupil, who becomes an un-married mother, and there is an element of truth in this. The girl who believes she has enough self-control will not take precautions in advance. Then, one evening, she may be carried away by the romantic atmosphere to find that she has gone all the way without using any contraceptives.

The same situation may occur among the boys. Someone who is always ready for sex is more likely to have a condom, or at least to know where he can get one at short notice. It is the boy who never intended to go as far as full intercourse who might get caught out. Contrary to the usual adult assumption, an unwanted pregnancy may indicate that the boy or girl had intended to avoid intercourse, rather than a sign of casual or carefree behaviour.

This thought may help us to be more tolerant and under-standing, but it will not be much help to the unwanted child. It is ironic, but not beyond belief, that the old convention that good girls hold out against sexual temptations may be the indirect cause of many unplanned pregnancies. The new conven-tion of only one sexual partner before marriage must curtail experience and limit sexual understanding.

Mutual Encounters

"Promiscuous sex is a good way of getting to know people." Put boldly like this, the statement may seem questionable. In fact many friendships have grown from casual sexual encounters. The quotation is from an underground newspaper (*Ink*, 23 Sep-tember 1971). It continues : " 'We can't make love, we barely know each other' should be replaced by : 'Let us make love, I want to get to know you.' " It is not always true that a sexual relationship cements a friendship. Indeed there are people who find it impossible to have sex with their friends. But this only applies to a small minority. If all other aspects could be dis-regarded (which is probably impossible for most people), it is true that a sexual relationship may increase understanding and affection between friends, and even acquaintances, in much the same way that it does for a married couple.

In some groups a new attitude to sexual relationships is emerging. This looks upon sex as a meeting of personalities in which each explores the other and at the same time discovers new depths in himself or herself. This may be a beneficial and rewarding experience without the necessity for continuity or exclusiveness.

Perhaps the strongest argument in favour of promiscuous activities is that it gives much pleasure to many people : in my research 85 per cent of those who did not have a regular partner said they enjoyed their sexual activities. Sometimes it was furtive, transient or uncomfortable but clearly it was enjoyable. Unfortunately there are some people who are suspicious of an activity that happens to bring happiness, and an activity performed solely for the purpose of giving pleasure is unwelcome. But any discussion about the advantages and disadvantages must take into account the pleasurable effects.

It is not unreasonable to ask why people have sexual intercourse. What is it for? Until quite recently many churchgoers would agree with the Bishop of Southwark who told the National Birth-Rate Commission in 1915 : "I have never been able to modify the view that the only thing that justifies ultimately the intercourse between the man and the woman is the purpose and the desire to have children." Times have changed and a more modern view is expressed by Elizabeth Janeway (1972): "... instant warmth, instant connection, instant pleasurable feedback...." It often seems to be overlooked that even promiscuous sex, like sex within marriage, is a two-way, give and take, activity. For very many people, the giving of pleasure is at least half the motive for going to bed together. Sexual intercourse is sometimes an act of generosity, a desire to give pleasure. Promiscuous sex can confer great physical rewards, but can also make intense physical demands.

In some way novelty also plays an important part. Three workmates were discussing their sex life; one said he had intercourse every night before he went to bed; the second said he preferred it in the morning; the third said he only had intercourse with his regular partner on Saturday nights, but if it was 'a bit of fresh', it would be three times a night. The others agreed that they would have intercourse more often if it was with someone new. Many readers must have heard similar conversations. But what is the strong attraction of someone new? Logically one would suppose that there are important disadvantages. Regular partners get to know what stimulates the other; a couple, used to each other's ways, should know exactly how to bring each other to a high pitch of excitement. Why should it be more fun with a stranger? Discovery, mystery, novelty, dissatisfaction with the existing situation—whatever the reason, a large number of people get extra stimulation from a new sexual partner.

It must be a similar drive that persuades many men and women to seek new sexual encounters after several years of married life. Sometimes a husband (or wife) grows discontented with his marital sexual life and wonders if he is not missing out on something. This is especially likely to happen to someone who has had no promiscuous experience before marriage. When he breaks out and tries sex with someone else, it may be unexciting and he returns reassured to his wife. But when the extramarital experiments turn out to be enjoyable, it may be the means by which a marriage is saved. By arranging to obtain sexual contentment elsewhere, the irrational resentment against his wife evaporates, the sexual side of the marriage is seen in proportion, and he is able to develop the many other non-sexual but satisfying sides of the union.

There is some evidence to suggest that monogamy is a difficult ideal for some people and they are not helped by the sexual stimulation they find all around them. Television, films, advertisements and fashions heighten their sexual attention and tempt them to be more adventurous. There have been occasions throughout history when men and women have rejected the accepted notion of pair bonding. The next section examines the communes in modern society where men and women live in a group without giving sexual allegiance to one particular person.

But it is important to note that the enjoyment of promiscuous sex, and particularly the mutual sharing which has been emphasized in this section, has only become possible since the changed situation of women. In the past, except in rare instances, the only females who were able to have promiscuous sex were prostitutes, servants, and fallen women. The full realization of mutual encountering and shared sexual enjoyment is only possible in a society where women have social and economic equality with men.

The New Youth Collectives

If there are so many advantages, it is fair to ask why everyone is not promiscuous. One reason is that many of the advantages noted in the first two sections of this chapter are logical and factual statements which are of limited value in circumstances where emotion and feelings are paramount. Furthermore there are palpable disadvantages and these are considered in detail in the three sections after this. But first we should try to understand those communities where the members have purposefully adopted this tolerant attitude to promiscuity and tried to put these ideas into practice. The new communes recently established by young people in several parts of this and other countries should provide us with what the sociologists would call a *model* to study, albeit the actual closed conditions make it more like a laboratory experiment.

Unfortunately very few worthwhile studies have been made on these communities, partly because there is some resentment towards outside investigators. This is understandable, for many of these men and women have not dropped out; they have opted out. They have decided to live together expressly because they wished to opt out of the larger materialistic society; consequently they do not feel inclined to co-operate with the agents of that society, and this of course includes social researchers. Many of them have also had some unfortunate repercussions after they have been interviewed by journalists. Even when they know you are not from one of the popular newspapers, it is difficult to get past the anti-intellectual climate that prevails in most communes. They tend to distrust the linear thought-sequences of the social scientist; they prefer bursts of insight to chains of reasoning. Nevertheless it has been possible to obtain a fair amount of information from some of the communes that have been established in south-east England.

Communes are not a new phenomenon. Communities founded as a protest against modern conditions became especially popular in nineteenth-century America where the climate is suitable for primitive living, but many other communes were established long before that. Most modern communes are disenchanted with the technological age and try to be as self-supporting as possible.

Many are looking for a particular kind of religious experience, not necessarily Christian, but based on mutual interests and living together as a large family.

The type of communes that are of particular interest in this section are those that have rejected the idea of pair bonding. In order to avoid the confusion with political communism, I will refer to these communities as youth collectives. The *Directory of Communes* lists about fifty of these collectives, most of them sharing the values and assumptions of the youth culture (Rigby, 1974).

In some cases these youth collectives have been founded especially as a protest against the old idea of the small two-generation nuclear family. The pursuit of independence extends to everyone's right to start and carry on sexual relations with anyone else without arousing jealousy or possessiveness. In a few cases the collectives include married couples who permit extra-marital sexual relationships and regard them as an indication of their ability not to possess the marriage partner. Promiscuous sexual intercourse within the collective, and sometimes with visitors, is to be viewed as normal, acceptable and a sign of group stability.

Obviously the backgrounds and personalities of the participants are various, but there are many similarities between these youth collectives, which is surprising, even ironic, because independence and doing one's own thing are thought of as the cardinal virtues. The furnishings of a typical collective tend to be the same—wall-drawings, candles, beads in doorways, mattresses on the floor, low furniture, equipment for rock music. Although the occupants wear a variety of different clothes, the personal attire tends to be drab, austere and asexual. The girls favour jeans or long skirts in rough weaves; the men wear patched jeans and grow beards. "I keep my material needs to a minimum," says one girl. "I only have one pair of jeans. When they wear out, I get another pair," says a man. No doubt the dress and hair styles are chosen because they are inexpensive, but ecological and conservationist reasons are also given.

Many of the participants in these youth collectives find it difficult to live up to their sexual idealism. Even in those specifically set up to get away from pressures of pair bonding, the members find it very difficult to live in a genuinely promiscuous way.

Many of them told the same story: the collectivization of
material things, about which they were most apprehensive,
proved to be the least difficult. They found they did not need
their own possessions, money, rooms, private lockers. But
attempts to give up the "oppressiveness of couples" often ended
in the establishment of unofficial but exclusive relationships.
Despite themselves, most admitted feelings of jealousy when
their regular partner had sex with someone else.

Although we may try to discourage and deny the possessive
element in romantic love, clearly this is not an easy thing to do.
Generally it was a case of serial monogamy: partners were not
shared or swapped until each moved on to a new relationship.
The usual arrangement seemed to be cohabitation for short
periods, then they parted, usually without rancour. But while
they were together, they tended to remain faithful.

In his study of youth collectives in America, Speck (1972)
came to this conclusion: "We did not find that the current
groups of nineteen to twenty-five-year-olds had solved the sexual
hang-ups of their elders. But there seemed to be less willingness
to cling to old conventions and old myths and more willingness
to experiment, with greater freedom and less inhibition. However, the young persons we talked to in their communes seemed
to have many of the same hang-ups which are seen in the larger
society. Most of the communes had a fairly rigid separation of
couples and singles. Similarly possessiveness, jealousy, and
paranoid-like immaturity reactions exploded the popular myth
that the youth of today have broken the intra- and interpersonal
defensive barriers to a freed love."

Perhaps the most surprising thing revealed in Speck's book is
that if the girl became pregnant, marriage usually followed
promptly. "We know that in seven of the nine marriages pregnancy preceded the wedding." Most of the girls in the English
collectives were on the pill and pregnancies were usually planned
when they occurred. It seems that a pregnancy was often welcomed as an affirmation of feminity and a confirmation of
masculinity without too much thought being given to the
upbringing of the child. In fact the pregnancy often hastened
the departure of the couple and sometimes led to the dissolution
of the collective altogether.

But there were children in some of the collectives who
appeared to be progressing healthily and happily. In a World

Health Organization volume, Margaret Mead (1963), the cele-
brated anthropologist, questions the assumption that the one-
mother-one-baby pair is the only satisfactory way to bring up a
child. In non-Western societies multiple mothering is common.
Babies are sometimes breast-fed by a number of different women.
Later there is joint responsibility for the growing child.

The Hutterites, a religious sect in America, is an example in
Western society of the situation where the children are brought
up most of the time in isolation from the parents. In the Israeli
kibbutzim the children are cared for in nurseries run by changing
shifts of women. Hutterite and kibbutzim children both appear
to thrive physically and mentally. It seems to be likely that a
child will grow up happily in a well-run commune. Children
need to associate with other children of about the same age. The
traditional family home is sometimes a lonely place for the child.
The commune may provide a useful peer group.

The parents are released from the continuous supervision of
their off-spring when the children become the responsibility
of everyone in the commune. Each child has the security of its
peer group and the presence of adults upon whom he can
model himself. Indeed it is possible that a child is less likely to
suffer the ill effects of emotional deprivation caused by the
death or absence of his own mother when he has grown up with
other adults he can trust. But most of the collectives studied
here are fairly temporary institutions and would be unlikely to
provide the stability that would be desirable for bringing up
children.

Some of the old communes based on religious or agrarian
principles have lasted very many years, but the new communes
of young men and women do not seem to be very durable,
although there are a few exceptions, especially among those
groups with strong political motives. Most of the youth collectives
which adopt the principle of sexual liberty seem to break up
after a short period, varying from a few months to about two
years. The casualty rate is particularly high among the "manna
from heaven" type who usually squat in an empty house await-
ing demolition where they will be turned out before long.

The winter climate in this country provides problems unknown
to communes in more fortunate areas where they do not need
heating. If they do not pay for electricity or gas, the services will
soon be cut off. Once they agree to pay for public utilities, rents

and rates follow and survival becomes improbable without organization, part-time jobs and mandatory contributions from earnings. Before long they are involved in all the mundane worldly problems from which they had intended to escape when they established the collective.

Cannabis was almost universal in these youth collectives, usually at a group meeting in the evening. It produces a sense of well-being and unity like the early Christians' love-feast. In the few collectives where the use of drugs was extensive, there seemed to be an incurious indifference to reality and an unfounded optimism that things will work out for the best even if no one makes any effort to do anything about it. Soon the agents of the larger society refuse to feed or support them and they are driven out into the cold world of reality.

It is possible that the instability of these collectives is one of their assets. They provide support and shelter to young people while they sort out their problems and test out their perceptions, values and social skills. But at the same time the collective does not become a permanent refuge and, gradually but inexorably, the participants are forced to move on into other facets of life.

Certainly, some people appear to gain from opting out and into a collective for a short period. Even the period of extensive drug experimentation seems to last less than two years in most cases. This experience of living in a small community may leave the participants with real lasting effects. Often they seem to embrace a new set of values which include gentleness, forbearance and serenity—the *marijuana agape* of which the ingredients are concern for the quality of life and rejection of the rat race, combined with an awareness of the harmony between man and nature.

It follows that young men and women who no longer feel the pressure for conformity and value freedom of choice are likely to stress equality between the sexes and tolerate a wider range of sexual behaviour. But sex within the youth collectives is not jumping from bed to bed or a long series of debauched orgies. It is usually a private matter between two people. It is not the place for unlimited sexual licence. The participants maintain that they have got rid of the exclusiveness and selfishness of the monogamous life and have embraced sexual relationships which are founded on a wider love and loyalty.

The slightly surprising result is that sexuality is reduced in significance. Many would go further and insist that the larger society's emphasis on sex symbols and its admiration of sexual conquistadors is a form of anti-feminism in which men, under the guise of putting women on a pedestal, are in reality forcing women to adopt an inferior role. The asexual mode of dressing, particularly the lack of flamboyance in the women's clothes and the denial of narcissism in the personal appearance of both men and women seems to reinforce this idea that the people in these collectives despise the over-selling of sex as a consumer commodity.

This is particularly noticeable in the gay collectives where they disdain the just-too-smart clothes of the about-town London queen. Interest in personal appearance and cultivating sexual attractiveness seems to be depreciated in the gay collectives. Members in these communities also disapprove of the hectic promiscuity of some other homosexuals, and in one gay collective it has become the custom to confine all sexual relationships to other members of the group.

It is interesting that many gay collectives have stayed together for a longer time than the straight communes. This is probably because the social hostility that homosexuality still ferments increases the bond between members of gay collectives.

In our society it is tacitly assumed that adolescents will reach sexual maturity, then after a period of chastity, they will fall in love and marry. In other cultures marriage is planned when the boys and girls are still children, before sexual maturation and before love; this arrangement assumes that love begins and matures with the sharing of the daily tasks and burdens, through a process of learning and adjustment. The new youth collectives seem to come somewhere in between these two arrangements.

The young men and women learn how to live together without having to make binding commitments and learn about sex and love without hurting each other too much. As one would expect there are certain disadvantages endemic to these collectives, especially the risk of withdrawal from reality and an indifference to the world and its problems. As noted, there are also advantages, not least as an experiment in living from which we can all learn and profit.

Perhaps without really knowing what they were doing, universities and other institutions of higher education have provided some of the youth of this country with these opportunities by converting single-sex student dormitories into co-ed hostels. Thus they have provided a kind of moratorium for students, allowing them a period to be held less accountable for non-integrative and nonconforming behaviour. From this may spring useful cultural innovations and the adoption of new basic values which will benefit all mankind.

I undertook this study of the new youth collectives because I thought it might provide a practical example of promiscuous living—a kind of laboratory setting for studying promiscuity in action. As we have found, members of these collectives are not particularly promiscuous. They change partners, but not frequently. It is almost like a miniature of the middle-class marriage system—a series of monogamous relationships lasting months instead of years. Consequently we have not learnt much about promiscuity from this section. However, we have learnt that, given the choice, only a minority will prefer out and out promiscuity to a series of short affairs.

We have also learnt, incidentally, that the experience of living in one of these new collectives, even for a short period, seems to have a lasting effect which includes a greater tolerance of other people's sexual behaviour and a greater concern for sexual equality. It seems probable that this is going to have a profound effect on future attitudes to promiscuity.

Physical Difficulties

It has been suggested more than once that the fear of promiscuity has exaggerated its possible harmful effects. Nevertheless there are deleterious effects and the next three sections are devoted to a consideration of these disadvantages.

The most quoted and most specific objection is that promiscuous activities are the direct cause of the spread of venereal diseases. This is undoubtedly true. If no one ever had intercourse with anyone except their husband or wife, VD would be at first contained, and probably eventually eradicated. Such a sexual utopia may seem to be an inspiring target, but it is so much against the prevailing trends that the idea can be of little interest to anyone who is concerned about the rather more immediate future.

Young people usually get most of the blame, but old people also live and love longer than in the past. One important reason for the rise in the VD rate is that more people go to a clinic and more cases are reported. Each case reported is a disease treated and eradicated, providing the patient follows through the initial treatment and returns to the clinic until he is told that he is free from infection.

Another factor that blurs the connection between promiscuity and the VD rate is that gonorrhoea is often found in one partner alone. Statistics and clinical experience have shown that some people who have intercourse with a person who has gonorrhoea will escape infection. Jelinck (1972) estimates that in contacts with acute gonorrhoea the chance of avoiding infection is 2:1, and in chronic gonorrhoea it is as high as 10:1. Clearly a person could be very promiscuous and escape infection if he was lucky.

Although it would be foolish to deny that the promiscuous stand a greater chance of catching a venereal disease, it is a mistake to use the rise and fall of the VD rate as an indication of the prevalence of promiscuous behaviour. Indeed it is possible that promiscuous activities are increasing at a faster rate than the venereal diseases. Everyone wants to reduce the number of people who get VD, but this is unlikely to be achieved by emphasizing the connection with promiscuity. This attitude only adds to the stigma already attached to VD and will make it more embarrassing and difficult for the infected to go for treatment before they spread the disease to others.

Many of the suggestions for reducing the extent of VD seem to subscribe to the curious belief that pregnancy is somehow incompatible with venereal disease. Lord Stamp's answer to the problem* is to exclude people under sixteen from obtaining contraceptives. Morton (1971) thinks the pill is to blame. Others think the new Abortion Act has been the cause of more VD. But an increase in the number of unwanted children will not affect the VD rate. What these people are really suggesting is that we should use the fear of pregnancy to stop people from having sex.

The fact remains that an individual gets a venereal disease, not by having sex with many people, but by having intercourse with one who is already infected. People make remarks about playing Russian roulette in bed, but this is not an apt metaphor. If the disease were deadly and incurable, it would be easier to understand the threats and dire warnings.

* In a debate on sex education in the House of Lords, 1973.

One other disease has been said to be directly associated with promiscuity. This is cancer of the cervix, but the evidence is complex and confusing. The most widely accepted theory until recently was that the wives of uncircumsized men were more likely to get cervical cancer. It was believed that the smegma under the foreskin acted as a carcinogenic agent and this theory received further support when it was found that cancer of the cervix was less common among Jewish women. But a recent research among Lebanese Christians (whose husbands were uncircumsized) and Moslems (whose husbands were circumsized) found no difference between the two groups in the incidence of cervical cancer (Feroze, 1972). It has also been suggested that there is an increased rate of cervical malignancy in the wives of husbands who have cancer of the prostate (Wynder, 1954) and of those who have had VD (Beral, 1974). It seems quite possible that some kind of sexually transmitted infection is involved in the development of this disease.

Other studies have suggested that cancer of the cervix is extremely rare among nuns (Towne, 1955) and "virgin females of any age" (Martin, 1967). It is also suggested that barrier methods of contraception (i.e. condoms and caps with spermicide creams or jellies) act as a protection (Feroze, 1972).

On the other hand it has been found that there is an increased risk of cervical cancer among those who have sexual intercourse at an early age, those who marry before the age of twenty, those whose marriages break down, those who re-marry, those who have had more than one sex partner and those who have a history of numerous pregnancies (Rodkin, 1967; Terris and Oalman, 1960). But all these factors are inter-related (Boyd and Doll, 1964). Before efficient contraception became available to single girls, teenagers who had sexual intercourse were likely to get pregnant and many of them were persuaded to marry the putative father. It has also been well known to social scientists (Martin, 1967) that teenage marriages are far more likely to break down than later unions, and of course those who marry again are very likely to have more than one sex partner. In other words early coitus often led to forced marriages because the young girls became pregnant; but efficient contraception and abortion is now more available and more acceptable, and so there is no longer such a strong relationship between early coitus and all these ensuing events (i.e. early marriage, marriage breakdown, re-marriage, numerous pregnancies and multiple sex partners).

It follows that the close association between cancer of the cervix and the age of first intercourse does not necessarily mean there is an association between cervical cancer and promiscuity. The number of sex partners may or may not be of some significance, but the factor that predominates in most large epidemiological studies of cervical malignancy (Rodkin, 1973; Terris *et al*, 1960; Wynder *et al*, 1954) is definitely the age of first intercourse. Singer (1974) writes : "All other variables seem to be 'dependent' on early coital age. For example, in an as yet unpublished study from Australia, 300 women with pre-invasive and invasive cervical cancer admitted to having a large number of premarital and intramarital sexual partners. When age of first coitus was standardised in the final analysis, the previously significant difference existing between women with cervical malignancy and the large control group (1200) with respect to multiple sexual partners completely disappeared." Furthermore cancer of the cervix is reported to be more common in married than in single women (Logan, 1953) and it is known that single girls are more likely to be promiscuous than married women. Consequently it is fair to say that the connection between cancer and promiscuity is uncertain.

One recent study (Malhotra, 1971) suggests that it is neither the age of first coitus, nor the number of partners, but the frequency of sexual intercourse that is of prime importance. He writes : "As the frequency of ejaculation increased the semen became more alkaline. The view is presented that it is not the smegma but the alkaline reaction, if the sex act is frequent, which may bear a causal responsibility for cancer of the cervix." This theory does not contradict the association with early coitus, because the sexual drive in men is very strong when they are under twenty and frequency of sexual intercourse among young couples is often very high. But my research (Schofield, 1973) found that promiscuous boys and girls have far lower frequencies than young married couples.

In conclusion, it seems that promiscuity, early marriage, re-marriage and multiple pregnancies are no more than secondary factors. Early coitus, high frequencies of intercourse and sexually transmitted infections appear to be the major factors in the development of cancer of the cervix. Consequently the earlier

onset of puberty and the more permissive attitudes towards premarital sex are likely to result in a marked increase in the
incidence of this disease in the coming decades.

Early detection is crucial. Corscaden (1962) has emphasized
that early diagnosis and prompt treatment is now possible and
can prevent the ravages of cancer of the cervix. Fidler *et al*
(1969) have reported that in a population already screened,
invasive cervical cancer develops at a rate of approximately 4.4
per 100,000, whereas the rate in the unscreened population is
about 29 per 100,000. A programme of inspection of those who
are thought to be vulnerable will be costly and will put a further
strain on the National Health Service, but early identification is
of paramount importance. The only other precautions that can
be taken against cancer of the cervix are : (1) the employment
of barrier methods of contraception from the very first experience of coitus, or (2) complete sexual abstinence.

The development of cervical malignancy seems to be associated
with the extent of sexual activity, but a distinction must be
made between the effects of having intercourse many times and
having intercourse with many people. The main hazards for the
promiscuous are still the venereal diseases and much more could
be done to reduce these risks. Far more use could be made of
contact tracing and much more could be learnt if these social
workers could provide better reports on the way infections are
spread. The VD clinics could be in more accessible places; for
example, there is no compelling reason for them to be part of
a hospital building complex. They should be open at more
convenient times, so that a person does not have to take a
morning off work to attend. There should be more venereologists
and para-medical supporting staff to reduce the waiting time in
urban clinics. An element of compulsion is used with other
infectious diseases and, providing strict attention is paid to
anonymity, powers under existing legislation could be used to
restrict the spread of the venereal diseases. Much more time and
money should be spent on research in the hope of discovering a
successful vaccine. The medical prospects of making such a
discovery are not encouraging, but in the end we shall probably
find it is easier to produce a vaccine than change the behaviour
of people.

Intolerance of other people's sexual activities is not going to
make much difference to the VD rate. What is required is a

massive, expensive and sustained campaign to eradicate these diseases. As Rosebury (1971) says in his book about *Microbes and Morals* in America: "It is anachronistic that the most 'advanced' nation on earth should have a flourishing epidemic of a nasty, ancient, curable disease."

Social and Psychological Aspects

Promiscuity is often given as the direct cause of the breakdown of marriage and so is seen as a threat to family life as we know it in this country. It is a valid accusation because a very promiscuous husband or wife is almost certain to put a severe strain on the marriage. The married partner who is not promiscuous will be left alone too often, will be expected to remain at home to mind the children, and will find that there is a large part of the other person's life that he or she cannot talk about and share. But the situation would still apply and the same strain would be put upon the marriage if the husband or wife is not promiscuous in the strict sense of the word, but has a single regular sexual partner outside the marriage. The threat to the marriage is caused, not by promiscuity, but by one of the partners having a consuming interest outside the home in which the other cannot share. It is a bit like being a 'golf widow', except that the emotional resentment is much stronger. If either one of the partners loses interest in the marriage and prefers to spend a large part of the time elsewhere, then it is quite likely that the marriage will deteriorate, and in some circumstances it is probably better for both that it should end in divorce or some other kind of agreed separation. But when the cause of the partner's waning interest in the marriage is sexual, then the indignation is much greater and the breakdown more probable. If the errant partner decides that he or she is 'in love', then it will become particularly hard to avoid the rupture. The promiscuous spouse is not so likely to fall in love as the husband or wife who is being unfaithful with one partner. The real objection, therefore, is to infidelity, not to promiscuity as such.

Most people would agree that the ideal sexual relationship is with a stable partner with whom one is in love. But it is not the only kind of sexual relationship and some people have found other solutions. There are some happy marriages that stay together although one or both have sexual intercourse with others. A quite common situation is when one partner has lost interest in sex and the other married partner is allowed to go outside the home for sexual satisfaction. In these cases it is often a condition that the errant partner should not become 'involved'; in other words, they feel more secure if the errant partner *is* promiscuous.

There is much to be said for the old insight that trust and emotional commitment has a very beneficial influence on sexual relationships. But it does not follow from this that sexual relationships cannot prosper unless they are exclusive and monogamous. As everyone knows there are exotic variations such as wife swapping, troilism (simultaneous sexual intercourse between three people), and sexual orgies.

Anthropology and history cite many instances of sexual events with large groups of participants. Mass sexual orgies took place in connection with fertility rites and religious ceremonies. They were social institutions and public occasions. Wayland Young (1965) speculates on what the presence or absence of orgies in a society can tell us about the society itself. "The first and most obvious fact is that if a society is doubtful or disapproving about all sexual activity, it will be even more so about orgies, because there's so much of it there. This is what happens in Christendom. But one can distinguish further. Take a husband and wife. If they live in a non-orgy society, their sense of identity is continuously buttressed by their monogamy; they both know who they are and are reminded of it by the fact that they are married to each other. . . . But if our husband and wife live in an orgy society things will work rather differently. Once or twice a year they will go out and eat and dance and get drunk and fuck absolutely anybody, without even knowing who they are. The whole point of an orgy is not to know who one's partner is. (Otherwise one starts thinking 'Do I love this person? If I do, would I rather not be alone with them? If I don't, what the hell am I doing here?') At an orgy, their own identity as individuals gets no buttressing from the identity of the unknown other."

These pastimes are not for everybody, but they seem to work for some, especially when both partners in the marriage are open and honest about them. It is when one or other is secret about his or her infidelities that trouble is more likely to occur.

The secret sexual adventurer soon finds himself involved in lies and deceit. The absences from the home have to be explained and the money spent has to be accounted for; sex outside one's own home always seems to require extra expenditure and careful timing. In some cases the errant partner finds that he is leading two lives and he must be careful his two worlds do not conflict. Friends from one of his worlds must not meet the others. He must have a store of convincing stories and become knowledgeable about transport and timetables so that his secret life should remain hidden.

I have used the masculine pronoun in the previous paragraph, but the situation may be even more embarrassing, socially and financially, when the errant partner is the wife. What with the strain, the suspicions and the upsets, it is no wonder that secret sexual adventures, whether promiscuous or confined to just one partner, are likely to lead to the breakdown of the marriage.

One of the most serious objections to promiscuity is the accusation that the children of the marriage will suffer. This, of course, is true if the infidelities lead to the end of the marriage. Children usually fare better when they grow up in stable surroundings. Many people marry in order to have families, but unfortunately others marry because they find out they are about to start a family. A forced marriage often throws two people together when they are too young, too immature, and perhaps unsuited to each other.

There are many cases where it is wholly praiseworthy for a couple to decide to stay together for the sake of the children. But it is not always a good solution. Children need a loving as well as a stable background, and if they are to be brought up in an unhappy home where the parents are forever quarrelling, then it may be better for the parents to part. But an unhappy home where the parents are at loggerheads is usually the result of many factors and an inimical sexual situation is more likely to be a symptom rather than the basic cause of disharmony in the marriage. No doubt there are circumstances when the children suffer because one or both parents are promiscuous, but it is unlikely to be the primary cause and much will depend upon the attitudes of the parents to each other, and to other non-sexual factors.

Sexual performance will be mentioned again a little later in this section. It is noted here in relation to the marital situation where one or both lack confidence in their own sexual capabilities and this may lead to a fear of promiscuity. As the Japanese say: "What does the faithful wife know about big or little penises?"

The husband or wife may fear that their own sexual inadequacies will be revealed if the other partner has intercourse with someone else. They fear that the other partner will enjoy the sex with the outsider so much more that they will lose him or her for ever. Their fears may be justified and this certainly happens. We put too much emphasis on sex with the result that we expect too much, and if our expectations are not fufilled, we sacrifice other very important things in the search for the perfect sexual partner. This paragon does not exist, but it is sometimes true that two people find they are sexually incompatible. The concept of sexual incompatibility has been over-stated and misunderstood, but it is possible that for physical or psychological reasons, two people may be unable to derive any kind of satisfaction from their sex lives. More often than not the cause of sexual incompatibility is because one or both partners have developed strong inhibitions which make it difficult for them to enjoy any kind of sexual congress. In such cases advice and help are more likely to be appropriate than outside explorations.

One of the most important disruptions caused by promiscuity is not the absences from home, the deceptions, the suffering of the children, or the fears about sexual capabilities, but plain straight forward sexual jealousy. Some readers may be under the impression that it is harmful to repress all human impulses but civilized life would be impossible unless people used repression. One impulse that could well be repressed is sexual jealousy. It appears to be a fairly basic instinct, for most people feel it at times and fits of jealous rage are to be observed among the higher primates. Sexual jealousy is a personally degrading and utterly unrewarding impulse, but it is very powerful and cannot easily be repressed.

It is interesting that excuses are often made for *crime passionelle* but usually when it is the woman who has been unfaithful. The murder of an unfaithful wife was known in the past as a "crime or honour". Until 1969 there was a law in Italy under which wives but not husbands could be sent to prison for adultery. In law sexual jealousy seems to be one-sided, but it is an impairment to be found in both men and women.

Promiscuous activities seem to arouse sexual jealousy in two ways. The most direct is when one of the partners feels rejected. It is hard to accept calmly that one's regular partner now finds someone else more attractive. It is particularly hard to take when the errant partner seems to prefer comparative strangers. It is small comfort to realize that we all grow older and tend to become less sexually attractive to others. Sexual jealousy can be very hurtful even when one knows it is irrational and stupid.

The other effect is more general. The older generations have reasons for being jealous of the young: they live better, look better, wear more sexually enticing clothes, have more opportunities for sex and expect a degree of sexual freedom quite unknown twenty or thirty years ago. In practice this undignified jealousy is disguised and interwoven with a concern for the health of the new generations, the puritan idea that one should have to work for what ever one gets, and a fearsome belief that the moral state of the nation is on the decline.

Akin to sexual jealousy is the possibility of hurt pride for anyone who sets out to be promiscuous. Some men would like to increase their sexual activities but are afraid to do so because they are held back by the fear of rejection. At the other extreme is the determined adventurer who has developed such a thick skin that he can shrug off sexual rebuffs on the theory that for every nine rejections, one will accept his proposition. Some would put the odds lower than this. Somewhere between the fearful and the bold comes the speculator who only makes an approach to the ugly girls which increases the chances of success and lessens the chances of a brusque rejection.

If fear of rejection hinders the promiscuous man, it is much more complicated for the woman. Some now feel liberated enough to make the first advance; these women lay themselves open to the same hazards as the man and may be rudely rebuffed. An added difficulty is that the man may indeed be sexually attracted to the girl, but feels annoyed or embarrassed because the girl approached him first. In many social circles this would still be considered unladylike and an affront to his male dignity.

Before the days of women's liberation the girl was expected to be coy and show no sign of concupiscence, no matter how interested she may be. If decorum was to be preserved, the seduction had to be preceded by a game of make-believe.

Of course even in the past when a girl waited for the man to make the first move, she might have to face rejection. But this was rejection by omission—he didn't call; he didn't invite her back; he didn't make any advances. But now when the woman calls, invites the man home and initiates sex, she risks a much more hurtful rejection.

It is complicated by the myth that the average man is always ready and willing to jump at any chance to have sex. Girls who believe this may make the mistake of being too direct. Many men enjoy flirtation and the ritual of seduction.

As well as the real rejection from people who dislike the casual approach to sex, there is another kind of rejection encountered at parties and other gatherings; this can be explained in the unspoken words: "Certainly not, but ask me again when we are alone." It is when this kind of rejection is confused with the genuine refusal that a man may go too far when he is alone with a girl. Promiscuity still invokes moral indignation and disapprobation. In all but a very few social circles the would-be promiscuous female has to tread warily.

Promiscuous sex can often be a fantasy which the man or woman does not expect to happen in reality. The man who eyes each girl and makes caustic remarks about her sex-worthiness may be acutely embarrassed if his suggestions are taken up by a girl. Similarly the flirt who has led on the boy may find she had taken on more than she bargained for and finds herself in a compromising situation. In these situations the sexually adventurous girl or boy who responded to the invitation finds that they are branded as lascivious seducers.

Women have been heard to complain about the sexual inadequacy of men with Don Juan reputations, and the man who is forever chasing after girls in search of a new sexual conquest may be hiding an inferiority complex about his sexual abilities.

Lack of confidence in one's own sexual performance is a common difficulty among young people. In my research it was the most often mentioned sexual problem in this group of twenty-five-year-old adults. Both men and women had this fear that they were not getting as much out of sex as they should. One girl said: "I must say I sometimes worry about my actual sexual performance. Whether I'm doing it right, I mean." A man said: "I do get a bit anxious about it sometimes. You get that feeling that she is not really enjoying it and it's my fault."

It must be said that sometimes this lack of confidence is justified and the sexual capabilities of some people, old or young, are unlikely to give much pleasure to anyone else. If they are married, the wife or husband may be prepared to put up with this lack of expertise and find satisfaction from other aspects of the marriage. Earlier in this chapter it was suggested that the partners of the sexually inadequate may be tempted to test themselves out with someone else. But this may not turn out to be a success. Much of the promiscuous sex that takes place is sordid and indelicate. The circumstances may be uncomfortable or dangerous and this may upset the man so that he cannot get an erection or, more likely, reaches a climax too soon.

The nature of promiscuity itself is changing and this is upsetting the man's idea of his own maleness. In the past promiscuity has always been a part of male aggressiveness. The male body was made for strength, but man no longer needs his muscles in modern society where machines can do the hard physical work more efficiently. So he finds to his dismay that his physical superiority over the female is of little account.* Similarly the male's image of his sexual functions are rapidly going out of date. The powerful stud who chooses a series of women to deflower no longer fits into the new situation. In the past promiscuity has been a male indulgence—part of the *machismo* myth. Now that women have caught on to the idea, men are not so sure that they like it.

For one thing it is becoming clear that they are not so well equipped physiologically as the female for promiscuous sex. Despite the conventional boastful attitude of the male, many men would not welcome an increase in their sexual activities and some of them feel unable to keep up with the sexual demands of the liberated woman.

Many men do not like the new situation and feel the new attitude to promiscuity puts too great a strain on their image of themselves as the hunter. They would prefer to go back to the old days when they decided when and how they were going to be promiscuous and it was up to the women-folk to oblige.

Another objection, often put forward more in sorrow than in anger, is that promiscuity is a second-rate kind of intercourse and will prevent you from enjoying the more euphoric experience of sex between real lovers. Of course it is true that sex with a stranger is unlikely to get much beyond the exploratory stage

* Although we are more aware of wife-battering, this is because in the past the husband's violence was regarded as a private matter, but now it is behaviour that society cannot tolerate.

even if they spend the whole night together. One girl observed: "A new man every night is always the same; the same man every night is always different." This may be an overstatement, but even on the level of sexual techniques, it is likely to be more interesting and exciting when each knows the other's preferences.

If sex with strong emotional ties is so much more rewarding, and most people would agree that it is, then it seems unlikely that people would choose to continue to be promiscuous. When love comes along, the promiscuous activities will cease. This is what happens to many young people who are promiscuous until they fall in love and get married.

The objection would only be convincing if in some way the promiscuous did not want to be promiscuous. If you continue to do something you don't want to do, you are sick. This is true of some mental illnesses where the patient becomes involved in repetitious activities which are obsessive but not pleasurable. There do seem to be some people who go from one sexual partner to the next in a compulsive way without apparently obtaining much satisfaction. This is the criteria; if they enjoy their promiscuity they are not sick; if they don't, maybe they are.

It is also said that some people are very promiscuous because one experience does not give them adequate release of sexual energy. But compulsive promiscuity is not usually the result of strong sexual cravings. On the contrary people who suffer from this disability are likely to find themselves in bed with someone they do not find sexually attractive. When a girl finds she is continually getting sexually involved in a situation that gives her no pleasure, then she requires help.

One of the reasons people engage in compulsive promiscuous behaviour is because they crave for physical contact, probably because they were deprived of such contact when they were young. Perhaps they really do not want sex, but they are willing to have intercourse so that someone will hold them closely and feed their hunger for physical contact.

Another explanation sometimes put forward is that there are some women who wish to destroy a man's erection. A quick way of getting rid of an erect penis is to get the man into bed. A more common cause of compulsive promiscuity is the frigid woman who will try man after man hoping to find the magic penis which will bring on the much desired orgasm. Similarly a man with a clumsy or inept sexual technique will have sex with many women under the impression that it is his partners who are to blame for his lack of satisfaction.

Compulsive promiscuity can also be a defence against homosexuality. Many men who find themselves attracted to other men try to assure themselves of their heterosexuality by going to bed with many girls. This is also true of some girls who think promiscuous acts will banish their sexual interest in other girls. It has been reported that prostitutes are often lesbians.

Others become promiscuous because they are lonely. Sometimes this may help to solve the problem of loneliness, but companionship requires more than physical contact if it is to develop into real friendship. Some of those who are compulsively promiscuous do not want close friends. They are promiscuous exactly because they are afraid of serious involvement. People who run away from friendships have complex psychological problems. Their promiscuity is only a symptom of deeper feelings of worthlessness and inadequacy.

Compulsive promiscuity may be a problem that requires treatment, but some psychiatrists interpret every kind of promiscuous behaviour as a personality defect of one sort or another. They make this interpretation because they are morally offended and feel it is their social duty to control this kind of behaviour. Some neurotic people become compulsive eaters, but that's no reason for putting everyone with a nervous complaint on a diet.

Compulsive promiscuity exists, but it is a rare phenomenon. Most people are promiscuous by choice. It has been argued that promiscuity acts like some sort of drug so that they become addicted to it and are unable to appreciate real love when it appears. A more likely explanation is that some people have never had the facility nor the opportunity to experience a real emotional commitment. On the whole people know what they like and like what they know. If an individual has never had the chance to know true love, must he be deprived of all sexual experience?

Any kind of obsession must be a severe disadvantage. Too much of anything is constricting. There never seems to be time to do all the many things one would like to do. Anyone who wants to do the same thing most of the time must be leading a life that is less than complete. But if he enjoys what he is doing, we should hesitate before we play the role of Big Brother and tell him that he is not as happy as he should be.

Moral Attitudes

The religious and moral objections to promiscuity are fervidly and deeply felt, but in some ways it is difficult to discuss them. They are more like rigid commands, not much like prudent advice. Consequently the discussion is not likely to be about the social benefits or possible detriments of these religious objections, but only about the received word and whether it is being interpreted correctly. If Paul said, "Flee fornication" (as he did in I Corinthians 6 : 18), what more is there to be said?

In fact there is more to be said, even from the strictly moral point of view, if only because promiscuity as it exists today has a very unpleasant side to it. Despite the advance of the woman's cause, more often than not promiscuity is the reflection of male aggression. In the jokes and in the stories of conquests, it is the male stud who is admired. The tough unfeeling hero—the James Bond syndrome—is still attractive to very many men, and to many women, too. But masculine boasts of exaggerated virility— the proportions of the stallion—are now antiquated and inapposite. The biological aspects of maleness have always been over-emphasized, but it is not necessary to accept that this will never change. Environment and culture can be powerful instruments of change if we want them to be. Poetry and ballet can be male attributes, and so can tenderness and sexual sensibility.

We can alter what is thought of as maleness in our attitudes to sex and in other ways. Some of the greatest and most respected men who ever lived, like Buddha or Jesus Christ, were filled with loving compassion. Indeed the biblical picture of Jesus is of a man who was not at all aggressive or sexually dominant. He extolled love and blessed the meek, attitudes that are a long way from the views of the typical male—not a bit like John Wayne.

Jesus was not married, but Christian teaching today advocates the integration of the individual's sex life into a close personal relationship with one other person. But there are some people of all ages who have never been able to establish a close personal relationship and there will be others who will be having sex as they search for this ideal. Consequently there is always going to be a large amount of impersonal sex taking place within the community, not least among married couples.

We must learn to live with this situation without taking offence. As we noted in the previous section, these people looking for impersonal sex have to be prepared for rejection; similarly, others (especially those who make a special effort to make themselves sexually attractive) must learn to reject solicitations with civility and tolerance. It is up to those who have been lucky enough to establish a successful close emotional relationship to afford others a little courtesy and kindness if one does not wish to grant their inoffensive sexual requests.

Another moral aspect which would certainly prove to be a major difficulty for many people is that real promiscuity would take little account of the sex of the partner. A promiscuous act is when two people come together for mutual sexual pleasure without commitment, so there is no logical reason why it has to be a member of the opposite sex. Promiscuity depends upon sexual attraction and so the participants may be exclusively heterosexual or homosexual, but most people are attracted in some degree to both sexes.

This would be too large an obstacle for some people, but this may be because they personalize the situation. There is no rule that says that because you are promiscuous, you must be bisexual. It is not logical to object to all promiscuous activities because some of them are homosexual. As homosexual acts between consenting adults are now legal, it is arguable that the sex of the partner is irrelevant in a promiscuous situation—irrelevant as regards moral attitudes, but obviously very relevant as regards an individual's personal preferences.

It is generally assumed that promiscuity is a temptation against which people have to fight, but in fact most people would find it difficult. Sexual jealousy so often intervenes that it seems to be almost a 'natural' defence against promiscuity. It is one of the attributes of love that we feel the need to devote ourselves exclusively to one particular person. This is admirable and praiseworthy, just as long as we are honest enough to admit that behind this selfless drive may be the fear of being alone, which in turn leads to possessiveness and jealousy.

One of the standard moral objections to promiscuity seems to be based on the belief in the wickedness of mankind. It is believed that a relaxation of the moral code would unleash such dissolute lechery and rampant lasciviousness that things would soon get out of control. It may be true that marriage, fidelity and the sexual taboos are all part of an intricate and elaborate structure assembled to keep our brutal passions in check. In the previous section I suggested that some repression of sexual impulses is necessary if we are to preserve the quality of life. But this does not mean that the moral code cannot be altered or the sexual taboos cannot be questioned. Circumstances change and each taboo should be examined to see how useful or helpful it is in the light of present conditions. The myth of inborn sinfulness is a Christian invention and has only a little to do with reality.

That other religion, psychoanalysis, has given support to the idea that we are all beasts who have to be kept in a cage. They claim that these taboos protect us from anxiety. According to the psychoanalytical view, as long as our perverted impulses are suppressed into the realm of the unconscious, they do not bother us. But if we meet sexual temptation, these impulses threaten to rise up into our consciousness and this we experience as anxiety. We require the support given by the sexual taboos to help us cope with this anxiety. Psychoanalysts also have this strange theory which they call sublimation. By this, they mean the procedure used to transform sexual energy into a force that is useful and beneficial to society.

These psychoanalytical beliefs have been repeated so often that they have become part of the twentieth-century mythology. But they lack all empirical support. Psychologists have been unable to show that individuals with strong sexual inhibitions are more capable of achievements in art, business or politics. Historians are unable to prove that nations with strong sexual taboos excel in the arts, technology or social organization. Freud's conjectures (and he was less dogmatic than his disciples) may have been useful to middle-class Viennese in the early part of this century, but that does not make them sacrosanct.

Religious and Freudian views on promiscuity are derived from dogmas that have become irrelevant in the conditions which exist today. But even in this era of efficient contraceptives, better health and a greater respect for individual liberty and women's rights, many people feel there are moral problems, even though it is hard to give them concrete formulation. A person suffering from strong feelings of guilt is in a distressed condition no matter how irrational the basic cause of the guilt. We should not be surprised that there are moral difficulties, just as there are physical and social disadvantages. All social changes will have a number of negative side-effects. Now we must compare the deleterious effects with the advantages.

A Question of Balance

Do the disadvantages outweigh the advantages? Before we try to strike a balance, it is sensible to leave out of the reckoning those who go too far. Almost any beneficial activity taken to excess becomes undesirable. It is absurd to use the compulsive collector of indiscriminate sexual contacts as an argument against promiscuity, just as it would be wrong to take the 200 deaths a year in swimming accidents as a reason for banning swimming, or even produce a fat man as an argument against good food.

Will the promiscuous harm themselves or others? Is promiscuity the cause of physical or mental illness? Will it make people unhappy? The onus of proof should be on those who wish to prohibit the activity. Even if they can show that it does cause a certain amount of damage, this is not necessarily an effective argument against it. The advantages may exceed the harmful effects.

In fact the answers to these and similar questions will depend upon the individual and the replies will vary from person to person. At my age and in my circumstances, I am not sure I would be happier if I were promiscuous. But I would like to feel that I had the right to be. Furthermore I am sure that for very many people the harmful effects are of a speculative character and are negligible in comparison with the great potentialities for happiness.

If a person chooses to be promiscuous, he or she will probably learn from his or her experience and develop skills which can be shared with others. He or she will become more understanding about other people's sexual interests. If unmarried, he or she may benefit from the opportunity to experiment and make mistakes before taking on commitments. It may make it easier to find a suitable marriage partner. She or he will be more likely to take precautions and avoid an unplanned pregnancy. It often helps a person to develop rewarding mutual relationships and to discover great depths in friends and in oneself. Sometimes an extra-marital experience has a stabilizing effect on a marriage. Promiscuity is often the means of communicating delight between human beings; not only does it give pleasure, but it enables people to enjoy the pleasure of giving.

The injurious effects of promiscuity have been considered in detail in the last three sections. There is the risk of infection and disease, especially from one of the venereal diseases. It is often the cause of disharmony among married couples, on occasions leading to the disintegration of the family unit. The children of the marriage may be the innocent sufferers. Sometimes it is the forerunner of deception and dishonesty which puts an impossible strain on any relationship. It may promote unwelcome, and perhaps unfounded, fears about an individual's sexual capabilities. It is a frequent cause of sexual jealousy and feelings of rejection. The urge to behave promiscuously may be no more than a fantasy which is better left as such and not put to the test of reality. It sometimes upsets a man's image of his own maleness (but perhaps this should not be listed among the disadvantages). It is often said to be less than the best kind of sex and a poor substitute for love. And for a few people it becomes an obsession which they cannot control.

Often the basic reason behind the objections is the fear that a tolerant attitude to promiscuity will disrupt the existing situation. Legislators and people in authority tend to oppose all suggested changes in sexual customs because any alteration in the existing moral code is regarded as weakness. They argue that a stable social structure requires a solid system of hard and fast rules. Most people would agree that some rules are necessary in a civilized society, but this does not mean that the validity and rationality of the existing rules should not be called into question.

In fact a study of this list of disadvantages reveals that many of the problems are caused, not by promiscuity itself, but by the social hostility that this behaviour excites. Promiscuous behaviour is deviant, using the word in its strict sociological sense. Sociologists use the word *deviance* to describe behaviour which provokes social hostility.

It is not the actual behaviour of the individual that makes a person deviant, but the reactions of others to that behaviour. Although homosexuals do not harm themselves or others, they are thought of as deviant because some people find their activities distasteful. Similarly smoking hash is deviant behaviour; the harmful effects of cannabis are insignificant, but the social hostility to using hash has a profound effect on the smoker. Even an illegitimate child is deviant in this sense of the word; he may have been brought up in a loving home by two parents who are not married and his personality may be unexceptional, but his illegitimacy will become a social handicap as he grows up (although much less so than in the past). If social attitudes to promiscuity could be changed, the effects would be less harmful and the problems less severe.

In fact attitudes are changing. The laws on divorce, abortion and homosexuality have all been reformed in recent years. The old taboo about sex before marriage appears to have been all but obliterated. And even attitudes to promiscuity have been changing. In the section on the new youth communes we learnt that few people want to be very promiscuous, but many will be more tolerant about it in future.

A certain level of semi-sexual promiscuity now seems to be socially acceptable in many quarters; for example, when wives and husbands flirt in different parts of the room at parties. Promiscuity involving full sexual intercourse is now accepted without guilt in certain social circles (often said to be the outer suburbs, although I know of no evidence that shows that these areas are particularly profligate.)

It is certainly not without historical precedence. As long ago as the second century there was a Christian from Alexandria named Carpocrates who advocated outright sexual promiscuity. In the seventeenth century there was a sect called the Ranters, one of whose chroniclers* wrote : "I pleaded the words of Paul, 'That I know, and am persuaded by the Lord Jesus, that there was nothing unclean, but as man esteemed it,' unfolding that was intended all acts, as well as meat and drinks, and therefore until you can lie with all women as one woman, and not judge it sin, you can do nothing but sin."

Cromwell thought that this was taking the word of the Apostle too literally and suppressed the Ranters. Just over a hundred years later the French aristocrats believed in promiscuity for fun. Wayland Young (1965) describes a typical French libertine.

"He put his grace, his learning, his chivalry and his wit to use, not in war, politics or conversation, but in bed. He regarded fucking as a continuation of conversation by other means. In this sunny outland, clear beyond the last fences of the Christian conscience, the French libertines were able to see fucking as a normal way of life, where personalities and motives were not suspended in favour of a red glow either of passion or of guilt, but continued to work as usual."

This very short diversion into the history of promiscuity may

* Laurence Clarkson who wrote the pamphlet *The Single Eye* in 1650.

help us not to prejudge the situation. Sometimes it is hard to believe that there is more than one side to a problem when a belief, previously accepted without question, is now being challenged. It may have appeared that too much emphasis has been given to the advantages of promiscuity, and not enough to the disadvantages. (To be fair, it is also true that a writer who is expressing an unpopular view is tempted to exaggerate as he tries to redress the balance.) The realization that promiscuity has been socially acceptable in the past may persuade some people that many of the ideas put forward in this chapter are not so new or outrageous as may appear at first sight.

No one is advocating promiscuity for all. It may suit some people to be promiscuous all the time, but for others it will be no more than an interlude or an incidental episode. For many more it will hold no interest at all. It would be deplorable if the tyranny of a new fashion made people feel that they had to be promiscuous. Earlier in this chapter we found that even in a situation designed to encourage promiscuity, most people did not wish to sleep around indiscriminately. Furthermore we found that in the new youth communes, the significance of sex tended to diminish.

Advocates of sexual freedom are inclined to forget that there are numerous people who regard sex as a very unimportant part of their lives. People who are responsible for sex education, at any age, should remember that those who do not want to have sexual relations should receive support and understanding.

Although there are advantages, promiscuous behaviour is not as easy as some people like to suggest. It is not for everyone. There are physical, social and moral difficulties. Many people will feel it is not worth risking the social hostility. It is, or should be, a matter of choice. It is not compulsory. Sometimes it does seem to be the Christian position that everything not forbidden must be compulsory.

But for those who do choose to be promiscuous, it is important that they know what they are doing, and for the rest of us, it is important that we know what they are doing to us and the community.

CHAPTER 7

MEANINGS AND REMEDIES

Misleading Words and Phrases

I have had to use the word *promiscuity* throughout the first
six chapters for the sake of clarity. But I feel sure my statements
would have seemed less contentious if I had been able to use a
more neutral word. One of the real problems of this subject is
that as soon as the word *promiscuity* is used, people think about
'loveless copulation' or 'unbridled lust' or 'a selfish man making
use of the body of a reluctant woman'. In reality both partners
are often sexually attracted to each other and eager to go to bed
together. If there was a term to describe sexual attraction without long-term commitment, public opinion would be more
tolerant.

Until quite recently teachers, following the text of nearly every
book on sex education, gave the impression that the choice for
the unmarried was between chastity and promiscuity. Now premarital sexual intercourse has become more acceptable because
housing and economic factors have made it difficult for young
people to get married and to get a home together. But if an
unmarried boy or girl has sex with more than one person, he or
she is still the subject of disapproval.

A girl may make love to the man she intends to marry but
after a few months they quarrel and part. Then she meets someone else and falls in love with him. If all this happens during
the course of twelve months, does that make her promiscuous?
And if it happens within three months, is that promiscuity or
not? How many months have to elapse between the breakdown
of one relationship and the start of the next? How long does
one have to know somebody before it becomes an approved
relationship? Questions like these indicate that it is going to be
very difficult to find a rigorous definition of promiscuity.

Some readers (including my publisher) may ask why I did not
start the book with a definition, instead of waiting until Chapter

7. But an attempt to find a precise definition does not *describe* promiscuity; it *explains* the confusion that surrounds the activity, because we all think we know what we mean by the word and we all mean something else.

In fact I did define promiscuity in Chapters 2, 3 and 4, but it was necessary to use a numerical definition—anyone who had had more than one partner in the last year was regarded as promiscuous. Obviously this is imprecise and distorts the real meaning of the word. There are many degrees of promiscuity from the husband who is occasionally unfaithful to the man who has six different partners in the week; from the chronically shy introvert who manages to find a willing partner twice in the last year to the casanova who enjoys the seduction more than the sexual intercourse. All these variations in behaviour have been lumped into an inexact aggregate.

A numerical definition gives no indication of the possible harm that may be caused. It would be wrong to assume that the very promiscuous are more immoral or cause more trouble than the less promiscuous. Compare the likely distress caused by an unmarried girl who has twenty or more sexual partners in a year, with that of the wife who once or twice in the year invites a man into her house while her husband is away.

One girl was most indignant when her doctor said that she was promiscuous because she had slept with fifteen men in the last year. She insisted that she was not promiscuous because she never went to bed with a man on her first date. Her definition of promiscuity was going to bed with someone she had just met that evening. The definition will vary according to the standards of behaviour considered acceptable in different social circles.

There are many other words and phrases which hinder clear thinking. An interesting one in the context of this book is the word *effeminate*. Qualities such as tenderness, sentiment and affection are acclaimed in a woman, but disparaged as effeminate in a man. Man still enhances his reputation in some social circles by exercising his genitals at random, whereas a woman is supposed to have no sexual desires that can be expressed openly. The artificially determined roles of male and female (developed during the Middle Ages) are quite unsuited to the latter part of the twentieth century. There is now a strong movement to discard and replace the traditional feminine roles. It is a pity that there is not an equally strong drive to discard and replace the traditional male image. In her book on modern marriage, Kathrin Perutz (1972) pleads : "Let men be sexy, not just genital. Let them touch other people, kiss them if they feel emotion, and not worry about the sex of the other person." A man who took that advice would be called *effeminate* and other uncomplimentary names.

It is often the case that understanding is impeded by an inexact term with misleading connotations. All sorts of injustices were done in the vain attempt to curb what was called *drug abuse* until it was realized that both words were imprecise. The word *abuse* was used to mean the use of any drug taken for non-medical purposes. In fact all of us take drugs of some kind and most of us take recreational drugs, like alcohol, tobacco, tea and coffee. Research reports showed that there were important differences between the various drugs (Schofield, 1971). For example, it can be shown quite conclusively that very few people who smoke cannabis will escalate to taking heroin. But until only a few years ago, people found in possession of cannabis were given prison sentences because the magistrate sincerely believed that he was preventing the pot smokers from going on to the very addictive drugs. In practice the magistrate himself was probably a drug abuser (i.e. he used drugs for non-medical purposes).

There are also specious magic words which produce bland complacency and this can be just as confusing as the words that evoke hostility. *Family life* is such a phrase and anything that is thought to be a threat to family life is castigated. When the authorities refer to the family in this way, invariably they mean the middle class family. In fact the far more numerous working class families, where the children do not go away to school, often have qualities of fellowship and unity which are a very powerful beneficial influence on the children, but not a bit like middle class family life. We also know that life in a middle or working class family can be a miserable experience.

There are, of course, many euphemisms for unpleasant subjects —nervous breakdown for mental illness, but terminal illness for dying. People who are in favour of abortion talk about terminations, but those who oppose it use the phrase abortion on demand. New words are used for old concepts in the hope that a change will refurbish an old idea. Nowadays sexual deviants are sick, not sinful. Measures taken against them are called care, not punishment. They are incarcerated in a therapeutic community, not a prison. Family planning has been a successful euphemism for contraception. Hopefully people suggest naturism for nudism, personal relations for sex education, sexually transmitted diseases for VD.

It is strange that the term venereal disease with all its dreaded stigma was once a euphemism : the malady of Venus. Statutory venereal diseases as defined by law are soft chancre, syphilis and gonorrhoea. Hardly anyone goes to a VD clinic with soft chancre; less than 2 per cent of patients have syphilis, and about 20 per cent have gonorrhoea. So the majority of patients attending the clinics do not have a venereal disease. The embarrassment and misery of catching a genito-urinary disease is exacerbated for patients who have to attend a VD clinic because of the emotional and moral implications of the name. If a general practitioner wishes to have a specialist opinion on a patient with a genito-urinary disorder, he must either refer him to a genito-urinary surgeon (now called a urologist) or send him to the VD clinic of the local hospital. If it is clear that surgery is not required, it would be better to send the patient to the VD clinic than to wait for weeks for an appointment with a urologist. Not surprisingly, many doctors hesitate before they suggest to a patient that he visit the local VD clinic. Most venereologists agree that a change in terminology would be an advantage because they could function more efficiently if they were able to avoid the moral judgements which tend to be made about a patient visiting a VD clinic even before a diagnosis has been made.

One of the more pervasive arguments used against the reform of the law on homosexuality was that homosexuals were a menace to children. The term *homosexual* was always used to describe men who molested small boys as well as people who were attracted to members of the same sex. Progress was held up until research reports (Schofield, 1965) made it clear that paedophilia was not the same thing as homosexuality.

Questions go unasked in sex education classes because the pupils only know the crude words to describe particular sexual activities. A teacher complained that if he used the word *penis* in his class, half of them would giggle and the other half wouldn't understand what he was talking about. Some people say it is better to use the vernacular because it is plain and straightforward, but this is not always true. The word *queer* is used for homosexual and the same word means *ill* in northern counties—"Mr Smith can't get in today because he's a bit queer". The more fashionable word for homosexuals is *gay*, but this is equally confusing :

> But the Child that is Born on the Sabbath Day,
> Is Bonny, and Blithe, and Good and Gay.

The word *fanny* is vulgar in England, but not in America, and the word *ass* has led to other confusions as epitomized in the limerick :

> There was a young girl from Madras
> Who had the most beautiful ass.
> It was not round and pink,
> As you probably think.
> It was grey, with big ears, and ate grass.

In Chapter 5 it was noted that the various meanings of love led to confusion in the minds of young people. People are said to fall in love free of all volition; but they are only permitted to fall in love at an authorized age, in certain conditions, and with the opposite sex. A young person is led to believe, and soon comes to accept that he or she has only so much love to offer and all of it must be given to one person. So there is no love left to give to others. As Cooper (1971) says : "If one operates with this naive algebra a corollary must be that any act of loving is experienced as loss of a certain inner quantity of love."

It is part of the ordinary process in the dynamics of language that meanings tend to get devalued. Sometimes the meaning is so wide that it becomes difficult to use the word with any precision. It becomes still more confusing when a word (and promiscuity is a good example) not only loses its meaning, but also provokes very strong reactions of disapproval. Perhaps we should abandon the word altogether and use a series of words for the different forms of behaviour which we now label as promiscuous.

Names and Categories

It is obvious that a numerical definition of promiscuity is too imprecise. As soon as we ask what the word really means, it becomes clear that many different forms of behaviour are being classified under the one heading. Some forms of this behaviour have undesirable consequences. Other forms produce strong feelings of guilt or regret as a result of the social hostility shown to all types of promiscuity. But some forms seem to avoid these hazards, for there is no denying that there are people who manage to be happily promiscuous without causing harm to themselves or to society.

For example, it is difficult to pinpoint the specific harm or the guilt feelings likely to be involved when two unmarried people openly and honestly recognize that it is possible to obtain intense sexual pleasure from each other without risking an unplanned pregnancy and without requiring any long-term commitment from each other. At all events there is not much sense in criticizing this kind of behaviour as if it were similar to indiscriminate sleeping around.

Another example of what would normally be termed promiscuous behaviour comes from a well-known woman journalist whose marriage was dissolved after nine years. "Having been married to one man for so many years, I now found it possible and preferable to love two, well, in truth, three. These relationships were grown-up ones and had, each of them, as fully much to do with minds as bodies. They were generous and warm and important. They were friendships, had nothing to do with my domestic details or children's education or paying the rates. They all deepened and withstood winter colds, strains of overwork, the putting on and taking off of weight and each lovingly endured year in, year out."*

After some hesitation I have decided to list the various types of promiscuity. I hesitated because human activities are so diverse and versatile that this kind of classification inevitably distorts the true situation. It is sure to leave out some kinds of promiscuity which do not fit easily into any of these categories. On the other hand some forms of behaviour will overlap into two or more categories. The list is not given in order of preference, nor indeed is it marked by degrees of moral turpitude.

Compulsive. This at least is fairly easy to name and define. It refers to people who have sexual intercourse even though they do not really want to and do not enjoy it. Sex has become an obsession but not a pleasure. This category would also

* Molly Parkin in the *Sunday Times*, 28 March 1971.

include inadequate people who find it difficult to make social contacts on any other level.

Impersonal. This is as capricious as compulsive sex but involves more freedom of choice. Those who think that novelty is more important than friendship would come into this category. So also would the sexual conquistadors who do not care or notice what is happening to their sexual partners. Impersonal sex might involve a different partner every night or the same partner for a longer period. It is a self-centred, masturbatory, kind of sex and the reactions of the other person are not important.

Extrinsic. The point has been made in this and earlier sections that some people can love and be totally committed to one person and yet feel sexually attracted to others. When these desires are put into practice, with or without the knowledge of the beloved, there may be genuine affection and sensitivity, but both parties recognize that there is no commitment. Into this category would come married couples who agree to exchange partners. People who enjoy extrinsic sex indulge their desire for change and variation whilst acknowledging that their prior obligation is to their union with one person.

Precursive. This refers particularly to young men and women who are learning about sex and about each other. It is the exploratory stage in human relationships and part of growing up. It is sometimes used as a way of sounding out a prospective wife or husband, although it is not usually a structured interview. In its longer version, it is sometimes called 'trial marriage'.

Transitory. This is much less cursory than impersonal sex because both react strongly to each other, but at the same time realize and accept that it is not going to be an enduring relationship. It is sex between two people who are really attracted to each other but for compelling reasons—social or geographical—are unable to be together for long. Holiday romances might come into this category. So might a loving relationship between two people who are unwilling or unable to enter into a permanent union.

Facultative. The term implies that the behaviour is partly optional and partly contingent. It is summed up in the words of the song : "If I'm not near the one I love, I love the one

I'm near."* But it involves a high level of mutual sexual attraction; if it is a case of *faute de mieux*, then it is closer to impersonal sex.

Therapeutic. Masters and Johnson (1970) have indicated that some marriages can be saved by arranging for one or both spouses to have extramarital experiences. Martin Cole† has suggested that young people who are unable to overcome strong sexual inhibitions can be helped by trained volunteers. In the American Journal of Psychiatry,‡ it is reported that one in twenty of psychiatrists in Los Angeles will engage in physical relations in the belief that "sexual therapy helps patients to overcome their sexual problems". More often the situation is less formalized, motivated simply by a desire to please or as a genuine act of kindness.

It would take much more than an expert in philology to find exactly the right word for each of these seven categories. *Transitory* sex sounds too perfunctory and does not describe the passionate feelings that may be aroused. *Precursive* sex fails to make it clear that these relationships may last for weeks or months. *Facultative* sex sounds very impersonal but may be an interim arrangement between two close friends. *Extrinsic* sex gives the idea of being outside or apart from the more important loving relationships, but sounds too casual.

No doubt some readers will have other words to describe the activities on this list. In some quarters no term of abuse is strong enough. Hardly anyone has a good word for promiscuity. Nerciat describes it : "A few excursions here and there are only swordcuts in water." The Marquis de Sade regarded sexual pleasure as "sneaking a few roses from the thorns of life" and Oscar Wilde as "purple hours one can snatch from that grey slowly-moving thing called Time". Ovid's description, "sweet lust" seems to echo both the pleasures and the problems.

I hope it has been a useful exercise to take the reader through this classification of promiscuity if only to emphasize the wide differences in behaviour all coming under the same label. It also shows how certain forms of behaviour are easier to understand when given other, less emotive, names. Even so, my own view is

* From *Finian's Rainbow* by E. Y. Harburg and Burton Lane.
† In the *Guardian*, 5 May 1971.
‡ October 1973

that such a classification is unworkable and should not be used. No doubt this list will be quoted without the addition of this qualifying paragraph, but I think it is right to abandon it.

As language develops new words are coined and old words alter their meaning. Hopefully new names will evolve to describe the various forms of behaviour now known as promiscuity. But for the time being I think we are stuck with the one word with all its subjective overtones. All we can do is recognize that the word has unfavourable connotations, which influence and bias our attitudes.

A New Sex Code

Not only are there wide variations in behaviour within one community, but ideas of what is morally permissible are changing all the time. The changes have been particularly rapid in the last three decades, brought about by the new technology, particularly improvements in hygiene, contraception, abortion (although the improved techniques have not been universally adopted), and the control of diseases, including VD.

The changes have not only been technological. There have been decisive changes in social values which have had a telling effect on sexual ethics. A particularly revealing example of this is the waning influence of *machismo*. This idea is still accepted in South America and it was a quite acceptable form of behaviour only a few years ago in this country.

It is vividly described in Oscar Lewis's book *Children of Sanchez* in the words of Manuel as he explains why his affair with Graciela must end. "Because of the eternal vanity, the *pendeja machismo* of the Mexican, I couldn't humiliate myself by going back to Graciela. I loved her with all my soul and deep down I really wanted to say, 'Come back to me—let's go together seriously.' But I set my pride and my vanity above everything else." Manuel freely admitted that he had gone with many different women, but Graciela, as he found out later, had only pretended to go with another man to test his reactions. Manuel explains his attitude when talking about another girl-friend. "As a matter of fact she was an expert and taught me a lot—different positions and how to hold back. That's when I learned that women enjoyed it too. But she wasn't for me because I wasn't the one who had dishonoured her. Women who have screwed others are not to my liking."

Dom Moraes (1974), the Indian poet, writes that *machismo*, pride in the penis, is "not as unique to Latin America as all that : I have seen it in Bradford and Bombay : maybe Spanish is the only language to have a name for it". There are probably many men in this country who secretly share the views of the Mexican Manuel, but anyone who openly expresses such views would now be told that he is out of sympathy with modern ideas on the rights of women.

Ecclesiastical and other authorities who think that sexual morality is changeless do more harm than they realize. If the sex code does not change, young people will see that it is quite irrelevant to present conditions and they will ignore it. Then we will be left without any moral or ethical guide lines.

One way in which the sex code is going to change is in the attitude to promiscuity. The present attitude regards it as the misconduct of an unfortunate minority, but it is an activity that concerns hundreds of thousands of people in this country alone. Indeed it would be reasonable to ask why there is not more promiscuity than there is, in view of the strong motivation for sexual satisfaction. We know that many people want to be promiscuous and we also know that many people want to love and be loved. What is not well known is that many people want both of these things. People have been brought up to believe that they are irreconcilable opposites but the evidence in this report suggests that both are possible, consecutively certainly and sometimes concurrently. I am not suggesting that we have to give our approval to all forms of promiscuous behaviour. I am suggesting that we should be realistic about it.

What should be our attitude to promiscuity? Some people seem to think it will herald the end of the British Way of Life and bring down the wrath of God. Others, like Dr Morton, think it will "precipitate emotional complications in the formative years and in the long term the institution of marriage and the family will be threatened". Most people, including many who are secretly promiscuous themselves, will not want to oppose the tyranny of the majority and will censure anyone who deviates : I don't (or can't) do it, so why should you? Some adopt a pitying attitude : you are not to blame because you are sick. Some blame the sick society we live in, like Dr Jelinck who writes: "Pop culture, with its anarchic, hip swinging idols, pop festivals, communes and underground literature, seems to conspire to encourage promiscuity in the young as an act of defiance to their elders, parents and society." It used to be a sin; more recently it was a mental illness; now it is an ideological weakness.

Tolerant liberals find themselves in an ethical dilemma; on the one hand there is the feeling that everyone should be allowed to pursue happiness after his or her fashion; on the other it is felt that one has a duty to try to save the promiscuous from the consequences of their own folly. In the face of all the evidence, they persist in believing that the promiscuous do not really want to go to bed with other people.

A rigid sex code does not take into account the wide variation of sexual behaviour within one area or one community. Research reports invariably report this diversity. My last research used a study group of less than 400 informants, all of them aged twenty-five, and yet there were some who had never had sex and some who started before they were sixteen; some had premarital inter-course and others were virgins when they married; some had only had one partner and some were promiscuous; some were exclusively homosexual, some were bisexual and some were ex-clusively heterosexual. It is unreasonable to expect uniformity, or seek to impose it, in such a personal matter.

When some people are confronted with something they dis-approve of, their reaction is to say, "there ought to be a law against it". There are laws against adultery and fornication in some countries and as late as 1948 there were 248 arrests for adultery in Boston, Massachusetts. In England the common-law charge of "conspiracy to corrupt public morals" had lain dor-mant for centuries until it was rediscovered in 1960, since when the judiciary has used it on several occasions to stop something which is not unlawful but which they think is immoral.

But people cannot be made good by Act of Parliament and it is not the job of the law to make people pure or to stop them being prurient. The function of the criminal law is the positive one of preventing harm to others. Where there is no need for protection the law should not intervene. It is not the law's busi-ness to prohibit promiscuous activities.

Of course this does not mean that promiscuity gets a stamp of approval just because it is legal. As the Right Rev John Robinson said to the Methodist Conference in 1972 : "The notion that 'anything goes' just because the law allows it reflects the pater-nalistic assumption that it is the function of law to tell people what is good for them and that what is not prohibited is thereby promoted. But it is precisely a sign of a civilised society that it progressively substitutes the free processes of social judgement for the sanction of penal suppression."

In fact contemporary social values have for many years severely censored promiscuity at one level whilst encouraging it at another. We are expected to be monogamous from the day of our wedding onwards, but our attention is drawn to sex every time we look at television, films, advertisements or fashions. Moral denouncements declare that all promiscuity is undesirable and girls who are promiscuous get a bad reputation. But at another level romantic love in films, plays and other fiction is shown as an irresistible force which explains and excuses the need to change partners.

The gossip columnists regard the sexual peccadilloes of the famous as news and it is understandable that we are interested in other people's lives. When Vienna was the centre of the world, if a man was seen on the Ringstrasse with a woman, it was assumed she was his lover; if he was seen with a male friend, he was thought to be homosexual; and if he walked alone, everyone felt sure he must be a masturbator. Gossip may be wicked and hurtful, but it is not at all like the hypocritical moral indignation we express when we find out that other people have sexual desires every bit as urgent as our own.

Tolerance as an Antidote
For the last 400 years sexual morality has been swinging like a pendulum. People say it will swing back and once again sexual freedom will be restricted as it was a hundred years ago, but this seems unlikely. As we increasingly value and respect the right of each individual to lead his own life in his own way, it seems more probable that there will be greater tolerance in all matters to do with sex.

For example, we no longer insist that young people should be chaste until they are married. Opinion polls show that most people now support free contraceptives and a national education campaign to publicize the advantages of birth control. Even among Roman Catholic women there has been a dramatic increase in the use of contraceptives and now more than two-thirds of married Catholics use birth control methods disapproved of by their church. In recent years the tide has been flowing in the direction of sexual tolerance and this includes changes in attitudes towards promiscuity.

Attitudes will become more logical and sensible when we learn to separate forms of promiscuous behaviour that are harmful from those that are not. Of course this distinction is blurred sometimes because too much of almost anything is harmful.

Physical exercise taken in excess is harmful. Too much food is bad for your health. All work and no play is said to make Jack a dull boy. Even love, when it is reduced to living in exclusive emotional isolation with the beloved, can be damaging for the individual and society. Similarly, anyone whose main preoccupation is finding someone new to have in bed each night is sex obsessed, besides missing many other delights.

Some forms of behaviour are not so much harmful as silly. But we must grant each individual the right to be foolish, unless we believe in a paternalist society run by an oligarchy of self-appointed guardians who always know what is best for us. Freedom, whether political, personal or sexual, must mean making as much room as we can afford for human folly.

This report has suggested that many of the more unfortunate consequences of promiscuity are not caused by the activity itself, but by the public condemnation of that activity. If there was an increase in tolerance towards individual variations in sexual behaviour, there would be a decrease in the harmful effects of promiscuity brought about by guilt feelings, deceit and secrecy.

It is part of youth to want to be extraordinary before learning how to be ordinary. The boy uses promiscuity to bolster up his independence from his parents' discipline and to show defiance to traditional authority. The girl who has had a few unsuccessful short affairs comes to believe that she is incapable of fidelity and abandons herself to thoughtless promiscuity. Intolerance encourages this all-or-nothing attitude.

When it is suggested in fiction and accepted in real life that sexual passion is so all-powerful, people believe that family, home, work, reputation and respect all have to be sacrificed to this uncontrollable drive. A more tolerant view would discourage this destructive belief. These tragic and wasteful sacrifices may be quite unnecessary in many cases. The husband who had been philandering may be the cause of distress and painful readjustments in the marriage, but it may not be necessary to leave his wife, give up his home, and break up the family. The wife who is unfaithful may have to make a special effort to rehabilitate her relationship with her husband (and assuage his hurt pride), but she should not immediately assume that the marriage has collapsed, that both lives must be ruptured, and that her children must suffer.

It is possible that these 'uncontrollable' passions would be less likely to take hold of a man or woman if there were not such a high premium put upon fidelity. It may all start as a mild flirtation, or the need to reassure himself that he is still attractive to women, but if he believes the myth that love is all-powerful, he can easily persuade himself that he is not to blame. In reality there may be other non-sexual reasons for the breakdown of the marriage and some kind of rehabilitation may be possible, but this will be difficult as long as one or both partners believe that the sexual passions override sense and sensibility. If there are no fundamental causes for the breakdown in the marriage, it is unnecessary and prodigal to allow a congenial relationship to fall apart because one or other partner develops a temporary sexual interest in someone else.

Research reports make it clear that a very large number of people will be promiscuous at some period of their lives and all the indications are that this proportion is going to increase fairly rapidly. It would be far more sensible to make promiscuous activities as harmless as possible, instead of trying vainly to stop them altogether.

It may take time to find a remedy for some of the harmful aspects. Vaccines for the sexually transmitted diseases are a long way off, but this should not prevent us from adopting a more sensible attitude to VD. Despite the improvements made in birth control methods and the efforts to make contraceptives more readily available, much more could still be done to help girls avoid an unplanned pregnancy. The director of the Family Planning Association has estimated that about 8 million women in this country risk unwanted pregnancies. Approximately seven in ten teenage births in England and Wales* are illegitimate or conceived before marriage. Statistics from the Registrar-General's office show that abortions were carried out on over 600 girls of fourteen or younger, two of whom had already given birth to one child before becoming pregnant again.

With progress in medical research and public education, it is

* Two out of three in Scotland.

possible to see how physical disadvantages can be minimized. The psychological and social problems need not be so formidable. We know that there are some people who have enjoyed promiscuous sexual pleasures without letting them spoil more important relationships; some of these people are happily married. The next move could be a well-planned research to discover why some promiscuous activities end in disaster, while others are manifestly successful.

Sexual behaviour is so diversified that any narrow sexual ethic is bound to leave a large number of people out of the reckoning. It is far more profitable to judge each type of behaviour as acceptable unless it can be shown that it is definitely harmful. The sexual code has always been restrictive. It is time to take a more positive view. This means we should be less concerned with stopping people from doing what they want to do, and more concerned with helping them to find the sexual pleasures they desire.

Part II

A POSITIVE VIEW OF SEX

CHAPTER 8

PHYSICAL AND PSYCHOLOGICAL HEALTH

Health Education

The suggestions made in the second part of this book are attempts to add something to people's lives instead of taking something away by means of social hostility or prohibitions. The educator's aim should be to help people to enjoy a good sex life, not merely to avoid sexual problems. Just as we would all like to learn how to enjoy good health, not merely how to avoid illness; similarly we would prefer to know how to establish warm human relationships, not just how to avoid being on bad terms with other people. Indeed good health and good relationships are an important aid to a good sex life.

Health education in the schools has made considerable progress in recent years, but it is still thought of as a subsidiary subject. This appears injudicious when one considers how much ignorance there is, how much there is to be learnt, and how important good health is to the future aspirations of all the pupils. Schools tend to concentrate on the old examination subjects, but real education should be preparation for life, not preparation for exams.

Arguably health education should be compulsory. It is hard to think of any school subject that is more important than hygiene, accident prevention and sensible ways of maintaining good health. The only compulsory subject in schools is religious education; we teach our children to prepare to meet their God, but not how to avoid a precipitous meeting.

Obviously it is not possible to suggest a complete syllabus in this section. That would require a book to itself because health education should be taught at all ages throughout the school years. I will merely mention a few items that are often left out of the syllabus—items that are particularly relevant to a positive view of sex.

The physical changes in the body as the child grows up are explained in some schools, but as girls and boys reach puberty at an earlier age, they have often started to experience many profound and puzzling changes before the school has found time to warn the children what to expect. In 1860 the average age of menstruation was between sixteen and seventeen; now it is between twelve and thirteen with a few starting even younger. There are still reports of cases where a girl thinks she is bleeding to death because no one has told her about menstruation, and of a boy being horrified because no one has told him about nocturnal emissions.

Many health education courses carefully avoid the subject of sex. This is regarded as a separate course, but it is much better if the courses on health education and sex education complement each other. Besides, the natural interest young people have in sex provides the motivation for the development of healthy habits. Good health means better sex; this point should be made so as to encourage the students to cultivate an interest in physical and mental well-being.

It is worth pointing out that sex only very rarely has a harmful effect on physical health. Boys and girls who are interested in sport should be told that Dr Craig Sharp, the medical adviser to the British Olympic team has written: "I can find no factual evidence either in scientific literature or in discussion with many athletes and sportsmen of world class at a wide variety of sports, that sexual activity in moderation up to and including the night before a match, has any detrimental effect on the sport in question." It used to be the custom of Italian football teams to insist that the married players spent the night before a match in a hotel away from their wives, but the managers came to the conclusion that it helped a footballer to relax if he could release tension through sex on the night before the game. Athletes say that sex on the night before competition is positively beneficial from the point of view of relaxation and sleep.

The NHS is really a National Disease Service. It comes to the rescue when the human body cannot cope; and so it would be a good investment for the schools to spend more time on the positive aspects of health education.

Human Relationships

A course in health education should include information about psychological as well as physical health. Students should learn that mental illness is neither rare, nor incurable. About a quarter of them in the class will probably have a mental illness at some period of their lives and in most cases they will make a satisfactory recovery. Mental illnesses are sometimes closely associated with sexual activities, or the lack of them. But though frustrating inhibitions and irrational obsessions may be due to faulty learning about sex, the more usual cause of mental illness is the inability to establish and develop satisfying human relationships.

'Human relationships' is a cumbersome term for the art of making friends and getting on with people. It is usually assumed that this is something that just comes naturally, but everyone has something to learn about making and keeping friends. It is hard to think of any part of education that is more important. In 375 BC Xenophon said: "Of all possessions the most precious is a good and sincere friend", and the only way to have a friend is to learn how to be one.

At this time of uncertainty most teenagers feel the need of support from a group of people of about the same age. Strong loyalties develop in these groups, not only when they are in difficulties, but also when they are enjoying themselves. As well as the obvious advantages to be gained from this group solidarity, there is also the drawback of a kind of mindless unquestioning compliance. This is where and how many of the myths about sexuality begin, particularly the *machismo* idea among the boys.

Young people should be made aware that an individual may behave in quite a different way when he is in a group. Girls scream at a pop concert partly because the singer looks sexy, but also partly because the other girls are screaming. Boys shout at a football match partly because the referee is a blind idiot, but also partly because their mates are shouting. This special kind of crowd behaviour develops because there is a *group will* which can be stronger and more powerful than the individual's will.

The converse of group solidarity should also be an important part of a course on human relationships. Pupils should learn that their behaviour depends to a large extent upon their group membership and so they should tolerate other people's behaviour which is different because they belong to a different group. This is particularly true of sexual attitudes and moral values. In the modern world there are considerable variations in people's views about sex and morals, and they are not necessarily wrong because they are different.

We share with all the inhabitants of Great Britain a large number of common ideas, beliefs and attitudes. We have the same background, technology, art, literature and history. This means there are certain social conventions that we expect from an individual simply because he comes from a particular area. If he came from somewhere else, these conventions would be different.

Foreigners not only speak another language, many of their unspoken actions have quite different meanings. Italian gestures are passionate expressions of emotion. Jewish gestures accompany words to emphasize the points made. French gestures are elegant and precise. The same gesture has quite a different meaning in other parts of the world. Sticking out the tongue means an apology in China. The Japanese smile when bringing bad news. Arab speech contains a good deal of exaggeration; an Arab will continue to pursue a girl who does not rebuff him vigorously enough, or will assume that a guest really wants more to eat unless he refuses three times; the English do not press their conversation like this and an Arab at an English meal is liable to starve because he is only offered the dishes once. South Americans stand much closer to each other than Europeans; at international conferences the British have been seen retreating backwards pursued by Latin Americans trying to get near enough to hold a friendly conversation.

Sometimes ordinary friendship groups are very competitive, which leads to disappointment and jealousy. In some groups every boy is trying to catch the attention of the most beautiful girl, and every girl is trying to outsmart the others by appearing to be more popular. Many of the things at school are based on competition, like exams, class ranking or sports. Friendship should not be competitive. It is more like the exchange of gifts. You give your friendly support and receive companionship in return.

Not many schools make much effort to teach this side of human relationships and those that do are inclined to gloss over the power of sexual attraction. Of course it is quite possible for a friendship to develop between girl and boy without either one feeling sexually attracted to the other. It is equally possible that sexual attraction may not include friendship.

Every course on human relationships must also include discussions on marriage, parenthood and love. The Romans thought of marriage as a privilege for the well-born and forbade it to their slaves. For hundreds of years it has been an institution designed to ensure the inheritance of property by the production of children. Only quite recently has it been thought of as a love match. Undoubtedly this is a change for the better provided that marriage is regarded as more than a licence to have sex together. It could be argued that sexual passion on its own may be a good enough reason for making love, but it is not sufficient reason for getting married.

Early marriage should be discouraged for several economic and social reasons, not least because all boys and girls benefit from a period of relative freedom before being tied down to the responsibilities of family life. People who marry young are twice as likely to be divorced.

Many schools now teach girls about mothercraft, but this rarely goes much further than playing with a doll and learning to change its nappies. Most adolescent girls are quite unrealistic about babies and they want a child because they want something small and dependent to cuddle. They forget that the infant quickly grows into the curious demanding two-year-old and before too long into the adolescent determined to live a life of his own. Schools could do a lot more to help pupils, including boys, to prepare for parenthood.

There is a misleading superstition about motherhood. It is usually assumed that women will automatically love their children and will instinctively know how to look after them. But experience does not bear this out. Indeed there is no reason why maternal feelings should be inherently different from paternal feelings. It may be that men find it convenient to encourage this superstition so as to infer that bringing up the children is not one of their duties. Adolescents, boys especially, should be taught about the responsibilities and problems of parenthood as an antidote to romantic notions of the quiet well-behaved little dolls whose main function is to be a source of pride and pleasure to their mothers and fathers.

The subject of romantic love has been given a section to itself in Chapter 5. The warnings given there may seem at first sight to be rather a negative view, but it should be remembered that this over-romantic mythology is made a prerequisite of sex and is used by the authorities to hamper the individual in his search for sexual pleasure. Fanciful talk from teachers about love only serves to reinforce adolescent misconceptions, because they are talking about two different things.

Passionate love is lovely and one of civilizations greatest inventions. It should be enjoyed for what it is, a feast of beauty and excitement. In the best circumstances it may develop and prosper. But to believe it will always continue on that same ecstatic level and to confuse it with the interlocking of personalities, which is the real self-giving love, is to deceive oneself and disappoint others.

Moral Education

Human relationships are part of what is sometimes called moral education. The aims of morality should be to make life as pleasant as possible for everyone. Sexual morality is an extension of general morality, not a special subject with special restrictions. The dangers of any course like moral education, or humanities, or civics, or personal relations is that it always seems to the pupils that it is one generation trying to tell another generation how it should behave.

It is to get over this difficulty that the new courses in moral education include a series of small case histories which are discussed in class and the pupils search for the best solutions. The advantage of this method is that adolescents learn more easily from each other. Their interest can be stimulated if the case material is well presented and appears relevant to their own lives. The pupils argue about the relative merits of the conflicting views as they try to resolve the ambiguities and complexities of what it is like to be a human being with that problem in those circumstances.

The one great drawback to teaching adolescents about morality or, for that matter, about anything to do with sex, is the tendency to assume that there is a *best* solution for everyone, which leads us to believe in uniform standards of behaviour. We laugh at an old Victorian standard like 'Be pure in thought as well as deed', but now we talk about 'the development of responsible behaviour' as if that is the same thing for everyone. Usually it means that everyone is required to repress individual aspects of their personality in the interests of this uniform standard called 'responsible behaviour'. But it can be argued that what many people need is less repression and more resolute determination to search for their own sort of happiness in their own way.

It is often forgotten that the reverse side of responsible behaviour is civil liberty. People have rights as well as obligations. Women's rights are particularly relevant in the context of sexual activities because they have been denied for so long.

The implementation of women's sexual rights implies that men must change their ideas about women, and indeed women will also want to alter their own conceptions of themselves. The works of Margaret Mead (1949) and Money (1955) indicate clearly that the 'woman's role' is not established at birth, but is learnt from the teachings and expectations of parents and other adults as they grow up. Modern social living does not fit in with the traditional idea of the male role (the breadwinner) or the female role (at home rearing the children). The younger generations are seeking new ways of sharing tasks and interchanging roles.

Recent changes in sexual knowledge, especially improvements in contraceptive techniques, have made it possible for a woman to have more choice about when and if she will have a child. But other practical, economic and legal provisions will have to be made before a woman can combine motherhood with a working career, and so lead a fuller and more varied life. There must be more day nurseries if women are to have a free choice as to whether to go out to work or not. The European Social Charter 1962 provides much better maternity leave provisions in EEC countries than exist in Britain. Sex discrimination starts at the primary schools level with children's books which show men and women in traditional roles and continues right through the school until the last year where fewer resources are allocated in girls schools to mathematics and science. Work discrimination against women starts from the earliest years; only 7 per cent of girls take apprenticeships compared with 42 per cent of boys, and only 10 per cent of young women get day release compared with 39 per cent of young men. The new laws on discrimination against women in employment contain so many permitted exceptions as to make it easy for an employer to avoid his legal obligations. The Church leads the field in upholding the conventional view that there are some occupations for which women are inherently unsuitable.

The rights of women are not the only civil liberties that every pupil should be taught to value and preserve. Any kind of moral education tends to over-emphasize the idea of regularizing people towards a uniform standard and fails to convey our need to accept ourselves as we are, and others as they are. It is essential to strike the right balance between social obligations and individual liberties. In no case is this balance more important than in sexual behaviour and at no time of life is it more important than in adolescence.

CHAPTER 9

LEARNING ABOUT SEX

The New Interest in Sex Education
During the nineteenth century the accepted method of dealing
with childhood sexuality was to deny its existence and to avoid
thinking about it; if it intruded upon adult thinking at all, the
behaviour was suppressed. To this day most courses of sex education are designed to suppress sexual behaviour although learning
and even discussion are now permitted.

There are only a few positive aspects in modern sex education.
One girl in my research group complained: "In mothercraft
lessons we got to know everything except how to have the baby."
A boy said they were not allowed to ask questions about sex
during a biology class because, the teacher said: "A third would
take it wrongly, a third would not understand, and the other
third would try it out." The only advice one girl received from a
teacher was: "Watch out where the boys put their hands." A
thoughtful adolescent remarked: "I wish some teachers would
stop confusing their sexual problems with ours."

The idea of sex education now receives official blessing. The
Schools Council is encouraging teachers to work out new courses
and the Health Education Council supplies materials and teaching aids. But the Department of Education still seems to take a
rather negative interest, particularly as to giving contraceptive
information in schools. Most of the schools now teach what
might be called the 'plumbing' side of sex with diagrams of
sperms swimming up tubes. This kind of sex education produces
the sort of boy who can name every part of the female genitalia,
but does not know the first thing about how to treat a girl.

The drawback of the predominantly biological approach to sex
education is that it tells the pupils everything about the sex act
except why anyone should want to do it. Perhaps the most important single aspect that is missing from most courses of sex
education is the obvious point that the purpose of sexual

intercourse is physical enjoyment. It is true that people also do it to get pregnant, or to cement a relationship, or to be kind to someone, or just to prove that they can. But all these are subsidiary purposes. Intercourse and other sexual activities are for pleasure and ought to be encouraged as such. It follows from this that part of sex education should be to help people to make it as enjoyable as possible.

Some teachers, concentrating solely on the bliss of married love, paint too rosy a picture of the sexual climate the students will find outside school. The prevailing sexual scene is very competitive and it would be over-sanguine to leave the impression that sex makes everyone loving and constant. Another important aspect which should not be left out is the woman's right to enjoy sex. Indeed the pendulum may have swung too far in some social sets and the girls should be told that it is not necessary to prove to the world that they are not frigid.

Obviously some information about masturbation must be included since it is the most important sex activity for males between the ages of ten and twenty. Those parts of the body that aid sexual stimulation should be noted and preliminary sexual activities leading up to orgasm should be discussed. Some people feel that unless sex is made dull, there will be too much of it. But the information will be picked up one way or another—if not from the teacher, then through clandestine and misleading chatter among children.

Even aspects which are not controversial, in the sense that they do not encourage the pupils to experiment, are omitted because they are too embarrassing. For example the subject of circumcision is very puzzling to both boys and girls and yet they will be required to make a decision about this when they become the parent of a son. Circumcision is one of those traditional customs scarcely affected by scientific thinking or medical knowledge. The family doctor generally leaves it to the discretion of the parents, who have no idea what to do. Many doctors regard it as nothing more than a religious custom practised by the Jews and Moslems and one gynaecologist has said that he disapproves of this "officious mutilation". But there are arguments in favour of it. There is the theory that the smegma—a secretion under the foreskin—can cause cancer of the penis and of the cervix, but the evidence is complicated (see Chapter 6). Occasionally the operation becomes necessary in adult life, and this is painful and embarrassing because of the necessity to avoid sexual excitement for some time afterwards. It is said the circumcised find it easier to clean the penis and they enjoy greater sexual staying power. Both these arguments are disputed by the uncircumcised; they maintain that it is perfectly easy for them to attend to their hygiene (although there have been cases of men who are otherwise scrupulously clean but have never retracted their foreskin and washed the area because they did not know this should be done) and learning to restrain one's orgasm is a matter of practice. Medical opinion seems to be swinging against circumcision as a routine operation. It seems to be more a matter of tradition than necessity. In Sweden they have never heard of it being done. In the USA they have never heard of it not being done.

Agents of Misinformation

It is really quite surprising that there is still some debate about whether information about birth control methods should be part of a sex education course. A United Nations report has affirmed : "Instruction in family planning should begin at pre-school age and continue concurrently with the general education of the child and juvenile, so that this information reaches him before he needs it."* While the debate goes on, the unplanned pregnancies continue. The British Pregnancy Advisory Service report that 87 per cent of the girls who came to them for an abortion had received no contraceptive advice at school. My researches have shown that very few schools made any attempt to supply information about birth control methods and in the few schools that did introduce contraceptive education, it was limited to the sixth forms after about two-thirds of the girls had left full-time education.

Many researchers have noted that the primary source of sex information for boys and girls is from their friends. In my research† among 1,873 teenagers, 57 per cent had learnt about sex from people of their own age and Gebhard (1965) found 91 per cent of working class men had obtained their information from their friends. Furthermore sex education is usually given too late, long after the boys and girls have heard other versions. Consequently

* United Nations, *Family Planning and Social Policy in Europe*, UN/SOA/ESDP/1971/2.

† Page 95 of *The Sexual Behaviour of Young People*.

it is an important part of a good course in sex education to correct misinformation.

Some of the misinformation will come from the parents. Stories about babies being found under a gooseberry bush or being brought by a friendly stork are usually to cover up the embarrassment of the adult. Few parents contribute anything towards their children's sex education. In my research 67 per cent of the boys and 29 per cent of the girls had never at any time had any advice about sex from their parents. In the research by Gebhard and his co-workers, approximately three-quarters of the parents had failed to give any direct sex information.

From about the age of eight children will start to give each other misinformation about sex. It is no surprise, therefore, that when teachers start to give sex education at thirteen or fourteen, the boys and girls think they know it all and do not listen. In several surveys* the teenagers complain that they are not taught anything about sex that they did not know already, but further questioning in these same surveys reveals large gaps in their sexual knowledge.

There is a strong tendency for fantasy to dominate the sexual life of the child, starting with the parents saying they were brought by the stork to the vague feeling that females have been castrated. The idea that sexual activities are dirty goes back to early elimination training when the genitals become associated with excretory functions. Add to this the emotional, irrational and evasive attitudes of many adults to sexual matters, and it becomes clear that a sex education course that relies on logical reasoning and the straight presentation of evidence has to break through thick walls of resistance.

As one confused child mininforms another, a bizarre folklore is spread around. Boys think that masturbation makes you blind or mad. Girls think it is safe so long as you do it standing up. No matter how thorough the course may be, plenty of time must be allowed for questions and discussion so that the more lurid myths can be explored and exploded. But no course can be complete if it relies solely upon the pupils to ask the relevant questions. No one can ask a question about something of which he is totally ignorant. Furthermore a question may be unasked in school because the adolescent does not know the polite words

* For example, the survey undertaken by the Opinion Research Centre for the *Sunday Times* in March 1972.

or, more unfortunately, because he genuinely does not want to shock his teacher.

The Right Time and Place

All this strongly indicates that sex education must be given in the schools far earlier than at present. The argument advanced against this is that children mature at different ages and some of them may not be ready to receive this information. The mistake in this assertion is to assume that a child is asexual until he reaches puberty. In fact the data obtained by the Institute for Sex Research in the United States shows that about 57 per cent of the males and 48 per cent of the females who were interviewed when they were adults remembered sexual play prior to puberty, with most of it occurring between the ages of eight and thirteen. In a small sample of boys interviewed before puberty, about 70 per cent reported such sex play, suggesting that it is an even more widespread phenomenon, and that memory of it is apparently often repressed by adults (Kinsey, 1948, 1953). So it is absurd to maintain that most young children are sexually naïve.

The alleged trauma that results from the child learning about his own body can only occur to someone who has already had an unfortunate upbringing and the specific age at which the child receives this information is of small significance. As Professor Gagnon (1965) has written in his monograph on Sexual Learning in the Child: "The child who is traumatized by the sight of a nude body, or by learning that intercourse occurs, or by learning that babies grow inside of the mother, had previously developed a background of experience such that sooner or later, in one context or another, he would have been unable to cope with similar sexual stimuli."

This fear about upsetting a child arises from the idea that sex education is a sudden revelation. In fact all such courses should be given to each class throughout the school years. This ensures that the information is given gradually, logically, and repeatedly, so that it is learnt and remembered when the time comes to make use of the knowledge. As one headmistress sensibly remarked: "You tell them, then tell them again, and then tell them that you've told them."

The information is important and the context in which it is learnt is still more important. The exchange of sexual information among children is fallible; information from parents reflects their own anxieties; ideas picked up from the media correspond to public attitudes which are not always the same as private behaviour. The schools have this unique opportunity to give a straightforward account of this useful information, which the pupils need to know about and which they would only stumble upon desultorily if they were left to find out for themselves.

At present sex education in the schools is too timid and too late. Consequently sex education for adults will be needed for many years to come. This may bring extra problems because it is much harder to correct misinformation and there are much stronger inhibitions to overcome when providing sex education for adults. Articles in the press and the specialist magazines like *Forum* show clearly that there is a big demand for more information. Advice columnists in popular magazines get hundreds of letters from married men as well as women. Sometimes the man is worried that his new bride will run screaming from the honeymoon hotel at the first sight of his penis, but a more common fear is that the girl will fall off the bed laughing.

Commercial enterprise fills the gap left by inadequate sex education. Hundreds of sex manuals—learning on the job—have been written for adults who feel they are not as well informed about sex as they should be. Publishers, film makers and others seek to turn the demand for sex information into saleable commodities; some of these products are good, some are misleading and some are inaccurate. Educationalists do not have much influence on the contents of this material because the main criterion is profitability.

It is still not uncommon for a married couple to have sexual relations over a long period without a word being spoken; these activities and their possible pleasures, satisfactions, disappointments or aversions are not discussed. It may not be knowledge about sex but the attitude to sex which is hindering these adults. The same may be true of the pupils who receive sex education in school. The information is important, but a more positive function of sex education is to create that attitude of mind which will enable pupils to make the most of their lives, including their sex lives. For example, all those who do not use contraceptives know about them, but they are unable to act on their knowledge for one reason or another. It is the task of sex education to provide the essential basis so that changing social attitudes to sex can be assimilated.

The rapidity of changing technology means that everyone leaving school this year must retrain for a different job at least once in his working career. The function of modern education is not just training for work. It is a far more important task. The teacher's job is to help his pupils to acquire the capacity to adapt to, and cope with, these rapid changes. And just as this is true of all education, it is certainly true of sex education.

Just compare the attitude to sex today with the ideas of five, ten or fifteen years ago. So what is it going to be like for the children who are now in school; in five years when they are married; in ten years when they have a family; in fifteen years when they will be called old-fashioned by their own teenage children? Sex education, if it is to be any good, must help the pupil to adapt to new conditions, new ideas, different ethics, different values.

One way to realize these aims is to encourage more open discussion which is helpful and realistic. There is plenty of discussion of a kind; the male to male interaction is usually tales about sexual prowess or scurrilous jokes; among females most of the discussion is about romantic love. But sensible open discussion is inhibited because, despite all that has been written, sex remains a very private and special thing.

Possibly this is the appropriate way to end this chapter. In spite of all the ignorance and all the possibilities of helping people, it should never be forgotten that for everybody sex is a part of their innermost being, and we must always be careful to respect the privacy and individuality of each person.

Chapter 10

ETHICS AND EPIDEMICS

Social Aspects of VD

The sexually transmitted diseases have been mentioned in Chapters 2 and 6, but it is necessary to consider them again in this part of the book because this has always been one of the most negative aspects of sex. The threat of VD has often been used to suppress sexual activity by moral authorities, including many medical men. For example the British Medical Association's report issued in 1964 entitled *Venereal Disease and Young People* received a horrified reception from the press and was described as one of the least satisfactory documents ever to come from a national professional association; according to Wayland Young, "58 out of 66 pages contain a lament about promiscuity which owes nothing to medical experience or insight and much to the sapping-the-foundations-of-our-national-life school of moralising".

Moralistic attitudes still prevail to some extent in the medical establishment, which does not universally welcome new methods of treatment and is not whole-hearted in its desire to eliminate the disease. Some doctors still believe that the best way to control VD is to frighten young people out of doing what leads to infection. This, as Germaine Greer has said, "is rather like persuading people not to eat as a precaution against food poisoning".

If the tactics are changing now, it is because it has become clear that the threat of VD has not been very successful in preventing people from enjoying sex. Even when the venereal diseases were harder to cure and the consequences of infection were much more serious, a study of history shows that syphilis and gonorrhoea were common illnesses. The August 1971 edition of the *British Journal of Venereal Diseases* catalogues an impressive number of notable people in the past who are thought to have been sufferers of these diseases. They include Boswell, Keats, Wilde, Dostoevsky, Strindberg, Nietszche, Schopenhauer,

Goya, Manet, Van Gogh, Schubert, Baudelaire, three medieval Popes and Cleopatra.

Now that gonorrhoea and syphilis can nearly always be cured without medical complications or permanent injury, there is a tendency among the impetuous young to say that VD is no worse than a common cold. This is not an apt comparison for two reasons: first, the common cold will nearly always disappear without medical treatment and this is not true of VD. Second, doctors know how to cure VD, which is more than can be said for the common cold.

My research has shown that it is not just the promiscuous who get VD. Reports from clinics reveal that one in three of the men who catch gonorrhoea does so from his regular sexual partner. It is, therefore, very doubtful ethics to withhold public money for research and extra facilities with the excuse that there will be more promiscuity if it becomes easier to cure VD. The logic is as doubtful as the ethics; if the reason for opposing promiscuity is because it is harmful, then it follows that every opportunity should be taken to make it less harmful.

The ethics are still more questionable when it is remembered that it is the young who will suffer. The statistics show that young people are more likely to catch VD; one-sixth of all new gonorrhoea infections are people under the age of twenty. Yet some doctors seem to think that young people should be allowed to catch VD because it will act as a warning against further sexual excesses. Dr Dalzell-Ward of the Health Education Council has said: "A visit to a VD clinic can have a valuable effect. It can be a warning and a preventative agent."* Others believe that VD is a fitting redress for the wicked.

Apart from the fact that the threat of VD probably never did much to curb the sexual passions, such an outlook is based on faulty values. It is better to have had the clap than never to have loved at all.

Sources of Infection
A more positive attitude to the problem of VD would start by trying to find out more about it. The main task of the contact tracers is to find the source of infection and persuade the infected to come to the clinic for treatment. But contact tracers, who should have undergone the full professional training of the health

* In the *Evening Standard*, 23 October 1972.

visitor (as many have), should also be trained to search system-
atically for information that will tell us more about the way VD
is caught. Obviously it is a disease which is more likely to be
spread by the young and unmarried, but it can be more complex
than this. For example, one thirty-five-year-old businessman with
syphilis named four women who might have given him the
disease, but he insisted that his wife could not have been the
source; all four extramarital contacts were traced and all proved
to be free of infection, but the wife had syphilis and, to her
husband's chagrin, a lover who had infected her.

When there is more information on the most likely sources,
then we can estimate who is taking the biggest risks. In this way
target groups can be identified and a special effort can concentrate upon reducing the prevalence within these groups. The
Health Education Council Research Unit at St Thomas' found
that the average number of recorded contacts of the male patients
was 1.4, whereas for the female patients it was 1.5. So the girls
have, on average, more partners than the men and therefore are
more likely to spread the disease. Homosexual males have an average of 1.6 partners, so they were even more likely to infect others.
These preliminary figures need to be sub-divided into small categories before specific target groups can be identified, but they
show how useful information can be gathered from the clinics.

It has already been noted in Chapter 2 that a considerable
proportion of infections come from abroad. Increased mobility as
a result of air charter international holidays means that one
person can infect two people in different continents in a single
day. 'Global gonorrhoea', as it has been called, may seem to
magnify the problem to a depressing degree, but it also gives us
the opportunity to find out where VD is more prevalent and to
study those societies to see if we can spot the reasons for this.

A study of foreign countries also enables us to evaluate other
methods of combating this problem. In the United States far
more money is spent on TV campaigns. In China they have
trained thousands of para-medical workers to take the treatment
into the homes of the people. In Sweden information about VD
is a compulsory part of the curriculum in schools. In Russia
there are legal powers to enforce partners who have been named
by patients to attend a clinic. A study of these various methods
should help us to evaluate our own efforts to see if they can be
improved. VD is a social disease and so attempts to lessen its

impact will require careful and elaborate sociological investigation as well as medical research. If, as we are always being told, VD is the most common infectious disease in Britain after measles, it is surprising how little sociological work has been done on this social problem.

Planning Future Campaigns

Until May 1970 anti-VD posters were liable to prosecution under the 1889 Indecent Advertisement Act. VD clinics could not be advertised on the public highway and the only posters permitted were in public lavatories, adding to the aura of dirt and shadiness. As many women never went into a public conveniece, they knew nothing about VD. This law has now been repealed, but there are still surprising pockets of resistance. Two years after the HEC launched its anti-VD poster campaign, the police at Newcastle upon Tyne removed some of these posters from a community advice centre because they were alleged to be indecent.

TV programmes and articles in magazines and newspapers often include photographs of someone in an advanced stage of syphilis. These pictures are irrelevant to the main problem and will have little effect on the young and adventurous who are most at risk, while they may disgust the old with stable sexual relations. Ponting (1963) tells the story about the boy who caught sight of an article on VD in the Sunday paper which his father was reading; the boy asked what it was, but the father hastily folded up the paper and said, "Nothing, son". The father did not know that the son had been attending the local VD clinic. That was some time ago, but it was not so long ago that horror was expressed when John Peel (the disc-jockey, not the ex-President of the FPA) admitted on radio that he had had VD; that was not all, for his probity as a witness at the *Oz* trial was impugned by the prosecution on that account although it was entirely irrelevant to his testimony.

The young are taught to engage in potentially dangerous activities such as climbing and sailing as well as possible and as safely as possible. The same attitude could be applied to sex so that the young are taught to set about their sexual endeavours as well and as safely as possible. As it is the new generations who have taken "ecology" as a battle cry and raised their voices against pollution, insecticides and food additives, it might also be good tactics to point out that regular injections of anti-biotics are a long way from the ecological ideal.

The message would be more likely to get across to the young if it were not felt necessary to be so threatening or so solemn. There are signs that it can be done. One HEC poster is headed: HOW TO CATCH GONORRHOEA and *Time Out's Book of London* (1972) advises: "Don't be shy or uptight about finding out— after all, it's just another germ, and its only distinguished feature is you caught it making love, which is OK, isn't it?" In 1972 a big extravagant TV show was produced in America and parts of it were transmitted by the BBC a year later. It included a rock group who sang, "Don't give a dose to the one you love most", and the urbane compère of the show held up a syringe and recommended: "A shot of penicillin for the man who has everybody."

This may raise a few eyebrows, but if people are to be persuaded to go to VD clinics, the stigma associated with these diseases must be decreased. If you get VD, you will probably have to go to a place named SPECIAL CLINIC, sometimes a building apart from the main hospital with a separate entrance so everyone who sees you go in knows where you are going. On entering you register and are then given a card with a number on it.* You are then asked to sit down and await your turn. This gives you plenty of time for looking at all the others and wondering what they have been doing.

Needless to say they will be wondering how you managed to get yourself infected. But in fact many of the people who attend these clinics do not have VD and may have been sent by their GP because they have some genito-urinary infection which may have nothing to do with sexual intercourse. VD clinics should be incorporated in the normal hospital out-patient departments with the same waiting rooms, instead of being separate premises.

The Medical Aspects
As well as all the sociological aspects mentioned so far, more money should be provided to improve the medical services.

---

* This is very important. A venereologist asked me to discuss my research findings with him and when I went to the clinic at the appointed time, the orderly said: "Number?" As I attempted to explain about my appointment, he said, "You can't come in here until you've got a number".

General practitioners are increasingly sending patients with minor genito-urinary ailments to VD clinics instead of waiting for weeks to see a consultant urologist and this is going to increase the pressure on the already overcrowded clinics. Furthermore those who have more than one sexual partner are sometimes advised to go to a clinic regularly for a check-up. For example, *It*, the underground newspaper, advises: "If you find you get tired of your sleeping partners and change them quite often, you should get into the habit of going along to your local clinic every so often, just to check (like going to the dentist, only not so painful)."

But if everyone heeded the good advice to have a regular check, the service would break down because the clinics would be unable to cope with the extra people. There is, therefore, the danger that a really successful campaign may so overload the clinics that they would be compelled to turn infected people away because they did not have the facilities to treat them.

Only about 175 doctors, of which fewer than a hundred are consultants, specialize in these diseases. This is nothing like enough. It is up to medical schools and the Department of Social Service to convince students that there is an important job to be done in this speciality. If there were an increase in the number of clinics, as there should be, this would improve the promotional prospects for the doctors.

Medical knowledge about non-specific genital infections (particularly NSU) is still deficient. The present techniques for diagnosing gonorrhoea are unsatisfactory. Even the best laboratory examinations may miss about 20 per cent of female infections.* The result is that many venereologists do not adhere to the strictly orthodox medical practice of 'diagnosis before treatment' and give antibiotics to all the sexual contacts of patients with gonorrhoea whether gonococci are found or not.

Although the most urgent need is a reliable serological method of diagnosis, it is a fact that no communicable disease has ever been eradicated until a preventative vaccine was discovered. It will be necessary to undertake considerable research which will require the use of the most modern techniques of immunology, bacteriology and epidemiology; and furthermore it will be very expensive. At present it does not have a top priority among

* According to the *International Journal of Health Education*, volume VI, page 75, 1963.

medical scientists. Even when it is discovered, tested and approved, it will be more difficult than usual to persuade people to be vaccinated because VD is one of those diseases which, it is assumed, happens to someone else.

If, as seems likely, about a quarter of a million will visit the VD clinics next year and if, as we have often been told, the sexually transmitted diseases have reached the proportions of an epidemic, then surely the search for a vaccine deserves a top priority in the field of medical research. Quite apart from anything else, think of the prestige and profit that is going to go to the first country that finds a successful vaccination. As a United Nations report has pointed out, the problem is world-wide. "The revival of the venereal diseases has engendered world-wide concern. It is estimated there are now in the world 30 to 50 million cases of venereal syphilis and more than 150 million cases of gonococcal infection." That was in 1967. The figures will have increased since then.

The age of puberty is lower than it used to be, so sexual relationships are generally beginning at younger ages. Not only are there more people in the world, but the proportion of young and sexually active people in the population has increased, so the number at risk is far larger. The problem of VD provides the perfect opportunity for abandoning a negative attitude and adopting a more positive view.

CHAPTER II

UNPLANNED AND UNWANTED

Contraceptives on the National Health Service

EVERY CHILD A WANTED CHILD was the slogan adopted by the Family Planning Association and it now receives almost unanimous support. The old pioneers of that movement must look back in amazement at the considerable shift of opinion in the last few years. Now that the government has decided to provide contraceptive advice and supplies, much of the controversy has abated although some people object to the service being free and ask why they should have to subsidize other people's love-making. There are good reasons for doing so, although people who ask this question are hard to convince. It is not just the young and promiscuous who have unplanned pregnancies. Many unplanned pregnancies occur among married couples who have already achieved their desired family size. A Government report* estimated that one in three of all unplanned pregnancies happens to women who enjoy a stable relationship with a man and it is further estimated that half of these unwanted pregnancies remain for ever regretted. It is also known that a large proportion of unwanted pregnancies cause much hardship because they occur in families that are already large and poor (Thompson and Illsley, 1969). Thus unwanted pregnancies are the direct cause of the continuation of deprivation from one generation to another.

But the argument that should most impress those who feel that free contraceptives are an unwarranted burden on the taxpayer is that the prevention of unwanted pregnancies would save the country considerable sums of money spent on medical care, supplementary benefits, child care facilities, sickness benefits, temporary accommodation for the homeless and other welfare

* *Family Planning Services in England and Wales* prepared by the Social Survey Division of the Offices of Population Censuses and Surveys in 1973.

services. A PEP Study on the Costs and Benefits of Family
Planning (Laing, 1972) has demonstrated that the financial
savings for the nation if unwanted pregnancies can be avoided
would be in excess of £250,000,000 per annum. Those who
protest about subsidizing free supplies of contraceptives should
remember that it is saving them from paying extra subsidies on
maternity grants, family allowances, more places in schools and
more demands on the National Health Service.

Improvements in Distribution

Most women see birth control as part of the medical situation.
The user of contraceptives should be discouraged from thinking
of contraception as a medical problem and from taking on the
role of patient as this suggests that only the doctor can help them.
This may flatter the competence of the doctor; Ward (1969)
enquired among general practitioners in Sheffield and found that
only 32 per cent had received training in contraceptive techniques, although 93 per cent advised their patients on birth
control.

Not all doctors are pleased to supply contraceptives on the
NHS because they used to make a little money on the side out of
prescriptions for the pill; many GPs regarded this as a perquisite
and did not declare their returns for tax purposes.

If contraception had been accepted as part of the NHS when
it started in 1948, the cost of supplying materials would be taken
as part of the capitation fee for which the doctor was expected
to provide total health care for each patient. But birth control
was not regarded as a medical service in those days. Now GPs
expect to be paid extra for supplying their patients with something which, in the long run, will probably reduce their work
load. It is ironic that the extra payment demanded by the doctors
comes at a time when people are beginning to realize that the
availability of birth control services is being severely limited by
the intransigence of the medical profession.

There are several reasons why some women do not like getting
their contraceptives from doctors. Some would prefer to discuss
birth control matters with a woman and, as the overwhelming
majority of general practitioners are men, it is often impossible
to grant this request. Some women, especially single girls, are
deterred from seeking contraceptive advice because their doctor
is a friend of the family; "He's too like your father", as one girl

said. The kindly doctor who has visited the small girl in her home when she had measles or chicken-pox is not likely to be the person in whom she can confide without embarrassment when she wants to obtain contraceptives. To the young the image of the family doctor today is of an over-worked, rather puritanical soul with old-fashioned ideas about sex and without the time or inclination to learn about the results of modern sex research. Furthermore there are still a few doctors who see it as their moral duty to refuse to prescribe contraceptives to girls who are not married, while others feel compelled to add a little moralizing to the prescription. Other women are worried by the apparent lack of privacy and the crowd in the waiting room. The consulting room of a busy doctor is not the ideal place for a diffident person to ask embarrassing questions. This must mean that there are some cases where information about contraception is not obtained or understood because the woman is not at ease. It is also the case that some women who receive adequate information about family planning from their doctor do not feel capable of passing on the relevant facts to their husbands.

It is so important to make contraceptives readily available that all possible methods of distribution should be actively considered. As over half of all births take place in hospitals, it is important that mothers be given family planning advice before leaving the maternity ward. It is obvious that there should be a systematic programme of contraceptive advice to girls after they have had an abortion. It is also a good idea to train midwives to give advice about family planning.

In 1973 the Central Medical Committee of the International Planned Parenthood Federation concluded that the limitation of oral contraceptives to doctor's prescriptions discriminates against those most in need of help. "When oral contraceptives were first introduced, it was reasonable to restrict the use of these unknown and relatively powerful drugs to medical prescription," the Committee wrote. However, more than fifteen years' experience and the tremendous increase in the number of users has demonstrated conclusively that "this method of family planning is highly effective, relatively simple to use, and that the health benefits almost certainly outweigh the risks of use in nearly all cases". The Committee believes that whoever normally meets the health needs of the community, whether doctor, nurse, midwife, pharmacist or store-keeper, can be an appropriate person to distribute oral contraceptives.

Despite the medical orientation that surrounds contraceptives for the female, it remains true that barbers and chemists help plan more families than all the doctor services added together. It is a good method of distribution, but there are some men who are too embarrassed to ask for contraceptives over the counter, like the man who was asked why he had four toothbrushes in his breast pocket and he explained that every time he goes into a chemist the shop assistant is a girl.

There is some doubt if chemists and barber's shops will continue to be a good retail outlet. The small independent chemists are disappearing and the big chains are becoming more like gift stores staffed mainly by young girls. Meanwhile the modish hair stylist establishments now frequented by smart young men feel that it would spoil their image to keep a stock of condoms.

It is still quite difficult to get advertisements for contraceptives placed in some newspapers, periodicals and on posters, unless they are so discreet that it is not clear exactly what they are advertising. Until 1975 the law regulating commercial television classified contraception with astrology as services which are not to be advertised.

One of the best ways of selling contraceptives is in a supermarket (not one of the sex supermarkets because many people would hesitate to enter such places), where the customer can simply pick up the brand he or she wants without having to ask for it. It is expected that these displays will also lead to a certain amount of impulse buying. But there is still resistance from retailers, although there is no law against displaying contraceptives.

Vending machines in public places have the same advantages as self-service stores, with the additional advantage that contraceptives can also be obtained in the evening when the shops are closed and at the hours when there is more likely to be a demand for them. To those who argue that this is pandering to the demands of the thoughtless and improvident, it is fair to point out that these are probably not the sort of people who should be encouraged to produce illegitimate children.

The authorities and others who fear that the moral state of the nation will decline if contraceptives become available too easily tend to forget that there is one very popular form of contraception that does not require a retail outlet. Furthermore it costs nothing. But withdrawal is not a very effective form of birth control and if the other types are difficult to get, the number of unwanted pregnancies and the demand for abortions will increase.

The Non-medical Methods

Sociologists tell us that we should pay attention to graffiti because it is often a cry for help from the frustrated. The writing on the wall of the women's lavatory at the London School of Economics* makes it plain that there is no contraceptive technique to suit everyone. "The pill made me fat." "Less acne with the pill." "Has anyone found a method they're happy with?" "Yes. Stop being fucked." "Diaphragm isn't as hopeless as it's made out to be . . . only hassle is that the jelly is *scented*." "I got pregnant with an IUD."

The old fashioned methods of birth control now seem a great deal less despicable than they did in the recent past. The attraction of the new methods like the pill and the coil is the very low rate of failure. But for some women these methods have unpleasant side effects and so they stop using contraceptives altogether. It is possible that the slightly less efficient but more popular methods might prove to be a better solution for many people. The popular but less effective methods make even more sense when they are combined with the new techniques of using vacuum aspiration as soon as the menstrual period is delayed.

The dangers of the pill have been exaggerated, but some of the side-effects which may be considered trivial in a medical sense, can be quite distressing. The slight discolouring around the mouth and eyes can be upsetting. Sometimes lubrication and sensitivity in the vagina is disturbed and this may spoil sexual enjoyment. Obviously it is worrying that some people put on weight when they start taking the pill. One woman said : "It is not the dangers that put me off. It is the fear of gaining a stone and coping with a size 40 chest."

Apart from the unpleasant side-effects, there is the business of remembering to take the pill no matter how distracted, exhausted or drunk one may be. Moreover the pill can get lost, dropped down the plug hole, or eaten by the dog. Germaine Greer suggests the manufacturers should append a supernumerary one like a spare button on a cardigan.

* According to *New Society*, 14 November 1974.

The coil is the other very effective method but this seems to be unsuitable for about one in four women. It is not known why this should be. Medical knowledge about intra-uterine devices is not very profound; indeed, doctors are not even sure how it works.

It is not really surprising that some people would prefer to do without the side-effects of the pill and the coil, and choose to take slightly greater risks by using the older methods. If it is easier to persuade someone to use a less effective method because it suits her, this is perfectly reasonable, especially when menstrual regulation (see Chapter 12) can be used as a remedy for the few cases when these contraceptives fail.

Even withdrawal, a birth control technique that is not usually recommended, is being reconsidered because it is popular with men and costs nothing. Known as the British Rail method— 'pull out on time', it is likely to be a frustrating experience for many women. There is, however, the chance that the man might impregnate his partner even if he withdraws and ejaculates outside because most men secrete (what has been called) 'love water' from the prostate before orgasm and this may have a few sperms in it.

But it is the condom which seems to be coming into favour again and there is a new sense of awareness among birth control campaigners that the old french letter can play a valuable role in family planning. This is partly because manufacturers have vastly improved the design and feel of modern condoms and there is much less consumer resistance to their use. Condoms are reliable, relatively inexpensive, require no medical examination or supervision, have no side-effects, provide some protection against venereal disease, and permit the man to share actively in planning his family. Latex condoms are manufactured on moulds dipped in rubber and they are rarely defective. The effectiveness of the condom depends far more on the way it is used than on the product itself and most of the reported failures are caused by the man allowing the condom to slip off while he is removing his penis from the vagina.

The Need for a Variety of Methods

Most women in this country choose the pill and it seems to be particularly suitable for the young and unmarried. But it is not generally known that it has a lower continuation rate than the coil. Doctors and workers in clinics get the wrong impression because they see the satisfied pill users returning for more supplies and the dissatisfied coil users returning for help or removal; the satisfied coil users do not need to make regular visits to the clinic or consulting room. Other people may find other kinds of contraceptives more suitable for their needs. In all cases it is important that the full range of possibilities should be put before each individual and each married couple.

It is important to realize that the fertile are not homogenous. They come from different backgrounds and sectors of society. What is appropriate or acceptable for one person is unsuitable for another. If a birth control programme is to be successful, it must accommodate these differences. The less effective contraceptive methods should not be despised, especially as they do not require medical supervision.

Most of the knowledge and work involved in contraception is technically simple and can be done by nurses and para-medical staff. Only a small amount of training is necessary for them to learn how to fit the cap or the coil. Peel and Potts in their *Text-book of Contraceptive Practice* write: "The prescription of the pill is generally limited to general practitioners, but this is more for administrative and legal convenience than for medically defensible reasons." There is now a growing campaign to scrap prescriptions for the pill and to sell it over the counter (Smith and Kane, 1975).

It certainly is not necessary for a woman to go to a doctor's surgery every time she wants some more pills, but of course she should be free to go when she wants help. She should be able to go when she starts to take oral contraceptives (although the routine examination given by most doctors seems to be very perfunctory and hardly contributes to identifying susceptible women in advance) and encouraged to see the doctor if she is worried about side-effects.

One place where medical skills will be increasingly in demand is for the surgical procedures of sterilization. Until fifty years ago, female sterilization was a major operation involving all the hazards of abdominal surgery and requiring days of hospitalization and weeks of convalescence. Today it can be performed easily with the aid of a laparoscope (a long slender tube with a series of lenses running the length of the instrument) as an outpatient procedure. It is offered gladly to women in developing countries and even forced on women in some countries, who are told to undergo the operation or be denied welfare. But in this country a woman who decides that she does not want any more children may have trouble finding a doctor who is willing to perform the operation unless she already has a large family. He fears she might change her mind or have it changed for her. If she is unmarried, she will find it impossible to get anyone to operate.

But male sterilization or vasectomy is usually considered a better solution for married couples who already have the number of children they want. There must be few operations that have such a high success rate (about 99 per cent) and offers so much relief from anxiety. There are over 10,000 operations each year. Family men have discovered that this once-only procedure can spare their wives or themselves a lot of inconvenience. Vasectomy is safe, simple, takes less than fifteen minutes, requires only a local anaesthetic and eliminates the need to buy contraceptives.

Most of the problems that occur after vasectomy are of psychological origin. It is rumoured that 'you can tell from a man's eyes' (or face) if he has had a vasectomy. Some men feel it is a blow to their pride and equate masculinity with the ability to make a woman pregnant. Some people even seem to confuse vasectomy with castration (the removal of the testes).

On psychologically well-adjusted men vasectomy does not significantly affect male hormone balance, sexual desire, capacity for erection or ejaculation of semen. Of 271 men who had undergone a vasectomy, 167 (62 per cent) replied that it had improved their sex life, ninety-two (34 per cent) replied it had made no difference and twelve (4 per cent) replied that it was worse (*Family Planning Journal*, January 1974). The friends of family men who have had a vasectomy sometimes ask : "What if one of your children died?" But children should not be regarded as replaceable and the womb is not a production line.

Motivation and Marketing
Despite the considerable improvement in contraceptive methods and provision, many problems remain and there is certainly room for a far more positive attitude towards birth control policies. Even free contraceptives will not be used by the people who most need them unless they are aware of their importance. The degree of ignorance among the young, even today, has to be heard to

be believed. Some think the safe period is in the middle of the month, or that nothing can happen the first time, or that it's safe if you do it standing up. Claire Raynor says she has come across people who think an energetic dance after intercourse will do the trick.

Perhaps it is not important that they remember all the details. Some courses in sex education spend too much time on genital anatomy and reproductive physiology. It is not necessary to pass a biology exam before one can enjoy sexual intercourse. But young people should know what kind of contraceptives are available and where they can get help when they need it. Meanwhile an educational campaign for people who have left school on family planning, ecology and population will reinforce and complement the knowledge that the pupils have acquired in school.

More time and thought should be given to the question of motivation and a far more lively approach is required if the large number of unplanned pregnancies is going to be reduced. Some people seem to think the problem is almost solved now that the Government provides free contraceptives. But there are other 'costs' besides the price of the contraceptive. There is the amount of physical or nervous energy that a customer is prepared to spend in order to acquire a contraceptive. Thus a free contraceptive may only be obtained by making a long journey to a clinic, or by submitting to an embarrassing examination, or by having to answer a lot of impertinent questions, or by waiting for over an hour at the doctor's. The wasted time and the inconvenience is an important part of the 'cost'. Free contraceptives usually have to be obtained in one's free time.

It is unfruitful to provide a service if it is not going to be used. Somehow the irresolute customer has to be convinced that it is worth the effort of using the contraceptives. The benefits are rather remote. One doesn't feel better because one has used a contraceptive. There is no immediate gratification and it depends upon an individual having the foresight to take precautions. Some of those who receive contraceptives will not learn to use them properly, like the woman who has had a child by every known method of birth control.

If one is sick, there is strong motivation to go to a doctor. People will attend the surgery because they are in pain and want to get better. But those who want contraceptives are not sick and consequently are not highly motivated to go to a lot of inconvenience on the promise of some future intangible benefit.

People who require contraceptives are customers, not patients. Contraceptives are consumer products manufactured for potential customers who must want to acquire these goods and services. In other words, it is a problem of marketing. The creed of the marketeer is that the customer must be provided with what he wants, even if the customer's desires are, on occasions, rather capricious. For example, elaborately packaged deluxe contraceptives are sometimes three times the price, even though the product itself is not so different and is in no way more effective. Retailers throughout the world note that the cheapest product is rarely the most popular and there is no demand for those marked 'small size' when condoms are sold over the counter.

To meet the psychological as well as the practical needs of the potential buyers, condoms may be opaque, transparent, almost any colour, reservoir-ended, lubricated, contoured, pagoda-shaped, spiral or flocked with a rough surface. Many imaginative schemes for selling condoms have been used in different countries and there is no real reason why similar sales promotions should not be tried here.

In Japan the advertising stresses colour: "Opal colour invites sweet dreams; the pink a delectable mood" (Matsumoto, 1972). In 1970 a new condom only 0.03 mm thick was introduced (Koyama, 1974). Saleswomen sell condoms door-to-door to Japanese housewives and these sales now account for 15–20 per cent of all sales (Potts, 1973).

In Sweden contraception has been openly promoted for several years. Posters and magazines carry advertisements for contraceptives. Cartoons explain how they work. Vending machines for condoms have long been a part of Swedish street furniture, department stores display them for sale and pharmacies are obliged by law to sell contraceptives. The Association for Sex Education (Riksförbundet För Sexuell Upplysing—RFSU, established in 1933) has its own 'Birds and Bees' shops and June 1972 was 'Condom Month' in Sweden. The latest condom is named *Black Jack* and its emblem is so well known that it is used as an imprint on T-shirts.

In Germany a relatively thick rough red condom has been introduced, obviously for sexual stimulation. One German manufacturer provides a twin pack of a hygiene towelette for the girl and a flocked condom for the man. All this may be too outlandish for some, but it would be a mistake to sneer at these promotions. Since the majority of fertile couples are young, contraceptives should be designed to appeal to this important market.

People who work in commercial enterprises also realize the importance of providing a good 'after sales' service. A similar service should be provided for those who use contraceptives. Not only should there be facilities for treating the side-effects when they occur, but when a birth control method fails, as it does from time to time, we must be prepared to offer a quick and efficient abortion service.

The Man's Point of View

Recently there has been a tendency to forget about the man's attitude to birth control and to underestimate his fears about loss of prestige when the contraceptive precautions are taken entirely by the woman. Masculine pride is one reason why more time and money should be spent on persuading men that contraception is also their concern. One of the more revealing results of my research into the sexual behaviour of young adults is that the man sometimes regards the pill as a threat to his dominant role. Gorer (1971) found that it is often the husband who decides that his wife should not take the pill.

When the husband refuses to allow his wife to take the pill, it may not be because he believes that oral contraceptives are dangerous. In my research 46 per cent of the men whose sexual partners were on the pill said that it spoilt their enjoyment of sex. In reality it has very little effect on the sex act except that it rids the couple of a certain amount of anxiety.

The most likely explanation for this negative attitude to the pill is that some men object to losing the initiative and wish to retain the power to decide whether birth control is to be used or not. The man is usually the initiator of sexual intercourse (in his opinion, at any rate) and it might be very embarrassing for a man after several years of marriage and a regular pattern of sexual activity if the woman suddenly started to make more demands. A woman can allow sexual intercourse to take place even if she is not in the mood for it, but a man may not be able to get an erection. A husband may resent not having complete control of the birth control situation because not only may he want to forbid his wife to take the pill, but also he may not know when she has not taken it. It is not difficult to envisage a situation in which the husband who does not want another child for financial or other reasons, is at odds with his wife who, perhaps unconsciously, forgets to take her pills because secretly she wishes to increase the family.

At present many women are not given a free choice because they are not sufficiently well informed to question the man's decisions. In a study among women who had undergone an abortion (Morton-Williams and Hindell, 1972), it was found that men, whether husbands or lovers, often had a marked influence on a woman's contraceptive behaviour, for example, by encouraging her to take chances, by lulling her into a false sense of security or by expressing prejudices against a particular method (mainly the pill) which deterred the woman from using it.

Advice given to the wife at a postnatal clinic, for example, may be ignored if she is unwilling to discuss such matters with her husband, or is unable to secure his co-operation. It is still not unknown for men to object to their wives using the pill because it makes them available for other men. (Wives sometimes try to prevent their husbands having a vasectomy for similar reasons.)

Although there has been impressive progress in medical knowledge, the contribution that can be made by the social sciences is only just beginning to be appreciated. Radical alterations in society will bring about changes in attitudes to contraception. The idea that a woman can only find fulfilment as a wife and mother has rightly been challenged by the Women's Liberation Movement. The occupational career of the wife may be as important as the husband's. In these circumstances family planning becomes an important factor in the domestic arrangements of married couples.

Contraception and the Single Girl

The fear of an unplanned pregnancy affects very many women and men, married as well as single. This fear is interfering with the sexual pleasures of many people on many occasions and inevitably causes one or both sexual partners to feel ill at ease and unrelaxed during intercourse.

This is bad enough, but my research shows quite clearly that those who are in most need of contraceptives are also those who are least likely to get it. It is the young teenagers and those who are least able to look after an unwanted baby who are most at risk.

The gap between the age when a girl first has sexual intercourse and the time when she begins to use contraceptives regularly is the cause of much distress and harm. This is the age when most girls are very fertile. Two out of three girls marrying under the age of twenty are pregnant on their wedding day and 22 per cent of all births to girls under twenty are illegitimate. An unwanted pregnancy can cause considerable difficulties to a married couple, especially among those who are poor and already have a large family. But the greatest distress for both mother and child occurs when an immature schoolgirl or student becomes pregnant.

Obviously we must do all we can to close this gap. Even when contraceptives are freely available, there will always be a gap of a few weeks, unless it is going to be official policy to encourage a girl to use contraceptives before her first experience of sexual intercourse. But any attempt to prepare these girls before they have had their first experience is likely to be misconstrued. Obviously the authorities and the general public are going to look askance at any suggestion that appears to be encouraging premarital sexual intercourse. But if the real concern is to prevent the individual misery and the social cost caused by unplanned pregnancies in young girls, the aim of the clinics should be to close the gap between the first experience of premarital sexual intercourse and the first use of contraceptive precautions. If the gap is to be closed completely, then the girls should visit the clinic before their first experience, not afterwards.

All things being equal, which they never are, one would expect a single girl to be more motivated to use a reliable contraceptive than a married woman because pregnancy is usually a far more serious problem for the unmarried. Research reports, however, show that the single girl is less likely to use birth control. Bone (1973) found that unmarried girls were less inclined to use contraceptives. Lambert (1971) found that 59 per cent of single girls compared with 17 per cent of married women did not regularly use contraceptives. In my research 54 per cent of the unmarried had never used birth control compared with 15 per cent of the married. If single girls continue to find it difficult to get their contraceptive supplies, there are going to be more illegitimate children and more abortions.

Contrary to the views of those who think that the pill is the direct cause of promiscuity, research reports show that the more casual the relationship, the less likely a girl is to use contraceptives. One reason for this is that it is more difficult for a promiscuous girl to get reliable contraception. If they go to a doctor or clinic, they are liable, under the guise of counselling, to be put through a long interview, which goes far beyond the necessary medical information, and are required to answer personal questions about their private life. It would be quite beyond the nerve of most girls to go to a clinic and tell the inquisitor that she had not got a regular chap but she felt it would be a sensible precaution to take the pill as she did occasionally have intercourse.

Why is there this gap between the first sexual intercourse and the regular use of contraceptives and why are the single, and especially the unmarried who are promiscuous, less likely to practise birth control? Many a teenage girl has become pregnant in that dangerous period after losing her virginity and before she has accepted her own sexuality. She will not go to the doctor or clinic to get contraceptives if she had not yet acknowledged her own sexual desires. It is the high level of guilt that prevents her from taking this logical and sensible step. When she accepts that she is going to have sex regularly, and is not put off by other problems (e.g. religious or moral fears), she goes on the pill.

The girl who accepts the notion of premarital sexual intercourse is more likely to take precautions. It is often the girl with high moral principles who gets into trouble. These are also the girls who think the solution to this lapse is to marry the father of the child. But teenagers do not make good parents and immature boys and girls who are forced to marry because of an impending unplanned pregnancy are far less likely to make a success of their marriage.

Some girls are put off taking precautions by the strange attitude of their parents, who are scandalized when they find out that their daughter is on the pill. For some reason there are parents who are much more upset by finding out that she is on the pill than when they discover their girl is no longer a virgin. Some are more understanding about their daughter having an abortion than taking the pill; somehow it is easier to accept that a girl can make a mistake than to admit that she is having a regular sex life.

But the main reason that makes a single girl reluctant to take the pill is this association of the pill with promiscuity. It is the fear of being labelled promiscuous that stops a girl from going to get her contraceptive supplies. And, of course, it is the self-righteous moralists who spread the idea that the pill is synonymous with promiscuity, and so it is these moralists who are the indirect cause of the illegitimacy and the abortions which they deplore.

Medical and Sociological Research

Medical research holds out several long-term possibilities. Experiments have been made with copper and medicated coils (Zipper et al., 1969; Pandya and Scommegna, 1972). The possibilities of a 'morning after' pill are being examined (Ball, 1971). Undoubtedly menstrual regulation (or very early abortion using the vacuum method) will be used more often (Karman and Potts, 1972) in conjunction with the less effective but more popular contraceptives. Some people see prostaglandins as the next step in fertility control; the hope is that these drugs might be self-administered when the onset of menstruation is delayed (Karim, 1971). Various attempts have been made to make vasectomy reversible (Mehta and Ramani, 1970); one way might be by establishing a 'sperm bank' to store frozen semen. Finally some scientists are working on a contraceptive pill for men (Lacy and Pettit, 1970).

The genetic effects of family planning have also been studied (Graham, 1972). There are three probable short-term effects if birth control is widely adopted. First, the age of parents will both increase and decrease. Unplanned pregnancies in the young will become rarer and it is hoped that this will lead to a big reduction in the number of forced marriages and teenage parents. But availability of free contraceptives will also reduce the number of children born to mothers aged over forty and it is hoped that this will result in fewer children being born with the defects which are common among the offspring of older parents, e.g. Down's syndrome or mongolism. Second, it will enable parents to increase the interval between births, which will be beneficial because the shorter the interval the higher the infant and maternal death rates. The third genetic effect of widespread family planning is the reduction in the size of the family. It is well known that children in large families suffer disadvantages not encountered in smaller families.

On the sociological side three factors will hasten the availability of contraceptives. One is the declining influence of the Catholic Church. In Britain, as in many developed countries, most Catholics have rejected the 1968 Papal Encyclical. A survey in the United States has shown that the majority (78 per cent) of Catholic women under forty-five who receive communion at least once a month are defying the official teaching of the Church which decreed in 1951 that the *rhythm method* (also known as the *safe period*) was the only permissible form of birth control. It is not always realized that the rhythm method is not an old traditional technique, but was first proposed by a Japanese doctor in 1930. It is not immediately obvious why this method was eagerly adopted by Catholic theologians, but presumably it is because it involves a period of abstinence every month. Most Catholic women have found the method ineffective and have turned to other contraceptives. There is a name for people who continue to use the rhythm method—parents.

Another important sociological development is the new awareness that the solution to all other problems depends upon our ability to defuse the population bomb. Many people in Great Britain think this does not concern them because the birth rate has started to decline. But the population in this crowded island is still going up and will continue to increase because there are a large number of girls who have not yet reached the age when they become fertile. The increased availability of contraceptives is certainly not a substitute for a realistic population policy, but it should help to reduce the problem.

A third sociological factor is that women are increasingly determined to assert their individual rights to live their lives in their own way. People of both sexes, including adolescents, are determined that the fear of pregnancy will no longer be a barrier to sexual happiness and fulfilment. Birth control is not just about avoiding an unwanted pregnancy. It is also about the development and preservation of rewarding personal relationships.

CHAPTER 12

NEW ATTITUDES TO ABORTION

Moral and Psychological Objections

There are signs that the opposition to birth control is waning, but this is not true of abortion where the opposition is determined and well organized. There have been improvements in medical technology as far reaching as those made in contraceptive methods, but the emotional impact of abortion has made it difficult to introduce these new techniques. Opinion polls show that most people now accept family planning and the opposition to sterilization seems to be evaporating. But the population remains deeply divided over the topic of abortion.

Religion continues to play an important part in the debate. The Roman Catholic Church is alarmed at the rate it is losing members and it is using the opposition to abortion as a way of rallying supporters. The Catholic press, notably *The Universe*, has actively backed the campaigns against all forms of abortion. The Society for the Protection of the Unborn Child (SPUC) is the strongest organization that campaigns for the repeal of the Abortion Act. It started as a specifically non-Catholic centre of opposition, but its leading speaker, Mrs Phyllis Bowman, has since been converted to Roman Catholicism and SPUC now works closely with the Roman Catholic church.

Pronouncements from Catholic pulpits, home visits by priests and organized letter-writing from Roman Catholics to MPs are part of the campaign. Girls at RC schools are asked to design anti-abortion posters. The Church is very specific about its opposition to all forms of abortion, even if it means two lives will be lost. "Any direct abortion whatsoever, even if it is performed in the presence of a manifest therapeutic indication to save the mother by its means, when otherwise she together with the child would perish, is immoral and forbidden by divine law" (Pius XII, 26, xi, 1951). Despite these strong words, the Institute for Social Studies in Medical Care found that Catholic women seek abortions as often as non-Catholics.*

The new method of terminating a pregnancy by vacuum aspiration is one of the least complicated and safest operations in medical practice. This is not to say that there are no dangers in abortion because all operations upon the human body involve some risks. But opponents of abortion no longer emphasize these dangers in their arguments, and concentrate on emotional and moral questions centred around the question of when life begins. SPUC shows a photograph of a baby and asks: 'Could you kill him in cold blood?' Use is made of gory magnified colour photographs of aborted foetuses—'left to die in the bucket'—and lurid leaflets are distributed to schools.

These arguments are often based on Roman Catholic theology, but not all Catholics agree. Pedro Calderan Beltrão, S.J., a professor at the Pontifical Gregorian University in Rome, wrote in 1973: "According to the latest biological data, the beginning of a new human existence cannot be pinpointed at the moment of fertilization. The presence of a full genetic code proves nothing since after fertilization two or more human existences (twins) can develop with the same genetic code. Neither can it be at the moment of implantation, because even after this, twin existences may also develop." So one cannot speak of the existence of a single human being from the moment of conception.

The opponents of abortion are more likely to emphasize the psychological effects than the physical dangers. A booklet produced by LIFE has this to say about mental disturbance: "Although a great deal is made of the mental strains caused by allowing a pregnancy to continue, little is said about the effect of terminating that pregnancy. Obviously in many cases the woman may simply feel relief. One cannot deny that. However a substantial number do feel deeply remorseful after an abortion and need a great deal of psychiatric support. Many will never completely forgive themselves, and a few even commit suicide." LIFE is an association opposed to all abortion and is "working for the day when the 1967 Act is repealed".

It is, of course, true that some women go through a period of depression, not unlike post-natal depression. Potts (1971) explains: "After an abortion, just as after a delivery, there are

* From the *Report of the Committee on the Working of the Abortion Act*, vol. III.

sudden changes in hormone levels in the woman's body. We would not interpret the familiar 'post partum blues' as an indication that this mother has made a mistake and should not have had a baby." This feeling of distress is a normal reaction and does not last for long.

It is the medical establishment that has in the past always insisted that a woman who has an abortion is very likely to suffer serious guilt feelings. As recently as 1966, the Royal College of Obstetricians and Gynaecologists expressed this view : "There are few women, no matter how desperate they may be to find themselves with an unwanted pregnancy, who do not have regrets at losing it. This fundamental reaction, governed by maternal instinct, is mollified if the woman realises that abortion was essential to her life and health, but if the indication for the termination of pregnancy was flimsy and fleeting she may suffer from a sense of guilt for the rest of her life."

If women do suffer guilt feelings or even serious psychological effects, we should look for the cause. Who has implanted these guilt feelings? A National Opinion Poll survey estimated that three-quarters of all abortions in 1966 had been illegal and writers were surprised to find that those women who had undergone illegal abortions had rather more pleasant memories about it than those who had legal abortions. It is not really so surprising when one remembers the censorious attitude of the medical profession in those not so far-off days.

Results from abroad seem to suggest that the more restrictive the laws, the more likely the woman is to suffer psychological harm. This is partly because family, friends and doctors look upon abortion as sinful or disgraceful and so make it far more likely that the woman concerned will be preoccupied with guilt feelings. But a restrictive law also means that the operation is likely to be delayed by the legal procedures. Emotional distress is more likely to occur in late abortions, after foetal movements have started and maternal feelings have been aroused.

Careful studies in this country carried out since the 1967 Act cast doubt upon the theory that women who have had abortions suffer from guilt feelings (Clark, 1968; Pare and Raven, 1970; Sclare and Geraghty, 1971; Morton Williams and Hindell, 1972). The Lane Report (1974) suggests that most women who have an unwanted pregnancy suffer some degree of distress, anguish or depression. The report estimated that legal abortions are followed by some form of psychological illness in about 2 per cent of the cases. A small minority are seriously disturbed before the abortion and the operation has very little influence either way on existing serious mental illness. But the Lane Committee suggest that in these cases when the woman is seriously disturbed, continuation of an unwanted pregnancy is more likely to be harmful than ending it.

Legal and Medical Procedures

Delay increases the risks, physical and psychological. All medical authorities agree about this, but as long as the legal procedures are cumbersome, it will be difficult to shorten the delay. The operation can be performed within the first few weeks of pregnancy in countries which allow abortion on request. These are the countries which show a very low death rate. For example, in Hungary, where abortion after twelve weeks is illegal, only nine women died among the 739,000 who underwent legal abortions in 1964–7—a mortality rate of 1.2 per 100,000. The mortality rate is far higher in countries where the process of granting abortions on medico-social grounds may take several weeks, and consequently a larger number of abortions are performed after twelve weeks of gestation. For example the mortality rate in Denmark was 40 per 100,000 during the years 1964–7. When pregnancies have advanced beyond twelve weeks, there is no totally satisfactory way of performing the operation; the risks to the woman increase considerably and medical staff find the ethical problems posed by the procedure more formidable.

In a study done in Britain, Chalmers and Anderson (1972) found that, contrary to their expectations, three-quarters of all women seeking termination of pregnancy approached their general practitioner at an early stage of gestation. It is not the women who cause the delay, but the doctors. Even those on the 'urgent' waiting list were usually delayed for more than two weeks.

In a survey carried out by the Medical Women's Federation, more than one in five who applied for a NHS abortion had to wait between two and three weeks before seeing a consultant. Not all of these women got an abortion even after this delay; 32 per cent were rejected; the consultant postponed a decision in another 15 per cent of the cases and the 53 per cent who were accepted had to wait, on average, another two weeks before they obtained the operation. There is less delay in the private sector and many women have to pay because they cannot, or dare not wait.

Research commissioned by the Lane Committee shows that earlier abortions tend to be obtained by married women over twenty-five who already have two or three children and are middle class. Single women and working class women usually have to wait longer and have later abortions. This is unfair and unfortunate, especially as some of these women are being needlessly subjected to abdominal operations because doctors are reluctant to recommend vacuum aspiration beyond thirteen weeks of pregnancy.

There is also some evidence to suggest that the medical profession has been slow to adopt the new techniques. It has already been noted that hysterotomy is more dangerous than aspiration. According to Kestelman (in a letter to the *Family Planning Journal*, January 1973), 35 per cent of abdominal hysterotomies were performed before thirteen weeks. There is considerable doubt if such a serious abdominal operation was necessary in all these cases.

Gynaecologists are trained as surgeons and it appears that some of them dislike vacuum aspiration. The Medical Director of the IPPF (Potts, 1973) has written: "Abortion has many paradoxes. One is that the most highly qualified surgeon operating in the best hospital is not always the best."

Perhaps the biggest paradox of all is that an efficient abortion service operating under a liberal law would reduce the moral and ethical problems about the sanctity of life which are of so much concern to the opponents of abortion. No one would claim that the present law makes for efficiency.

From the start there was dissatisfaction about the way the Act had operated. Some doctors were making fortunes and many people could not afford the very high prices charged for an abortion in the private sector. After criticisms in Parliament the Lane Committee was set up to enquire into the operation of the Act. The fifteen members of the committee, including ten women, reported that the Act had relieved "a vast amount of individual suffering" and unanimously recommended that the Act should not be amended in a restrictive way. "To do so when the number of unwanted pregnancies is increasing and before comprehensive services are available to all who need them would be to increase the sum of human suffering and ill-health, and probably to drive most women to seek the squalid and dangerous help of the back-street abortionist."

A common jibe is that London has become the abortion capital of the world—a strange remark because many countries have more liberal abortion laws than Britain. Most of these foreign women go to the clinics run for profit and are grossly over-charged. At a conservative estimate 54,000 abortions at over £100 each were performed on girls in 1974, which adds up to at least £5 million of foreign currency and must put these doctors in line for the Queen's Award for Exports. In the *Release Progress Report* (d'Agapeyeff, 1972) it was stated that during a period of twelve weeks, one doctor received £12,065 from girls referred to him.

The Committee seemed to undervalue the effects of the new out-patient abortion techniques, widely practised in America with success and increasingly used in this country. Aspiration of the uterus was first tried in Russia in 1927, but the procedure was little discussed until the Chinese reported on the successful use of this method in 1958. The first English reports were in 1967 (Kerslake and Casey). Now vacuum aspiration is being used all over the world with success and it seems likely that menstrual regulation (MR) will soon become equally widespread.

MR is the term used to describe vacuum aspiration carried out within a few days of the first missed period. Some women prefer the term 'over-due' treatment because its main effect is to bring on a period. MR may be used before definite diagnosis of pregnancy is possible. If the woman has conceived, legally it is an abortion, but neither she nor the doctor who performs the operation will know for sure. A woman's monthly period is basically the shedding of her womb lining and this is what is removed when MR is used, whether or not the lining contains the fertilized egg. Some women prefer not to know if they have conceived and this may also be true for some doctors.

There is some concern that MR will be used not in addition to, but *instead* of birth control. Present-day contraceptive methods require foresight, whereas MR is a question of hind-sight, so some women may be tempted to go for MR when they miss a period instead of taking the pill each day. In the present state of our knowledge, MR is probably best regarded as an intermediate step between contraception and abortion. But men and women have traditionally used many methods of fertility control despite strong medical and legal disapproval and birth control remains very much a matter of individual choice. The doctor's task should be to provide several different procedures, pointing out the advantages and disadvantages of each, but the final choice should be left to the individual.

As MR is a simple and relatively safe procedure, it has been suggested that paramedical personnel can be trained to perform the operation as effectively as gynaecologists or other doctors. In most countries there is a shortage of doctors. In developing countries, midwives traditionally performed abortions even before the procedure was legal. Karman (1972) studied the capabilities of paramedical staff and concluded that "in a supervised clinic setting they are capable of performing safe abortions on certain carefully selected patients".

In America some groups of unqualified women have been trained in the techniques of MR and have opened self-help clinics. Some have maintained that women can be trained to perform MR on themselves—"It is so simple, you could learn it from the instructions on the packet", one of them remarked. The doctors, of course, are very much against this. The equipment is virtually fool-proof, so the main danger is infection. If prudent aseptic precautions are observed, MR could certainly be used by trained paramedical staff. If the service is good enough and is widely available, untrained women would not be tempted to try MR on themselves or their friends.

An Adjunct to Birth Control

In spite of religious and legal sanctions, abortion has been practised since time immemorial. Ways of terminating pregnancies are mentioned in early Chinese and ancient Egyptian writings. Since then all manner of materials have been tried including camels' saliva, the chopped tail hairs of a deer, a paste made from crushed ants, and emulsion of goat dung and fermented vegetables.

There are still pills and remedies on the market which are supposed to induce abortion. Nathanson (1970) and Loraine (1970) reviewed these preparations and both concluded that there is no safe and reliable drug which will induce an abortion even when the recommended dose was considerably exceeded. Some of these remedies were merely purgatives (e.g. castor oil, cascara), but some were poisonous (e.g. argot, quinine) and dangerous if taken in large amounts. Despite this unpromising history, legal abortion today is as safe and effective as any medical operation can be. It should be regarded, therefore, as a useful adjunct to birth control, not as a last resort in an emergency.

Even at the present time no method of contraception is completely reliable and even the most effective methods (except sterilization) are subject to mistakes and forgetfulness of the user. Consequently it will still be necessary in the future to provide a second line of defence against an unwanted pregnancy. It is reasonable to suppose that eventually the rate of abortion will be reduced as contraceptives become more readily available, but it is utopian to suppose that abortions will cease to be needed. A rational birth control policy involves not only free access to contraceptives, but also to abortion as an additional safeguard.

Many couples now decide to plan their families and use birth control. Nearly everyone prefers contraception to abortion. But if the woman becomes pregnant involuntarily, the husband and wife are unlikely to abandon their desire to control the size of their family and so the woman will resort to abortion. One cannot logically oppose abortion and at the same time support family planning.

The Rights of Women

Now that the medical technicians have made impressive improvements in the methods available, we need to adopt a far more positive and practical attitude towards the termination of pregnancies. Employers have often justified the restricted job opportunities and unequal pay offered to women by holding out the possibility that female employees may become pregnant. In the present situation it is difficult for a woman to guarantee that she will not become pregnant and so her employer is reluctant to give her a responsible position. But if we accept menstrual regulation and out-patient abortions as a necessary safeguard against the possibility of contraceptive failure or misuse, then women have the chance to escape the primordial yoke of being the bearers and rearers of children.

Over the years the fear of an unwanted pregnancy has had an inhibiting effect on the sexuality of women. In my research over half the women (53 per cent) had thought that they were pregnant when they were not, and nearly half the men (45 per cent) had been told by their wives or girl-friends of a pregnancy that turned out to be a false alarm. Add this to the number of times when the fear of pregnancy proves to be well-founded, and it becomes clear that this fear is interfering with the sexual pleasure of many people on many occasions and inevitably causes one or both sexual partners to feel ill at ease and unrelaxed during intercourse.

Some people think it is a woman's duty to produce children and are hostile to those who decide against terminating a pregnancy. There is a punitive attitude to those who want to have an abortion, implying that they are careless or promiscuous or both. But if a woman is denied abortion facilities when she needs them, she is being denied the right to decide what should happen to her own body.

The main purpose of abortion is to provide the woman with one of a number of options. She should not be persuaded to undergo an abortion, but neither should she be prevented from having one if she wishes. At present she is being exposed to avoidable risks, partly due to inefficiency and even intransigence in the medical profession, but also because she is unaware of her right to choose.

Abortion has been considered sinful and shameful for so long that some women do not even think of it as a possibility. Those women who do wonder if it could be a possible solution may not know where to go for advice. The Health Education Council and local health authorities are charged with the duty of making family planning facilities known to the public. The dissemination of information about abortion should also be the duty of these bodies and the HEC should be allowed to advertise so that the public know where these facilities are available; then the operation can be carried out early in the pregnancy when the risks are still small. Women who go for an abortion are told how to get contraceptives, but women who go for contraceptives are not told how to get an abortion if the contraceptives fail.

Abortion on request can be obtained in this country, but only if the woman lives in the right area and is prepared to go through a minor charade to satisfy the legal requirements, or if she is rich enough to have it done privately. A woman cannot be said to have a free choice until we provide a service which ensures that she knows where to go and gives her the opportunity to consider all the options. Then if she wishes, and providing there is no

7—P • •

complicating disease and she is in the first twelve weeks of pregnancy, she should be able to go for an abortion as an out-patient the very next day.

Even people who adopt a liberal and sympathetic approach to abortion tend to view every request for a legal termination as a 'sign of a life crisis' or a 'cry for help' in a wider context. This is to make too much fuss about a fairly commonplace event. Women have been having illegal abortions for many years without much emotional trouble. Now that abortions are legal and far less risky, all that is needed in most cases is sympathetic counselling and medical efficiency.

The positive attitude is to get away from the idea that abortion is 'an admission of failure'. If, for example, a woman prefers to use one of the less effective contraceptives plus the safeguard of MR, this is a reasonable choice. It is the counsellor's duty to put other options before her and to explain the possible consequences of her decision. But no one is entitled to restrict her choice or to insult her with authoritarian pronouncements.

CHAPTER 13

EROTIC VARIATIONS

Law and Morality

The complaint about the (so-called) permissive society is that activities are being permitted which should be stopped. The charge is that standards have slipped. The implication is that certain members of society have the right to control the behaviour of others and, if necessary, they have the right to use legal sanctions in order to enforce the morality of those who know best. In the past when the church had its own set of ecclesiastical laws which were enforced just as rigorously as the civil law, it was accepted that our moral guardians should prescribe what we should read or do or think, and there was a 'moral police' to stop us from doing what was wrong.

In more recent times the feeling has been growing that Acts of Parliament should not, and cannot, control the moral side of our lives. It was put forcibly in a perspicacious sentence of the Wolfenden Report (1957): "Unless a deliberate attempt is to be made by society, acting through the agency of the law, to equate the sphere of crime with that of sin, there must remain a realm of private morality and immorality which is, in brief and crude terms, not the law's business."

It is often said that the law must reflect public opinion and certainly the legal system does not exist in a vacuum; nor can the law be changed without reference to general opinion. In some cases the law does not reflect public opinion so much as the attitudes of a more restricted group. This is an élite circle composed of editors, writers, TV personalities and others in the media, including public relations men who are paid by groups with special interests. All these people try to influence the politicians who are (or should be) the law makers.

On occasions Members of Parliament and others who decide about social policy have a mistaken view of public opinion. In the controversial area of sexual morality there is often quite a wide gap between what the public are supposed to think according to the views of politicians, and what they really think.

This difference is very apparent when authorities speak and write about sex as a very serious matter, never to be undertaken lightly, and only when certain non-sexual conditions have been fulfilled. But in reality the majority think of sex as a pleasurable activity, not necessarily linked with other commitments.

Despite restrictions imposed by various laws and traditional customs, sex is mankind's most delightful and enduring recreation. The great educationalist, A. S. Neill (1962) wrote: "Everything is loaded against our young people. Circumstances compel them to convert what should be lovely and joyful into something sinister and sinful, into smut and leers, and shameful laughter."

The signs are that attitudes are changing rapidly and people are becoming more and more determined to make sex lovely and joyful. Christian teaching, which for so long has advocated a positive appreciation of marriage with a negative distaste for sex, now recognizes that sex may be for pleasure as well as for reproduction. Even the Second Vatican Council declared that sexual expression is "decent and worthy" and allowed that a married couple may "with joyful and grateful spirit reciprocally enrich each other"—the Catholic way of saying that husband and wife may enjoy having sex together.

Masturbation

If sex is also for pleasure and not just for procreation, this weakens the arguments against other forms of sexual expression besides intercourse. In the past masturbation and other sexual activities that did not involve the man penetrating the woman were regarded as perversions because they could not bring forth a pregnancy.

Homosexuality was forbidden for the same reason because it was important for the Jews surrounded by hostile tribes to produce and raise large numbers of children. God commanded them to go forth and multiply. It was also necessary to maintain a high birth-rate in those days because the communities were threatened by the ravages of disease and war. Hence the story in the Old Testament (Genesis 38) of Onan who was struck down by God because he "spilled his seed upon the ground" instead of having sexual intercourse with the widow of his brother, which he was expected to do in order to provide children for the tribe.

It is now thought that what Onan did was withdraw from intercourse before he ejaculated, but for hundreds of years it was believed that God destroyed him because he masturbated and this activity was called Onanism. The Jewish Talmud regarded masturbation as a more serious sin than premarital sexual intercourse. Today there are only a few people left who still say that masturbation is sinful or harmful, but people often refer to it as self-abuse.

Most research results indicate that women masturbate less than men. Kinsey (1953) found only about 35 per cent of women had masturbated by the age of twenty. There was no sign of change two decades later when Davis (1971) reported that 34 per cent of his group of girls aged under twenty has masturbated. It has been speculated that many more women do masturbate but do not label it as such; Klausner (1961) in his study of middle class Israeli youth found most girls (81 per cent) had masturbated by the age of twenty-one. The extent of masturbation among females is open to doubt, but clearly it is not a rare occurrence. It is commonly agreed that nearly all men have masturbated by the age of twenty-one. No one really knows why there is this difference in frequency between men and women and no one has put forward any convincing cultural or biological reasons to account for it.

Some psychiatrists have expressed fears that masturbation will make it more difficult for the individual to achieve a normal adjustment to heterosexual intercourse. But Ellis (1958) and others including Kinsey have noticed that women who have inhibitions about masturbation are more likely to have later problems with achieving orgasm during intercourse.

Masters and Johnson (1970) report that the orgasm that results from masturbation is more intense physiologically. Perhaps there is a danger that personal fantasies will cut an individual off from reality. In the play, *The Boys in the Band* (Crowley, 1968), a character says: "One thing you can say for masturbation . . . you certainly don't have to look your best." But there is no real cause for concern if a person occasionally prefers to masturbate instead of having sex with someone else. Certainly there is no need to produce children as there was in the days of the Old Testament. People retort that the human race will die out if everyone preferred masturbation to sexual intercourse, but there is absolutely no danger of that happening.

For many people masturbation seems to satisfy a purely physical need, but others enjoy elaborate fantasies. In another play, *The Philanthropist* by Christopher Hampton, someone says: "Masturbation is the thinking man's television." Others with less imaginative powers like to use pornography while masturbating. But there is no evidence that masturbators make an attempt to realize their fantasies. On the contrary, they tend to use masturbation as a substitute and are more likely to be embarrassed or inhibited if the chance came to act out their fantasies in real life.

It is often argued that pornography is harmful, but there are occasions where it may be beneficial. As Mr Justice Frankfurter* sensibly remarked, the point about pornography is that it must be sexually stimulating. It may be helpful for men who have difficulty getting an erection, or for couples who have lost interest in the sexual side of their marriage.

Masturbation may be the most sensible outlet for people who for a variety of reasons find themselves in situations where heterosexual and homosexual activities are discouraged. For example, this might apply to individuals who are young, who live in a hostel, who are away from home or who have recently been bereaved. It can also be a valuable outlet for people who are invalids or who have physical handicaps. Far from making life more difficult for such people, it would be humane and helpful to provide them with adequate pornographic stimuli if this is what they require.

Inceptive Activities

Any form of sexual expression before intercourse was regarded as a perversion until the beginning of the century when the writers of the early sex manuals (Stopes, 1918; Van de Velde, 1926; Havelock Ellis, 1925) emphasized the importance of foreplay. The first of the English sex manuals was *Married Love* by Marie Stopes who used high-flown language which is now outmoded,

* Mr Justice Frankfurter made this observation in the US Supreme Court and it was soon re-interpreted into the slogan: 'It is not pornographic unless it gives Mr Justice Frankfurter an erection.' As he was over seventy at the time he made the remark, this provided a memorable but not really a very practical yardstick by which to judge whether something was pornographic or not.

but it was the first book that attempted to describe the sexual needs of a woman.* In effect Dr Stopes was explaining that it takes time and some stimulation before a woman can reach the same level of sexual excitement as a man. Similar advice had been given in an earlier century by Marie Theresa's doctor when she was worried about sterility: "I am of the opinion that the vulva of your Most Sacred Majesty should be titillated for some time before intercourse." Later she had sixteen children.

Although *Married Love* ran into twenty-eight editions and was translated into thirteen languages, thirty years later Kinsey noted that the effort devoted to foreplay was generally brief and perfunctory. Since then millions of sex manuals have been sold and now the message seems to have got across that there is more to sexual intercourse than putting the penis into the vagina. In some sections of society the wheel has turned full circle and the man who does not indulge in foreplay before coitus is thought to be rather unsophisticated.

But many people still regard these activities as unacceptable if they are not a prelude to coitus. Inceptive activities (what the Americans call 'petting to orgasm') are often condemned as mutual masturbation, a description which should not have negative connotations in any case. The woman may have deep feelings of oneness with her partner when the penis is inside the vagina, but the physical gratifications of coitus are less sensual for the woman than for the man, and a woman is likely to find stimulation of the clitoris by a finger or the tongue to be just as exciting. It is the man who has always insisted that penetration is essential and some of the women liberationalists have claimed that intercourse has been foisted upon women by men who care only that the vagina provides a voluptuous massage for the penis.

It is no longer an unmentionable secret that it is possible to obtain intense pleasure and excitement beyond the point of orgasm without the male penetrating the female. Young people, especially students, have questioned why there are taboos on other forms of sexual expression which do not have such high

* Dr Stopes describes an orgasm in these exotic terms: "The half-swooning sense of flux which overtakes the spirit in that eternal moment as the apex of rapture sweeps into its flaming tides the whole essence of the man and woman and, as it were, the heat of the contact vaporises their consciousness so that it fills the whole of cosmic space."

potential risks as heterosexual coitus. Consequently they enjoy
inceptive activities and regard this kind of love-making as a
legitimate and satisfying endgame.

Inceptive activities can be justified for their inherent sensuality
as bodily enjoyment and need not be regarded as preparation for
coitus. Women, especially, see the advantages of inceptive techniques because they provide a release from tension, while maintaining a profound intimacy and allowing the relationship to
develop without the act of intercourse, which may have special
significance for some girls. As a result of faulty education or cultural conditioning, there are still some girls who have feelings of
fear or self-reproach following coitus which they do not feel after
inceptive acts.

Inceptive techniques using the hand or mouth have the advantage that they do not depend upon the man maintaining his
erection. It can be a relief for the man (although he may be the
last to admit this) to know that the woman's satisfaction does
not depend upon his powers of sexual endurance.

One of the most influential of the early sex manuals used to
be *Ideal Marriage* by Van de Velde. Although he was a refresh-
ing and liberating voice in his day, this book also contained
quaint advice which, unfortunately, has lived on in hundreds of
subsequent manuals that have echoed his beliefs. As well as
frightening women by asserting that orgasm was a matter not
only of pleasure but of hygienic necessity, he also warned that
excitement without orgasm would cause women permanent injury "to both body and soul". This is quite wrong. Sexual
arousal that does not lead to orgasm can give a man a pain in
his testicles, but this is not thought to be harmful. A high level
of sexual excitement may cause tensions that create an urgent
desire for orgasmic release, but there will be occasions when this
will be inconvenient, embarrassing or messy. It may be dis-
appointing but there is no cause for alarm if sexual activities do
not end in orgasm.

Two possible reasons why inceptive activities are not always
popular are (1) because there are strong inhibitions about oral-
genital techniques and (2) because men and women are unin-
formed about the erogenous zones of the body. Although there
are probably more germs in the mouth than most other bodily
areas, kissing on the mouth has long been acceptable. But many
people are repelled by the idea of kissing other parts of the body.

But now many of the sex manuals recommend oral-genital contacts. As Kinsey (1953) notes: "It is not so strange that the two parts of the body that are the most sensitive erotically, namely the mouth and the genital organs, should be brought into contact with one another."

When a young couple have just got to know one another, everything is exciting and sexually exhilarating. But there are parts of the body which are particularly responsive—many of them 'forbidden' areas. Girls and boys usually have to discover these for themselves because it would be a brave teacher who supplied this useful information during a sex education class. Consequently it is not surprising that there are some myths about what is supposed to be sexually stimulating. Men, for example, are often disappointed to find that most women are not as interested in having their breasts fondled as men are in fondling them.

Fisher (1973) asked nearly 200 women to rank six areas of the body according to the degree of response to sexual stimulation. The terms used were precisely defined so that the women clearly understood the meanings. The body areas were ranked in the following order:

1. Clitoris
2. Vagina near clitoris
3. Inside lips of vulva
4. Inside vagina
5. Breasts
6. Outside lips of vulva

Fisher makes the following comment: "It is striking how relatively constant the ratings were. The 'clitoris' and 'vagina near clitoris' were designated as the most excited of all areas. Also, 'outside lips of vulva' was usually designated as the least excited. One notes too how relatively low is the excitement attributed to the 'inside of vagina'. The fact that high excitement is ascribed to the clitoris and low arousal to the vagina is nicely congruent with the observations of Kinsey (1953) and Masters and Johnson (1966) that the vagina is relatively low in its sensory arousability, with just the opposite holding true for the clitoris."

Clearly the most important area of sexual stimulation in the woman is the clitoris. During intercourse the man's pubic bone —and in some cases the root of the penis—can stimulate the clitoris by pressing against it. As muscle fibres connect the clitoris to the smaller vaginal lips as well as to the muscles around the entrance to the vagina and the rectum, pressures brought to bear elsewhere can also be stimulating. But the clitoris is the focal point of erotic pleasure in the woman and it is the direct stimulation of this area that is most likely to produce an orgasm.

Some psychiatrists have held that petting to orgasm is likely to distort the response to coitus. This belief is based on Freud's false distinction between clitoral and vaginal orgasm. It was argued that inceptive activities must be inferior (and therefore perverse) because they could only involve stimulation of the clitoris. In order to get 'deep orgasm', it was necessary to stimulate the vagina and this could not be done without penetration during intercourse. But modern sex research has established that even during coitus, sexual arousal is achieved by clitoral rather than vaginal stimulation. In the passage from Fisher's study just quoted, he referred to Kinsey (1953) and Masters and Johnson (1966), who considered that their data demonstrated only a little response to stimulation of the vagina and they attributed a large part of sexual arousal in the female to the direct or indirect stimulation of the clitoris. It must come as another disappointment for men to be told that the presence of the penis in the vagina is nothing like as stimulating for the woman as it is for the man.

Masters and Johnson (1970) have also shown that orgasms achieved during coitus are physiologically indistinguishable from those achieved during inceptive activities. This is not to say that all orgasms are the same. Indeed it is important to make the point that they cannot really be classified into types. As Singer (1973) says: "There will be as many variations (of orgasms) as there are emotional responses to another human being at the moments of physical and psychological intimacy. One might almost say that this is true of all human consummations. How many ways are there to see a sunset or to enjoy a great work of art? Such responses may be analyzed into categories, but our analysis must never forget that consummatory events are always unique—never the same and often very different."

Inceptive activities, far from being a perversion, develop the individual's capacity to relate to another person and to take pleasure in his own body. The conclusion of this section is simply to say what many people know, but hardly ever admit, that inceptive activities can be just as much fun as coitus.

Hedonism and Homosexuals

Fisher's ranking order of erogenous zones (listed in the previous section) can be confusing if taken too literally. Everyone is different and almost any area of the body is potentially capable of arousing sexual passions for someone. Without doubt the clitoris and the penis are the focal points of women and men, but the stimulation of other areas a long way from the genitals can bring on an orgasm for some people. The ears, the hair, the inside of the thighs and of course the mouth are frequently mentioned as sexually exciting parts of the body. Conversely some of the areas often mentioned in sex manuals may not be particularly stimulating for some people.

One of the more striking changes in attitude in the last few decades has been the notion that the sexual act is not confined to the genital area but includes other parts of the body. The younger generations have taken a special interest in the philosophies of Hinduism, Buddhism and Taoism. In the sexual yoga of the eastern philosophers, males and females enjoy a spiritual sharing of sensory pleasures throughout the whole of their bodies. Much emphasis is put upon the sensuous enjoyment of touching and feeling. Watt (1973) puts it like this: "One finds out what it can mean simply to look at the other person, to touch hands, or to listen to the voice. If these contacts are not regarded as leading to something else, but rather allowed to come to one's consciousness as if the source of activity lay in them and not in the will, they become sensations of immense subtlety and richness." This is not at all like following minute instructions about positions and techniques of the sort to be found in modern sex manuals. It is an activity that requires a high level of concentration and sophistication directed towards obtaining the maximum amount of sexual pleasure.

There has been considerable resistance to this hedonistic attitude to sex and it is frequently condemned as unnatural or immature. In the western world man has developed the conception of 'perversion' because he likes to believe there must be a right way and a wrong way in all matters of importance. The wrong sort of sexual activity is one that cannot result in pregnancy, and so heterosexual coitus is seen as the only normal and natural activity and any variation is defined as a perversion.

This ill-judged and intolerant attitude caused much unhappiness to many people, especially among homosexuals, who form a very large group in the community. Estimates on the number of homosexuals in Great Britain vary considerably, but the lowest figure is 5 per cent and if all those who have at some period of their lives had homosexual experiences are taken into consideration, the proportion is very much higher. So there must be millions of men and women who were told (and many of them believed) that they were immoral and inferior because they preferred homosexual activities to heterosexual coitus, which was deemed to be the only natural form of sexual response.

Not only is there nothing to warrant this concept of perversion, but there is something that many heterosexuals could learn from homosexuals, who seem to be more interested in sexual techniques and more concerned about the reactions of their sexual partners. Homosexuals are more likely to take a pride in their sexual performance. This fascination with their sexual capabilities can go to absurd lengths with (for example) too much emphasis on the size of the penis or the number of orgasms in a single night. But there is nothing wrong with being very receptive to the sexual responses of one's partner or with wishing to give as much sexual satisfaction as possible.

Westwood (1960) reported that some of the male homosexuals in his study-group complained about the sexual competence of their non-homosexual partners. One of them said: "A normal's technique is often dismal." Another explained: "Normals are so bad in bed. The homosexual develops a sexual technique so much more quickly. The girls I've slept with tell me it's the most marvellous sex they've ever had. That's not because I'm some super Don Juan. But men are naturally more experimental and when two men get together they learn from each other, so a homosexual is always improving his technique."

The rabid opposition to male homosexuality can often be traced back to the repugnance engendered by anal intercourse (also known as buggery or sodomy). In law it was referred to as the 'abominable act' which was punished by death in the past and even today still arouses the strongest feelings. In 1974 a judge told the jury: "If you have but a passing acquaintance with the Bible, you will know what happened in Sodom when Jehovah called forth fire and brimstone to punish the inhabitants for their unnatural practices. It has always been in this country, and in every civilized country, a serious offence to commit sodomy, which is punishable by life imprisonment. It is as serious as committing manslaughter, or grievous bodily harm."

Many people assume that all homosexuals engage exclusively in anal intercourse. But in reality most of them develop an extensive range of sexual techniques and only a minority prefer anal intercourse. Bergler (1956) wrote: "Popular ideas notwithstanding, most homosexual practices consist of mutual masturbation, intercrural movements, and licking of the genitalia (fellatio), not of anal intercourse."

Westwood (1960) concluded that most homosexuals "start with mutual masturbation and gradually learn other techniques. In time some of them develop definite preferences and objections, but many homosexuals do not develop a set pattern because they feel that affection and love-making are more important than the actual technique".

Chesser (1958) reported: "From my own clinical experience I doubt if more than 15 per cent of homosexuals are sodomists and I believe that most psychologists would confirm this. What tends to be overlooked is that in heterosexual marriage the practice, or the desire to practise sodomy, is probably more than 15 per cent. In an investigation which I carried out in a provincial town many years ago, this practice was accepted by many wives as an insurance against the possibility of pregnancy."

Robertson (1974) reports several recent cases where individuals have been given jail sentences for heterosexual anal intercourse. The 1967 Act enabled males over twenty-one to be lawfully penetrated, but consenting ladies and their lovers are still liable to life imprisonment.

CHAPTER 14

CHANGING ATTITUDES

Premarital Sexual Intercourse

The change in attitude towards premarital intercourse has been noted in earlier chapters. There is little doubt that more people have sex before marriage than in the past, but the biggest change is in attitude, not in behaviour. Premarital sex has been quite common in this and other societies for hundreds of years, but it is only recently that the authorities have admitted that in certain circumstances this may be acceptable.

Murdock (1949) found evidence of premarital sexual intercourse in 70 per cent of the 158 communities throughout the world that he studied. Henriques (1963) has pointed out that some sections of the British community have long gone in for sexual activities before marriage and what he calls "covert permissiveness" is in fact part of our tradition. In some country districts it is understood that the couple will have premarital intercourse after they have publicly announced their intention to marry.

In small communities, the inheritance of property and the survival of the group were important considerations. Therefore the man wanted to ascertain whether the girl could become pregnant before he married her. When she did conceive the wedding ceremony was performed. In this century these considerations are not so important, but the tradition continues. The earlier researches into sexual behaviour (Hamilton, 1929; Terman, 1938) found that about half the men and a third of the women had sex before marriage. Kinsey's information was collected in the 1940s and this showed increases of about 20 per cent. The most recent research (Schofield, 1973) reports that 80 per cent of the men and 61 per cent of the women had experienced premarital sexual intercourse.

During the last fifty years boys and girls have become physically mature at an earlier age with the result that they are ready for coitus before they are ready to look after a family. The unfortunate consequences of this is that young people are marrying at an earlier age because the girl is pregnant. Two-thirds of all the girls marrying before the age of twenty are pregnant on their wedding day. A large proportion of these marriages break down because these boys and girls are forced to marry before they are able to cope with the obligations and stresses of married life.

The advent of efficient methods of birth control has lessened the chances of an unwanted pregnancy and now the young question the need for this old taboo. It is noteworthy that the biggest change in attitude towards premarital sex occurred among student groups in the first place. Not very long ago students were less likely to have premarital sex than working class adolescents, but now it is the other way round. This suggests that the reasons for the change were not only more freedom and less decorum, but also, in part at least, it was an intellectual decision : the arguments of the older people against premarital intercourse were not sufficiently convincing. Indeed it is clear that the economic and social arguments have evaporated, providing the couple take adequate contraceptive precautions. Only the moral arguments remain and these can only be sustained by the belief that moral laws have eternal validity because they are the result of divine instigation.

In practice this new tolerance is qualified because most religious leaders and moral authoritarians still insist that premarital sexual intercourse is only acceptable as a prelude to marriage. This is based on the unspoken assumption that if anything goes wrong (i.e. if the girl becomes pregnant), they can always bring forward the date of the wedding, which is an unfortunate attitude because a boy and girl should not be forced into the responsibilities of marriage before they are ready.

The real reason why people only accept premarital sex as a prelude to marriage is the fear of promiscuity. It is still not acceptable for a boy and a girl to go to bed together simply because they are sexually attracted to each other. The old question the teenage girls used to ask was : 'How far should I go?' Now the question is more likely to be : 'Does he really love me?' What she is really asking is : 'Does he intend to marry me?'

Unfortunately the confusion between sexual attraction and marriage suitability is the cause of many wrong decisions and much unhappiness. This confusion will continue as long as people are encouraged to think that a licence for sex can only be obtained in exchange for a promise of marriage.

But these views will change because young people are becoming increasingly critical of this attitude. In my research over half (58 per cent) of the young adults did not agree with the principle that premarital sex was only acceptable between couples who intended to get married. Less than 8 per cent disapproved of premarital sexual intercourse in all circumstances. Before very long most people will share the conviction of Anatole France, who once shocked his readers when he wrote that of all sexual aberrations chastity is the strangest.

The Sexual Response of Women

Another change in attitude, which has not been accepted in all quarters but which is gaining ground rapidly, is the realization that women enjoy sex as much as men. William Acton, the eminent doctor of the Victorian era, thought that this was 'a vile aspersion'. In his book *The Function and Disorders of the Reproductive Organs, in Childhood, Youth, Adult Age, and Advanced Life, Considered in their Physiological, Social and Moral Relations*, he wrote: "I should say that the majority of women (happily for them) are not very much troubled with sexual feeling of any kind. . . . As a general rule, a modest woman seldom desires any sexual gratification for herself. She submits to her husband, but only to please him; and, but for the desire of maternity, would far rather be relieved from his attentions."

Old traditions die hard and perhaps there are still blushing brides who are told by their mother that something rather dreadful is going to happen on the honeymoon but she must learn to put up with it because it is a part of marriage.

In his searching analysis of the sexual response of women, Fisher (1973) produces convincing evidence that they do enjoy sex. He summarizes his findings as follows: "When the women were asked how much gratification they obtain from sex, the average response fell close to the category 'Highly gratifying'. Similarly when the women were asked to indicate how much they preferred a series of seven activities (drinking alcoholic beverages, eating, sexual intercourse, sleeping, sports, talking to friends, watching television), they designated sexual intercourse

as their first choice. .... Additional information about the importance of sex to the women was supplied when they were asked
how frequently they think about sex. The average response was
just short of the 'often' category. Apparently, sexual themes are
not an inconsequential part of the stream of thought of these
women."

These findings challenge many of the assumptions which have
been held by men who write books about sex. They also indicate
that women may have problems in making known their interests
during the rituals that precede sexual interaction, for it is a
strongly-held tradition that the male is supposed to take the
initiative. The girl who makes it too obvious that she wants sex
is apt to frighten off the man. In the past the woman has had
the begrudged right to say 'No', but she has not had the
privilege of asking the question. As the pendulum swings, it
may be necessary to speak up for the right of the man to say
'No' without seeming to be a sissy.

It is often said that sexual intercourse for the woman is indis-
solubly linked with the desire for children and a home. In the
past this was true and in some cases it is still true because the girl
has been brought up to believe that this is the main purpose of
the sexual act. When she discovers that she likes it, this may be
confusing because she did not expect such a serious act to be so
very enjoyable as well.

In communities with Christian traditions (and in many others),
the reproductive role of sex has always been over-emphasized.
Women are brought up to believe that motherhood should be
the highest achievement and sole aim. But this is to under-value
the talents of women. For their sake and for the sake of everyone
in the community, it is important that women should not be
content to be stuck in the home. There are good economic and
demographic reasons why women should be encouraged to find
other satisfactions besides childbearing. They are a valuable part
of the work force and modern society needs women in senior
positions as well as in routine jobs.

This emphasis on the woman as the full-time housekeeper is
unlikely to change as long as women are denied equal opportunities. For many women the type of work they are required to
do is so far below their real capabilities that they regard it as no
more than an economic fringe benefit. To prove their value as

people and to feel wanted, they think they must concentrate on playing the role of wife and mother.

At present the husband is still regarded in reality, if not in law, as head of the household. But if the wife is as well educated as the husband and is holding down a job which is just as important, then clearly there will have to be changes in the archaic marriage laws and customs; and the wife should have equal influence in all family decisions, not just those which involve the children. Not only would there be equal status in marriage as regards matters such as finance and ownership, but there would also be a change in the sexual rights of the wife.

The Women's Liberation Movement will not just affect conjugal rights and relationships. It will also change the situation of single women whose sexual rights are very limited at present. Even in this so-called permissive age, the single girl who openly enjoys sex will meet more social disapproval and will be the subject of more gossip than an unmarried man with similar appetites. There are social pressures on girls to get married and there are considerable economic disadvantages in remaining single for all but a few women with well-paid jobs. As Bridget Brophy says: "Celibacy is a luxury uneducated women can't afford." Women will not really have freedom until they have the acknowledged right to enjoy sex without being committed to a lifelong union.

Promiscuous Men and Faithful Women

It is generally said that men want to be polygamous and women monogamous. Women as well as men believe that this is a biological fact of nature, but even a cursory knowledge of sexual physiology contradicts this idea. After a man becomes sexually excited and reaches orgasm, he is exhausted and cannot easily be aroused again for some time. But a woman can achieve orgasm and be ready to start making love again within half a minute. Therefore the needs of a man can be satisfied to exhaustion point by one woman. But, biologically speaking, one woman could continue for a long time at a high point of sexual excitement exhausting a series of men. It is more 'natural' for a woman to be more promiscuous than a man.

In this country women are expected to be more reticent than men, but there are dozens of examples in other societies which show that women will readily commit adultery if given the opportunity. In many communities extramarital sex was permitted on special occasions such as religious ceremonies or festivals. In some modern countries the same tradition is carried on at annual fiestas when the women are allowed a few days of sexual license.

Hospitality was another excuse for adultery. Sexual hospitality was extended to visitors sometimes (as noted in Chapter 3), but more often it was confined to special members of the tribe and became a way of expressing group solidarity. The exchange of wives was also found in many societies. Wife swapping among the Eskimos had a practical basis; for example, a man would borrow someone else's wife if she had the type of skill he needed on a hunting trip.

Wives also had sexual intercourse with priests and gods. In some societies priests were paid to copulate with the wives because it was believed that the child of such a union was bound to be virtuous. In other societies infidelity was sanctioned if there were doubts about the fertility of the married couple. This is allowed in modern society under the name of AID (artificial insemination donor, i.e. someone other than the husband).

There is also another reason for doubting the belief that it is natural for men to be irked by fidelity but for women to be suited to it. After all monogamy is an essential part of our social, religious and legal systems; these have been devised and administered by men. So it is the men who have invented the notion that they are free to seek sex elsewhere but women must remain faithful to one man. Obviously there is a measure of self-interest in this male attitude to fidelity, but it was not entirely selfish before the days of efficient contraception. As well as all the problems of illegitimacy and inheritance which might have arisen if women had been allowed the same kind of sexual freedom as men, it should not be forgotten that child-birth was dangerous until quite recently and the men could protest that they were protecting their women-folk from additional dangers by disallowing adultery. Birth control has now eroded the one-sided male control of sexual relations.

Much of the fanatical opposition to adultery has very little to do with the concern of one partner for the other. In 1665 La Rochefoucauld wrote "There is more self-love than love in jealousy". Henriques (1959) noticed that strong manifestations of jealousy are absent among tribes where extramarital intercourse is permitted; one example he gives is the Marquesan Islanders in the Pacific; extramarital sex was common among the Marquesans, but sexual jealousy was met with ridicule. Another tribe, the Todas of Southern India, used to despise a man who begrudged his wife to another; they believed that 'grudging people' would experience difficulty in getting to the next world after death.

The psychoanalysts regard sexual jealousy as rooted in the Oedipus situation—the child loves the parent of the opposite sex and thus the conditions are present for the arousal of jealousy towards the parent of the same sex. But the anthropological evidence and the very varied manifestations of jealousy in different places and at different times makes it seem more likely that social factors play the most important part in its formation. This is not difficult to understand. When extramarital activities are institutionalized, feelings of jealousy may not be so easily aroused because there are compensations: you may sleep with my wife, but I may sleep with yours.

It is an argument in favour of extramarital relations if it is true that a more tolerant attitude to adultery can moderate sexual jealousy, a very destructive emotion. As Bertrand Russell (1958) has written: "Jealousy must not be regarded as a justifiable insistence upon rights, but as a misfortune to the one who feels it and a wrong towards its object."

Although it is possible to show that the difference between male and female attitudes towards adultery is essentially cultural with only a little biological backing, women hold these beliefs just as strongly as men. One of the major objectives of the Women's Liberation Movement must be freedom from psychological constraints, particularly freedom from the ideas that women have about themselves.

Of course it is a mistake to dismiss the opposition to adultery because it is not God-given but merely the result of social conditioning. Even if this antagonism is what might be called an acquired taste, none the less it is felt sincerely and fervently. My research among young adults revealed a permissive attitude to premarital sexual intercourse, but not to extramarital sex. Only 7 per cent of this group had committed adultery—a small minority, albeit not insignificant. Even in Sweden, famous as the land of free love,* a recent survey ordered by the Swedish government

* This reputation owes more to the liberality of the Swedish cinema than to any objective assessment of Swedish sexual life.

reported that 87 per cent of men and 91 per cent of women thought that marital fidelity was an absolute necessity.

Most people condemn infidelity because it results in the breakdown of many marriages. But it is difficult to separate cause and effect, for it is this attitude to adultery that produces the bitterness which occasions the breakdown. It is the condemnation as much as the infidelity that causes the unhappiness, especially for those individuals who believe that divorce is the only respectable conclusion when one partner of the marriage has been unfaithful. This is to act on the principle that no bread is better than half a loaf. Divorce is often a very inappropriate solution for an affectionate couple who enjoy each other's company, even if there are sexual problems.

In some ways the situation has been aggravated by the modern attitude to sex. Many couples now believe that lasting sexual fulfilment is an essential ingredient of a happy marriage and domestic companionship is not enough. The emancipated woman demands more from the sexual side of marriage. Sometimes both women and men expect too much. Youthful passions cool and boredom, ineptness or curiosity may tempt one or other partner to look elsewhere. Need this spell the end of the marriage?

It would not be so difficult to find an amicable solution if sexual attraction could be seen as something which may occur quite apart from friendship, affection and love. The pity is that when the crisis comes, the sexual side is over-emphasized, and the more important aspects like companionship and affection are under-valued. Friendship is more fulfilling and harder to find than sex. Young upstarts have been heard to say it is easier to find someone to have sex with than someone to talk to.

There are a few signs that a new attitude is emerging and some married couples now view adultery as a problem that can be coped with and not as a sign that the marriage has collapsed. In time it may be possible to achieve a new kind of sexual relationship within marriage which is free from possessiveness and jealousy. This does not mean that everyone will be having sex with everyone else every night. Most people will still prefer a one to one relationship and they will see marriage as a convenient method of legitimizing the situation for economical and social reasons. It can be safely predicted that however great the development of sexual freedom, most people will settle down into marriage after a period of experimentation. They will continue to see marriage as the best family structure throughout the child-bearing and child-rearing years and, for many, throughout the whole of their lives.

But it does not follow that those who find their greatest sexual satisfaction with one person are therefore superior to the many others who enjoy sex with a number of people with whom they have no deep emotional ties. Each person should be encouraged to find fulfilment in his own way as long as no one else is harmed in the process. Who sleeps with whom should be of no concern to anyone except the people directly involved.

In some cases the arrival of a third party has unexpectedly revived and enriched a marriage. In all cases the institution of marriage is strengthened when it is a freely chosen partnership, not just at the beginning but throughout the relationship. Loving couples usually have to learn how to cope with dissimilar intensities of sexual desire. One solution is to make sacrifices; another possibility is to assent to extramarital sex.

No one is suggesting that a more tolerant attitude to extra-marital sex will be easy or painless. Most couples, whether faithful to each other or not, inevitably go through periods of distress and difficulty. There are no infallible solutions where sexual feelings are involved. But when one partner is unfaithful, it is better for the other to try to understand than to turn automatically to divorce, the legal modification of monogomy, which may mean losing the company and friendship of a loved one to the disadvantage of all concerned.

Compulsory Permissiveness

It is sometimes said that attitudes change like the swing of a pendulum from restrictions to liberality and back. But it is misleading to think of changes in attitudes proceeding along a restrictive-permissive line. An example of how attitude changes can be quite complex is to follow recent fashions in the clothes of young women.

In most periods of history women have dressed to be sexually attractive to men and most girls made some effort to awaken or re-awaken sexual desire in the men they are keeping company. At less frequent periods of history men have also taken a special interest in clothes; for example, young men have been through a peacock phase (1950–70) and this obviously had explicit sexual overtones.* But this has changed recently and a new generation of young men in their dirty jeans have shown a marked lack of interest in clothes. Similarly many young women now follow the fashion for long flowing clothes that do nothing to accentuate their sexual attributes. There may be economic and conservationist reasons for this (as suggested in Chapter 6). Liberated women also protest about the way men treat them as sexual objects, and for this reason sexual allurement is not such an important part of their dress.

It is interesting that authoritarians are upset when men dress in a way that emphasizes their sexuality, but women are expected to wear sexually provocative clothes. The theory behind this tradition is that the rudimentary sex act cannot take place until the male has an erection and the role of the female is to increase masculine desire. But the modern woman thinks that sexual arousal should be by mutual caressing in private, not by wearing coquettish clothes in public.

A positive attitude to sex should certainly include tolerance, but there are some rather shabby aspects to what is now known as the permissive society. There seems to be an element of compulsion about it—the feeling that people should be enticed into gazing at more sexually explicit advertisements, inveigled into watching public performances of simulated sexual intercourse even if they are not interested, and coaxed into cultivating a sexual sophistication which suggests that everyone should try everything and everybody at least once.

Far from anyone being compelled to behave in a prescribed manner, it is important to realize that there is no such thing as natural sex of a uniform sort. Modern research does not support the doctrine, unfortunately fostered by psychoanalists as much as by churchmen, that nature indicates an ideal direction for human sexuality and that all who fail to live up to it must be inferior. Human beings cannot be expected to live the same lives, share the same standards or think the same way.

For example, sexual response and loving affection can be just as intense when the recipient is a member of the same sex. Sexual attraction depends upon a great many variables including one's innate disposition, hormonal forces, psychological

* Tight pants are said to be the cause of infertility in the male and one doctor has said the fashion for tight trousers is having a greater effect on the birth rate than the pill!

development and social conditioning. Some people will obtain love and/or maximum sexual satisfaction within a homosexual relationship; most people will not. Even those who will obtain more satisfaction from a heterosexual union may want an occasional homosexual experience. We cannot tell someone else what is the most suitable sexual relationship for him or her.

Attitudes are changing, but still there are blocks and inhibitions in all of us, some more than others. This is as it should be. Social stability requires that people do not easily change their views about important things. But attitudes about sex change particularly slowly because it is a private matter. As these intimate details and problems cannot easily be discussed in ordinary conversation, the writer about sex (whether as fiction or otherwise) has an important function as an educator because he is giving information in public about a very private matter. In this way the novice can learn about things that other people will not tell him in a face to face situation, while those who have been misled can correct their misconceptions without embarrassment.* Many people want to know if their secret sex life is deficient, harmful or abnormal. This is why any form of censorship that limits what can be said about sex in books and the visual arts will hinder the spread of useful knowledge. Even the demand for pornography is often educationally motivated; many readers are not looking for lascivious excitement; they are seeking information.

Most people would agree that sex has been over-sold: the mad search for orgasms; the confusion between love and passion; the belief that it is impossible to lead a full life without a regular supply of sex. People are left with the impression that everyone else's sex life is more exciting than their own. It is no solution to outlaw other people's enjoyment, to ban private activities or to restrict unusual sexual outlets. But it might be a good idea to lower the temperature.

We are apt to take our sexual behaviour a little too seriously. Sexual intercourse, as often as not, is no more than an incident —very enjoyable, but soon forgotten. People worry about trivializing sex, but this is because they are comparing it with love and marriage, which should be taken very seriously indeed. Love and marriage often includes strong sexual attraction, but

* This statement makes the unwarranted assumption that the writer is always well-informed.

it is the deep involvement, one person with another, that is paramount.

Sex by itself is a different matter. It is basically playful—the innocent enjoyment of the body. In a sense it is easy-going although it can also be quite skilful. It is an expression of human happiness, whether it is limited to inceptive activities or goes on to coitus, whether it is heterosexual or homosexual, whether it is between old lovers or new friends.

CHAPTER 15

FACILITIES AND OPPORTUNITIES

The Sex Life of the Handicapped
The positive attitudes to sex noted in the previous Chapters (8–14) will bring forward demands for changes. Sometimes this will be a demand for law reform, but legal changes are not enough and tend in any case to come about in response to social pressures. As sexual behaviour is bound by tradition and custom, it is not the deliberate actions by governments and law-makers that will induce changes. Far more important are the social pressures created by small groups and organizations with roots in the local community.

A new enlightened attitude to sex will improve the quality of life for many individuals within the privacy of their own homes. In general this will only apply to couples living together in relative comfort; these are the lucky people who have already found a measure of sexual fulfilment. More help will have to be provided for the handicapped, the immature, the timid and those with unusual sexual drives. Unfortunately it is only the sexually orthodox who have benefited from the new age of permissiveness. There is less need to be concerned about those who are hetero-sexual, healthy, presentable and under forty. They are the sexually privileged. But there are many others who do not get the same opportunities to satisfy their sexual interests.

One of the earliest sex manuals, *The Perfumed Garden*, attempted to help people who were suffering from various physical handicaps (including instructions on "how to make small members splendid"). But modern sex manuals contain no help or advice for the physically, mentally or sexually handi-capped. Even two otherwise excellent handbooks published for the disabled* cover the aids and apparatus to assist the domestic

* *Coping with Disablement* (The Consumers Association) and *An ABC of Services and General Information for Disabled People* (The Disablement Income Group).

lives of the physically handicapped, but do not mention their sexual problems.

We have a moral obligation to help the handicapped to experience some kind of bodily satisfaction. Sexual interests become especially rewarding for those whose physical experiences are restricted by disablement. Unfortunately many kind and caring people appear to think this is an unsavoury subject better ignored, but sexuality for the disabled may be the only equivalent of breathless excitement followed by pleasurable relaxation that others get from sports and other pastimes.

There is very little provision for privacy among residents in homes for the physically or mentally handicapped. They sleep in dormitories in some homes. The staff who look after them, often with great devotion, tend to care for them as if they were children and they do not feel it is necessary to provide for their sexual interests. Most of these homes for the disabled have been set up by religious foundations and there are no opportunities to meet and mate with the opposite sex. Some of these residents will spend the rest of their lives there. It is a cruel mistake to assume that these long-term patients have no sexual needs.

People who are paralyzed below the waist (i.e. paraplegics) may still have sexual feelings. Even if the genital organs are totally numb to the touch and orgasm has become impossible, there may be forms of caressing and massage which are sexually gratifying. It is wrong to assume that those with severe disabilities do not desire to have some kind of sexual dimension to their lives. It may be possible to make use of sex aids like vibrators;* and erotic books, pictures or films might be helpful in some situations.

Of course this will provoke all sorts of practical difficulties and confused fears for the staff who have had no training in the sexual problems of the disabled. But there are exceptional cases where the staff of a home have provided succour for the handicapped by helping them to masturbate. This may be a labour of love, but it is likely to be misunderstood. Not long ago a dedicated male nurse in a home for severely handicapped teenage boys received a five-year sentence for helping them to find sexual relief through masturbation; his 'crime', the judge said, was all the more reprehensible because he was a member of the staff.

* Sex aids are described in more detail in the last section of this chapter.

But who has more need for release from tension than the disabled who are necessarily cut off from many of the ordinary pleasures of life? Members of the staff who help them to develop interests in life and encourage personal exploration should be praised, not penalized.

Most of the disabled live at home and here it is likely that they are over-protected by relatives who treat them as if they have no sexual feelings. Many parents try to avoid the problem by emphasizing a kind of ethereal love and by refusing to admit that their handicapped children ever experience any sexual desires. But there are a few who have faced up to this problem. For example, some parents of thalidomide boys are teaching them to masturbate because they feel that it is wrong that they should be denied all sexual gratification.

Handicapped teenagers who live at home rarely get the chance to meet other boys and girls. Some of the physically handicapped are so deformed that they are unlikely to attract partners of the opposite sex. Here the problem is not just deprivation but also humiliation. Even people who are kind can be repelled by the ugly and the abnormal until they take the time to get to know and appreciate the personal qualities of the deformed individual. People tend to assume that the physically handicapped are sexually incapable and try to persuade the disabled that sex is not for them. But nearly all the physically handicapped can experience some from of sexual gratification and they should not be denied.

The Sexual Minorities
The previous section has been concerned in the main with those who have physical or mental handicaps, but there are others who are sexually handicapped because they have unusual erotic interests. The plight of those with homosexual interests is not as bad as it has been in the past, partly because people now realize that it is not a particularly unusual sexual activity, and also because the various homophile organizations (for example the Campaign for Homosexual Equality, The Sexual Minority Group and the various splinter groups from the original Gay Liberation Front) have been fairly successful in demanding the legitimate sexual rights of this minority.

In villages and country districts an individual is liable to become the subject of gossip and ridicule if his homosexual interests are discovered, but most large towns now have places where homosexuals can meet. People with less common minority interests find it far more difficult to meet others with similar sexual drives. There are very few facilities for those who are interested in transvestism, sadism, masochism, exhibitionism, scoptophilia, fetishism, troilism, or other specialised erotic interests.

It should be possible to establish introductory bureaux so that people with the similar sexual interests can arrange to meet each other. This will produce advantages for both the community and the individual. Those with minority sex interests will refrain from bothering or embarrassing others who do not share their particular sex drives; and they will be able to avoid the humiliations of sexual rejection. These bureaux could be run by private enterprise or by the local authority. If the former is preferred, there would have to be special regulations and an agreed code of practice in order to protect the clients from the duplicity and trickery commonly found in the less reputable marriage bureaux and computer dating services.

Specialized periodicals should be encouraged to introduce personal advertisement columns for people looking for sexual partners with similar tastes. In *Gay News* there are about a hundred such classified advertisements in each issue. Here are three examples: "Fair slim 26, average looking, discreet, living Kent, short distance London, hopes for lasting friendship with active male 28–40 who feels the need for love and affection. Genuine only please." "Rocker with bike, leather jacket and jeans seeks mates in denim, leather etc. Photo for exchange." "Masculine young teacher with own car and bungalow wants to meet good looking friend 21–27 in SW Surrey, Haslemere area."

Gay News head their personal advertisement columns with a quotation from Chaucer, "Love Knoweth No Laws", but it seems likely that these advertisements are against the interpretation of the law according to the House of Lords (15 June 1972) when the judges decided that it was unlawful of *It* magazine to publish advertisements in which homosexuals indicated their wish to meet others. The offence of the publishers was to "debauch and corrupt the morals as well of youth as of divers other liege subjects of Our Lady the Queen". This archaic language makes one wonder if it would still be an offence if the advertisers were trying to meet homosexual foreigners who were not subjects of

Our Lady the Queen. The judges expressed the view that the Sexual Offences Act 1967 had made homosexual conduct "merely exempted from criminal penalties" but did not make it "lawful in the full sense".*

The more specific the advertisements are, the more people object to them. But no one is obliged to read these advertisements and there is not much point in doing so unless one is looking for a friend with similar interests. It follows that a detailed and descriptive advertisement is more likely to reduce the chances of disappointment among those who respond, but avoids misunderstandings and wasting the time of those who do not share the sexual interests of the advertiser.

There are special clubs for homosexuals, although it is not easy for a lone homosexual to find out about them, because any attempt to make these places better known meets legal and social restrictions. It is even more difficult for people with less common minority sex interests. Transvestites or fetishists, for example, could have special clubs where they could meet others with similar inclinations.

No doubt the provision of these facilities would provoke much opposition, but the result would be that fewer people would be offended and there would be fewer public manifestations of sex. All the activities would take place in private and the existence of these bureaux would make it less likely that the public would be inconvenienced by people looking for sexual partners with specialized erotic interests.

But bureaux, clubs and similar facilities are quite clearly not a practical proposition as long as the law interferes with the private sex life of the individual and the authorities believe that they have the right to tell other people how to behave in private.

Prostitution as a Social Service
Recently it has been suggested that brothels could perform a

* Not only is this a direct affront to Parliament, but it is difficult to be sure what else the Law Lords may decide is not "lawful in the full sense". There is no way of knowing beforehand. The decision is made *ex post facto*. At some future date a teacher giving sex education, a critic reviewing a film, a social worker advising a client or a speaker at a conference on deviation may be judged to be conspiring to corrupt public morals.

useful social function if operated by the medical services as a therapy for the sexually handicapped and as a substitute for those who are temporarily deprived of their usual sexual outlet. In fact prostitution has always provided a limited social service, even though the main objective has been strictly commercial.

In the past it was believed that it was necessary to have prostitution because the sex drive of the male was so much stronger than the female's; in order to prevent adultery and illegitimate pregnancies or avoid the dangers of child-birth, highly-sexed men were allowed to gratify their carnal appetites with prostitutes. The Roman senator Cato remarked that he was pleased to see a man emerge from a brothel because "otherwise he may have gone to lie with his neighbour's wife". Even the Church has not always been opposed to prostitution. St Augustine once warned : "Suppress prostitution and frivolous lust will ruin our society."

In present day Western civilization prostitution is no longer a growth industry, partly because the more liberal attitudes to premarital sexual intercourse has diminished the demand for the prostitute's services, and partly because it is more difficult to delineate the boundaries of the profession; models, actresses, young housewives and girls who work for escort agencies and occasionally receive presents, gratuities or payments for sexual favours do not regard themselves as whores because it is only a part-time occupation. If there is to be an expansion of prostitution, it is more likely to be in the establishment of male brothels to provide for the needs of those women whose husbands cannot satisfy them.

Meanwhile in London and in other large towns there are still several girls who are full-time prostitutes or call-girls, working regular hours, advertising their services on little cards in news-agents shops or on small lighted bell-pushes at the entrance to their flats. The police seldom harass them and they are no longer in the news because the popular stories about golden-hearted tarts, wicked ponces, vice rings, and pitiable girls who have been dragged unwillingly into the business are no longer realistic, if ever they were.

Even when operating on a commercial basis, prostitutes provide an indirect social service for many men. Their services are sought by :

(1) Men who feel the need for relief from sexual tension

when their wives or girl-friends are ill, pregnant or not available for other reasons.

(2) Men who do not have the time to court a girl (e.g. when they are in a big city for only a few hours).

(3) Men who want sex without commitment because they are emotionally involved with their wives and children.*

(4) Men who want a variety of sexual experiences.

(5) Young men who want to learn about sexual intercourse without seeming to be a novice before their girl-friends.

(6) Men who are too shy to date girls and to take them out.

(7) Men who are old, ugly or deformed.

(8) Men who have physical difficulties, such as impotence or premature ejaculation, which would be a cause of concern to their wives but immaterial to the prostitute.

(9) Men who need to experience an orgasm which they cannot obtain from their wives.†

(10) Men with special sexual drives (e.g. fetishists).

In addition many of the clients have non-sexual needs, which the prostitutes find embarrassing because they are not prepared to offer companionship or advice as part of their price. Few prostitutes have the intelligence, training or inclination to offer help to the lonely or the handicapped (Rolph, 1955). In his book on the future of marriage Bernard (1973) notes: "Prostitutes report that bottlenecks in production of their work are the men who want to linger and talk."

Nearly all these girls work for themselves, although they probably do not stamp their cards or make an income tax return. Some of the girls are really employers because they have a maid and pay commission to the taxi drivers, waiters and doormen who send them clients.

* Benjamin and Masters (1964): "A large number of men want to avoid obligations, are afraid of impregnating a girl, or want to avoid emotional entanglements. . . . A visit to a prostitute may be, for all of them, simpler, safer, and even cheaper."

† Humphrey's (1970) investigation into sexual activities in public places revealed that many of those who were having impersonal sexual contacts with other men in public lavatories were not homosexual, and were on their way home to their wives; his conjecture is that in the past these men would have visited the old 'twenty-minute' whorehouses, which have largely disappeared from the American scene.

These girls are likely to be exploited by newsagents, who charge high prices for taking what is obviously a call-girl advertisement, and by landlords or property agents who charge exorbitant rents when they realize the flat is being used for prostitution. But there are no so-called vice kings who recruit innocent girls and turn them into prostitutes.

No one wants to go back to the days of the Messina brothers, the London operators who took the girls' earnings and paid them a weekly wage. But there are some disadvantages to this independence and some girls find they cannot cope on their own. Indeed, many girls would prefer to work in a brothel, as they do in Hamburg and in other foreign cities. A properly run bordello would provide fair working conditions and terms of employment. If such establishments were legally permitted, higher standards of hygiene could be enforced and there could be regular medical check-ups which would restrict the spread of VD. Arrangements should be made to have doctors and social workers available at short notice so that the brothel could provide a comprehensive social service which the self-employed girls cannot offer at present.

Officially recognized brothels would also provide protection for the girls—not only from pimps, ponces and vice-merchants, but also from the clients who occasionally cause a disturbance because they are drunk, aggressive, or overcome with feelings of shame. When it is accepted that prostitution can be a useful public service, it will be possible to eliminate the association with the criminal fringe that tends to latch on to this profession while it operates in the twilight zones of the big cities.

The main function of these establishments would be to cater for the needs of those who cannot find sexual satisfaction for themselves because they are old, ill-favoured, fearful or handicapped. Sexual therapy could be provided for those who have special difficulties along the lines advocated by Masters and Johnson (1970). They provide what they euphemistically call 'surrogate partners' who are women trained to help and have coitus with men who are sexually inadequate.

Dr Ullerstam (1967) thinks we should provide mobile facilities for clients who are unable to leave their homes and for patients in hospitals. His name for these people is "erotic Samaritans" and he hopes that "cheerful, generous, talented, and

8—P * *

morally advanced persons with a knowledge of the joys of giving would feel attracted to this humanitarian profession".

I am not sure what he means by "morally advanced persons", but it is quite reasonable to suppose that recruits to the ranks of the oldest profession would be of an entirely different character if a more positive attitude were taken towards prostitution. If we thought of them as medical auxiliaries, instead of whores and harlots, it is probable that the calibre of the recruits would improve and young people of both sexes would not be ashamed to enter the ranks of a worthwhile professon. They would be trained in social welfare and part of their job would be to attend to the non-sexual needs of their clients. Courtesy, conversation and a good knowledge of inceptive techniques would become important aspects of the work. This would make the job more interesting and this is important, because the usual complaint from London prostitutes (Rolph, 1955) is that the work is intensely boring.

Some men will dislike these suggestions because it is making 'whoring' too clinical and dull from the client's point of view; part of the attraction, it is said, is that it is all rather clandestine and naughty. But it will not be necessary to forbid the old style of prostitution; indeed, there will be fewer harassments when the laws have been changed. The independent prostitutes, however, will have to lower their prices if they hope to compete with the new style of prostitution.

Although people in this profession should get a fair reward for their work, the charge for this service need not be anywhere near the ridiculously high prices that self-employed prostitutes demand at present. The Exchequer would also benefit from a more rational method of providing for the sexual needs of the community because prostitutes do not pay any income tax although their earnings clearly are taxable.

It should not be assumed that all prostitutes will always be female, because services should be provided for sexually handicapped women who wish to have male partners and for homosexuals of either sex who are finding it difficult to find a suitable partner.

The principal reason for legalizing brothels and for prostitutes working away from the old red light districts is to provide an effective therapeutic service for the sexually handicapped. But this does not mean that other people need be excluded from using this social service. Many young people pass through a period when they are more interested in sexual gratification than in personal relationships, and there would be social advantages in allowing them to use these services instead of pressing their unwelcome attentions on girls who do not find them sexually attractive. If prostitution was run as an efficient social service, the number of hasty ill-judged marriages because the girl is pregnant would be reduced, the situations where a girl is left to bring up a child on her own would decrease, and the risks of sexual assault or rape would be lessened.

Restrictions and Objections

Marketeers and salesmen now accentuate the sexual side of products which did not appear to be in the least erotic until recently, and sexual stimulation is now part of the everyday commercial scene. But there are still people who find it difficult to get the kind of sexual experience they seek even when their sexual desires are not unusual. It is not only the sexually handicapped who require more facilities. The young, the old, the divorced, the bereaved and many other people find they are leading sexless lives in the age of sexual affluence.

In Chapter 6 it was noted that the new attitude to premarital sexual intercourse might actually make it harder for young people to meet others of their own age. When they do meet, it is difficult to find a place that is comfortable and private. Young couples have to express their love for each other in the cinema, in the dark corner of a back alley, or in the front room after the parents have retired upstairs. Far from providing facilities for the young, the present policy is to restrict their opportunities. If by chance a new place is discovered, such as a lonely beach or a club with a sauna, as soon as it becomes known as a place where young people can meet and make love, it will be raided and new restrictions will be imposed.

A new tolerance may be extended to courting couples if it seems likely they will marry, but not to the younger teenagers even though the lower age at which they reach puberty means that their sexual drive can be strong from about fifteen onwards. In some ways we expect a higher standard of behaviour from adolescents than we do from ourselves. A young girl who is having sex with more than one boy can be brought within the Care and Control provisions of the Children and Young Persons Acts, even though she is over the age of consent and has not broken any law; she may be required to live in a hostel with other girls who have been convicted of criminal offences, but the law does not penalize an adult woman who is sleeping around with several different men. If homosexuality is mentioned at school at all, it is usually said to be permissible only when it is a passing phase on the way to exclusive heterosexuality; this makes it difficult to explain why an adult man can have homosexual relations with another adult, but a teenager who does this is liable to be arrested and charged with committing an offence. There are, of course, good reasons for providing a certain amount of protection for the young, but some of these prohibitions look like adult hypocrisy to a teenager.

The old also need more opportunities and facilities. It is a mistake to assume that most people over sixty have lost interest in sex. Many people seem to think that it is rather tasteless of an old age pensioner to want sex. In fact there are many instances when a woman well past her menopause appears to take on a new lease of life because she finds a man taking a sexual interest in her.

Older people, including married couples who are disappointed that their sexual desires are waning, should be encouraged to experiment with sex aids. As these are made and distributed by people whose main concern is to make money, many of these so-called aids are unhelpful, but not all of them. Some women have experienced orgasm for the first time when using a vibrator. Others have found a new interest in sex after their partners have started to use shaped condoms that act as clitoral stimulators. Desensitizing creams and aerosols have helped men who suffer from premature ejaculation. Contrary to popular belief the artificial penis (often known as the dildo) is not often used by homosexual women, but by heterosexual men suffering from impotence. Temporary impotence is quite a common affliction, but rest and reassurance is probably more effective than a dildo. Some of the more fantastic sex aids are dildoes with scrotum sacks that cause ejaculation when squeezed, mechanical penis enlargers, and artificial vaginas which "fit into a briefcase when deflated".

Most people think that sex aids are a bit of a giggle and there is no harm in that as long as it is realized that there are a few people who are not amused because, for one reason or another, their sex lives are joyless or defunct. If sex aids can help these people, they should be encouraged to use them without feeling ashamed. Marriage guidance and other counsellors should recommend them in appropriate cases and doctors should prescribe them on the National Health Service.

There are some people who feel the need to participate in group sexual activities. Experienced practitioners say that group sex requires a certain amount of discipline and unselfishness, for the group pleasures can easily be spoilt by a few ruthlessly egotistical men. The trouble with orgies is that it is not always clear who does what to whom with what and in what order. Group sex activities which occur as a ritual within the framework of a festival, when the usual taboos break down for a few days, seem to be more successful and seldom give rise to strong feelings of guilt or jealousy. It could be argued that the community would derive important social benefits from officially recognized festivals that provide periodic sexual catharses.

Apart from this last suggestion (i.e. that there may be some advantages in establishing uninhibited festivals in this country), none of the proposals made in this chapter needs to be publicly offensive. But as soon as it is suggested that brothels and other facilities should be provided, there are always very strong objections. The reactions are so hostile that it almost seems as if the objectors are going to be forced to become involved themselves. But those who do not wish to make use of these facilities need hardly be aware of their existence; in fact, they only become the subject of public discussion when those who object try to impede the freedom of those who wish to use them.

This does not mean that these facilities should only be found down back streets. Furthermore it is essential that people are *told* where they can find these services through advertisements and official announcements. The rent rebate scheme was of little value at first because hardly anyone knew about it, and similarly these services will be of no avail if they are only used by people who already know their way around the red light districts of urban areas.

It is precisely because there is such a sordid atmosphere surrounding them that prostitution, sex aids and other sexual services are far more expensive than they need be. People are persuaded to pay high prices because they are secretive and shameful. When the provision of these facilities is recognized as a useful social service, the prices will be lower and the standards of hygiene will be higher.

Attitudes to sex have altered considerably during the past few years and this change has created a demand that is not being met. The gap is being filled by the commercial entrepreneurs, who have found a ready market for a sordid version of sex, whether it is poorly written sex manuals, useless sex aids, expensive flats for prostitutes, or badly produced pornography.

A good example of how a change in public opinion without being backed-up by the provision of new facilities can lead to misunderstanding and disappointment is illustrated in a report on a mass media advertising campaign to increase the use of contraceptives (Udry, 1972). The advertising was successful in the sense that it changed attitudes and created a big demand for contraceptives. But no extra facilities were provided by the local clinics so the main result was that the waiting time between making an appointment and seeing the doctor stretched from one to eight weeks. Consequently the rate of kept appointments dropped as low as 50 per cent and most of the interest in contraceptives created by the campaign was lost before the new recruits even started to use them.

It is not advertising, but a more fundamental change in attitudes that is creating the need for more and better facilities. This new positive attitude to sex requires that these services are provided at a reasonable price, at accessible locations and in a suitable way.

CHAPTER 16

SEX AND SOCIAL POLICY

A Review of the Results

The fear of promiscuity has hindered the development of sensible attitudes even among those who have welcomed the new interest in sex education and the increased availability of contraception and abortion (Chapter 2). Promiscuous behaviour has been found in all societies throughout history and there probably is not much more of it today than in the past. But the future is a different matter. The sexual revolution has only just started (Chapter 3).

Four questions were asked about the promiscuous. When we asked where they were to be found, the short answer was everywhere. When we asked who they were, we discovered that they were not deprived in any way; on the contrary they tended to be better educated and better paid; this, we suspect, gave them more opportunities to be promiscuous. When we asked what sort of people they were, we found they were extrovert, gregarious and tended to be critical towards the traditional moralities. We gave up trying to answer the question why because there are many different kinds of promiscuity and the search for a single cause is likely to prove unrewarding (Chapter 4).

The physical effects of promiscuity were found to be limited, but the social and psychological consequences could be more serious. Even so it was found to be less of a threat to family stability than other forms of infidelity. Apart from rare cases of compulsive promiscuity, the harmful effects to the individual were not so much the direct results of the activity itself, but were caused by secrecy, duplicity and guilt feelings. It is clear that promiscuity will provoke social hostility for some time to come and this is bound to produce alienation and other problems for the individual (Chapter 5). Most people know about the physical, social and psychological ill-effects of promiscuity, but there are also a number of important advantages and there are many instances when these outweigh the disadvantages (Chapter 6).

The word *promiscuous* covers many different forms of behaviour and this is the cause of much of the current misunderstanding. It does not solve a problem to coin new words, but it helps to clarify the situation when we realize that we have attached several different meanings to one word. Many of the unfortunate consequences of promiscuity are caused by public condemnation. It is clear that a large number of people will be promiscuous at some period of their lives and this proportion is going to increase. It is more sensible to try to make these activities as harmless as possible instead of trying vainly to stop them altogether (Chapter 7).

In the second half of the book I have suggested that more emphasis should be placed on the positive aspects of sex. Health education courses in schools should make the point that a healthy body means better sex. Some forms of moral education seem to work quite well, but moralizing education does not (Chapter 8). Although sex education is now accepted as a legitimate task for the schools, it is usually too timid and too late. It hardly ever tells the pupils what they want to know or what they need to know (Chapter 9). Not enough emphasis has been given to the sociological aspects of VD, which is, after all, the most social of all diseases (Chapter 10).

There has been a rapid improvement in family planning services over the last few years and now it is part of the NHS. But problems remain, particularly because (1) there is no ideal contraceptive method; (2) the medical aspects of contraception have been over-emphasized; (3) single girls start to have sexual intercourse before they begin to use birth control (Chapter 11). Improvements in the techniques used to perform an abortion have been as far-reaching as the advances in contraceptive methods, but the opposition is much more determined. The new techniques have blurred the line between contraception and abortion; one cannot logically support the former and oppose the latter. Abortion is not 'a cry for help' or 'an admission of failure' but a human right (Chapter 12).

Men are beginning to realize that there is more to sexual relations than putting the penis into the vagina, and women are beginning to demand more and better sex (Chapter 13). The fear of promiscuity arises again in our attitude to premarital sexual intercourse because it is regarded as a prelude to marriage and not as a legitimate method of obtaining sex experience. Most people are still utterly opposed to adultery, even though the case against extramarital sex is not as bad or as formidable as it is usually made out to be. But attitudes are changing and women are now asking why promiscuity should be the man's privilege. But sex in the permissive society has been over-sold. Simultaneous orgasm is just a beautiful coincidence, not an indispensable stipulation (Chapter 14).

The new attitudes to sex have created a demand for services and facilities which is not being met and I have suggested various ways that these can be provided without giving offence to those who do not need them (Chapter 15).

The previous paragraphs are not intended to be a summary of the many points made in the first fifteen chapters. They are a brief review of those results which show how the fear of promiscuity is bound up with other changes in the sexual scene. I have suggested that this fear is only rarely justified.

One day, not so far away, the act of copulation will not involve any risks or hidden dangers. The last risk to be abolished will not be an unwanted pregnancy, or VD, or any other physical danger. The last risk will be psychological because we take it all too seriously. Most sex is little more than two (or more) people coming together to share mutual sensory pleasures.

Other Acts and Attitudes
I must apologize for referring to my own researches so often. In a way this book is a compendium of many of my researches. The attitude to promiscuity is very similar to past attitudes to homosexuality, which were derived from learned papers based on very untypical groups of sick homosexuals. There are also similarities in our attitudes towards those who smoke pot, where we have over-reacted and over-punished those people who use what is really a fairly mild and relatively harmless drug. It is also similar to our recent attitudes to sex among the young, when just a few years ago we thought premarital sexual intercourse could be controlled by forbidding them to do it. More recently my research into the sexual behaviour of young adults has shown that our attitudes to contraceptives for the unmarried, abortion and VD have made the situation worse by inflating the stigma attached to these problems.

The similarities are unmistakable. Psychiatrists generalize from a few cases of promiscuous girls in trouble. We have over-reacted to a relatively harmless activity. We force young people who have sex before marriage into premature commitments in a fruitless attempt to ban promiscuity. And we have amplified the problems of contraception for the unmarried, of abortion, of VD, and now of cancer of the cervix, by implying that anyone who comes up against any of these difficulties must be immoral because they are promiscuous.

I have emphasized that the moral code cannot be changeless because many of the reasons for the prohibitions no longer apply. We must expect the barriers to come down if the foundations are crumbling. Nor can we expect to impose the same standards for everyone in a pluralistic society. One man's obscenity is another man's bed-time reading. In hundreds of homes there are small private collections* which delight the owner but would shock his neighbours, who do other things that would appal him.

But perhaps the biggest change in the moral code is that most people now accept that sex is for pleasure as well as for reproduction. In practice human coitus is usually afertile. It is not physiologically related to procreation (as in most other animals) and can take place when fertilization is impossible (e.g. during pregnancy and after the menopause). If the sole purpose of coitus is to produce children, then the average couple has sexual intercourse about 2,000 times more than it is necessary.

Even the religious authorities now accept that people can have sex for pleasure and not just for reproduction. But they have not yet woken up to the fact that once you separate fun sex from biological sex, many other strongly-held beliefs lose their support. If it is agreed that the human genitals are not designed solely for procreation, but may be legitimately regarded as a source of pleasure, then all sorts of non-coital activities can be encouraged and enjoyed; for example, it is no longer rational to maintain that homosexual and inceptive activities are unnatural or second-best; nor is there any logical objection to masturbation. If sex for pleasure is acceptable, then it is not necessary to insist that sexual intercourse is only permissible when the couple are in love and committed to each other. It can no longer be maintained that the emotional commitment of women is usually deeper than that of men for biological reasons, because girls want sex for pleasure

* The largest private collection of pornography is in the Library of the Vatican in Rome where there are 25,000 volumes and some 100,000 prints.

just as much as men and the question of which partner has to bear the child becomes irrelevant when efficient contraceptives are used. If sex does not have to be within the context of marriage and child-rearing, then it need not be taken so seriously, and we can take our sexual pleasures more casually and lightheartedly.

Sexual Ethics

Understandably there will be strong opposition to these ideas. I have argued in this book that promiscuity is not an unmitigated evil. Inevitably I shall be accused of saying that promiscuity is always acceptable, even laudable. Many people have erected a set of values around the assumption that promiscuity is always wicked. For some, the language that would persuade them to change their minds simply does not exist, and if it did, and if I had used it, I should merely have made them angrier than before. All they will remember after reading this book is that I am in favour of compulsory promiscuity for everyone over the age of fourteen and especially for happily married couples, who are quite content with each other!

Some will concede that there are people who appear to be both promiscuous and happy, but they will insist that the risks are too great. But there are always risks. It is a question of balancing them against the advantages, and the disadvantages of trying to restrict people's behaviour. After all, the chances of having a heart attack during sexual intercourse are much greater than at most other times of the day. "Nothing worth having is to be had without risk," wrote Shaw in the Preface to *Blanco Posnet*. "A mother risks her child's life every time she lets it ramble through the countryside, or across the street, or clamber over the rocks on the shore by itself."

Others will say they do not very much object to promiscuity as I have described it, but it is promiscuity combined with selfish irresponsibility that must be stopped. But almost anything combined with selfish irresponsibility is bad. There is no disagreement about that.

Perhaps the strongest opposition will arise around my words on infidelity. But the point I would make is that it need not lead to disaster. It is the way we deal with it at present that is disastrous. Infidelity leads to the break-up of a marriage and family because that is what we seem to want. But it need not always end in tragedy. As Lizzie Miles, a blues singer of the twenties, used to boast: "He may be your man but he comes round to see me sometimes."

I have suggested that we may be attaching too much importance to promiscuous sex. Dante placed the lustful in the least uncomfortable part of hell. Langland, in his parade of the seven deadly sins, gives 9 lines to Pride, 53 to Anger, 57 to Envy, 87 to Gluttony, 91 to Sloth, 115 to Avarice, but only 5 lines to Lust.

Sexual attraction in itself is innocent. It only becomes injurious when it is mismanaged or when other people decide it is scandalous. How it is consummated in private should not be important. There are probably as many kinds of love-making as there are lovers. It is man's intolerance that is remarkable, not the variety of his sexual expressions.

It is obvious that there are some people who do not want (or cannot have) an exclusive sexual relationship with one person only. This does not necessarily mean that they do not want (or cannot have) a close emotional affinity with one person. It does mean that a certain amount of promiscuous sex will always be present in the community, not least within marriage. The biographies of famous men frequently show that politicians do not always practise what they preach. Many people, famous and otherwise, enjoy promiscuous sex although most of them are reluctant to admit it. As far as promiscuity is concerned, it is not our behaviour but our ideology that needs to be changed.

People in authority tell us how we ought to behave—always an agreeable task. Their mistake is to think that there is only one solution. Those who want several partners, those who want just one, and those who do not want to have sex for the time being, should all feel assured that they will receive understanding and support.

Those who want to be promiscuous could abide by a simple code:

(1) You should not force yourself upon another—either sexually or in any other way.

(2) You should be careful to avoid an unwanted pregnancy or the spread of disease.

(3) You should judge the sexual behaviour of men and women by the same standards.

(4) Your own sex life should not be offensive to other

people, and others should not be allowed to intrude into your private life. ✗

The extent to which the law can enforce this code is very limited. Social convention may be more effective. Good sex is a question of good sense and good manners. A higher standard of loving will depend upon the care and consideration one person gives to another. Living things do not flourish when they are short of what gardeners call the TLC factor. Even promiscuous sex needs a ration of Tender Loving Care.

There is no reason why promiscuity need ever be publicly offensive. Personally I am *against* the so-called permissive society, which encourages any amount of sex stimulation but frowns on sexual satisfaction. I am *against* what might be called the sexual counter-revolution, which interferes with the private sexual expression of the individual. I am *in favour* of privacy and modesty, which can flourish at the same time that sex is exciting, beautiful and abundant.

REFERENCES

ANDERSON, RACHEL, *The Purple Heart-Throb*, Hodder and Stoughton, 1974

ASHDOWN-SHARP, PATRICIA, "The Engagement Pill", *Sunday Times*, 27 February 1972

BALL, M. J., "The 'morning after' Pill", *Canadian Medical Association Journal*, 1971, 108, 240.

BELTRÃO, PEDRO, "Ethical and Religious Aspects of Family Planning", in *Population and Family Planning in Latin America, The Victor-Boston Report*, 1973, 17

BENJAMIN, H. and MASTERS, R. E. C., *Prostitution and Morality*, Julian Press, New York, 1964.

BERAL, VALERIE, "Cancer of the Cervix: A Sexually Transmitted Infection?", *The Lancet*, 1974, 1, 1037

BERGLER, EDMUND, *Homosexuality: Disease or Way of Life*, Hill and Wang, New York, 1956

BERNARD, JESSIE, *The Future of Marriage*, Souvenir Press, 1973

BLACK, TIMOTHY, "A Marketing Perspective of Family Planning", *Family Planning*, 1973, 22–3, 59–61

BOAS, F., "The Central Eskimo", in *Sixth Annual Report of Bureau of Ethnology (1884–5)*, 1888

BONE, MARGARET, *Family Planning Services in England and Wales*, HMSO, 1973

BOWDICH, T. E., *Mission from Cape Coast Castle to Ashantee*, 1819

BOYD, J. T. and DOLL, R., "A Study of the Aetiology of Carcinova of the Cervix Uteri", *British Journal of Cancer*, 1964, 18, 419

BURTON, J., "VD. The Protection of Youth Through Health Education", Proc. xxivth Gen. Ass. of I.U.V.D. Lisbon, 1965

BURTON, SIR RICHARD, *Perfumed Garden of Shaykh Nefzaivi*, Putnam, New York, 1964

CARSTAIRS, G. M., *This Island Now*, Hogarth, 1963

CARTER, MARY, "Knowledge About Sexual Matters in Delinquent Girls", *British Journal of Psychiatry*, 1969, 115, 221–4

CARTWRIGHT, ANN, *Parent and Family Planning Services*,
Routledge and Kegan Paul, 1970

CATTERALL, R. D., "The Problem of Gonorrhoea", *British
Journal of Hospital Medicine*, 1970, 56

CAUTHERY, PHILIP and COLE, MARTIN, *The Fundamentals of
Sex*, W. H. Allen, 1971

CHALMERS, IAIN and ANDERSON, ANNE, "Factors Affecting
Gestational Age at Therapeutic Abortion", *Lancet*, 1972,
1, 1324

CHESSER, EUSTACE, *Live and Let Live*, Heinemann, 1958

CLARK, M., "Sequels of Unwanted Pregnancy", *Lancet*, 1968,
2, 501

COMFORT, ALEX, *Sex in Society*, Duckworth, 1963

——, *The Anxiety Makers*, Nelson, 1967

COOPER, DAVID, *The Death of the Family*, Allen Lane, 1971

CORSCADEN, J. A., (ed.), *Gynaecologic Cancer*, Williams and
Wilkins, Baltimore, 1962

CROWLEY, MART, *Boys in the Band*, Penguin, 1968

D'AGAPEYEFF, JEREMY, "Relase : A Progress Report", *Release*,
1972

DALLAS, DOROTHY, *Sex Education in School and Society*,
National Foundation for Educational Research, 1972

DAVIS, KEITH, "Sex on Campus: Is There a Revolution?",
Medical Aspects of Human Sexuality, January 1971, 128–42

DUBOIS, J. A., *Hindu Manners, Customs and Ceremonies*, 1947

DUNWOODY, JOHN, SERVICE, ALASTAIR and STUTTAFORD, TOM,
A Birth Control Plan for Britain, Birth Control Campaign,
1972

EKSTROM, K., "One hundred Teenagers in Copenhagen Infected
with Gonorrhoea", *British Journal of Venereal Diseases*, 1966,
42, 162

ELLIS, ALBERT, *Sex Without Guilt*, Lyle Stuart, New York, 1958

ELLIS, HAVELOCK, *Studies in the Psychology of Sex*, F. A.
Davis, 1925

ERMAN, A., *Travels in Siberia*, 1948

EYSENCK, H. J., *Psychology Is About People*, Allen Lane, 1972

FEROZE, R. M., "Cancer of the Cervix", in DEWHURST, C. J.
(ed.), *Integrated Obstetrics and Gynaecology for Post
Graduates*, Blackwell, 1972

FIDLER, H. K., BOYES, D. A. and WORTH, A. J., "Cervical Cancer Detection in British Columbia: A Progress Report", *Journal of Obstetrical Gynaecology British Commonwealth*, 1968, 75, 392

FISHER, SEYMOUR, *The Female Orgasm*, Allen Lane, 1973

FORD, CLELLAN S. and BEACH, FRANK A., *Patterns of Sexual Behaviour*, Eyre and Spottiswoode, 1952

FOX, ROBIN, *The Family and its Future*, CIBA, 1970

GAGNON, JOHN H., "Sexuality and Sexual Learning in the Child", Psychiatry: *Journal for the Study of Interpersonal Processes*, 1965, 28 (3), 212–28

GAGNON, JOHN AND SIMON, WILLIAM, *The Sexual Scene*, Transaction Books, Chicago, 1970

——, *Sexual Conduct: The Social Services of Human Sexuality*, Hutchinson, 1974

GEBHARD, PAUL, GAGNON, JOHN, POMEROY, WARDELL and CHRISTENSON, CORNELIA, *Sex Offences: An Analysis of Types*, Harper and Row, New York, 1965

GORER, GEOFFREY, *Sex and Marriage in England Today*, Nelson, 1971

GRAHAM, JOHN, "Genetic Effects of Family Planning", *Family Planning*, July 1972, 27–9

HAIR, P. E. H., "Bridal Pregnancy in Earlier Rural England", *Population Studies*, 1970, 24, 59–70

HAMILTON, G. V., *A Research in Marriage*, Boni, New York, 1929

HARRIS, ALAN, "Sex Education in Schools", *New Statesman*, 28 February 1969

HENRIQUES, FERNANDO, *The Pretence of Love*, Panther, 1962

——, *The Immoral Tradition*, Panther, 1963

——, *Love in Action*, Panther, 1964

——, *Modern Sexuality*, Panther, 1968

HOLLIS, A. C., *The Masai*, Oxford, 1908

HOLMES, M., NICOL, C. and STUBBS, R., "Sex Attitudes of Young People", *Educational Research*, 1968, 11 (1), 38–42

HUMPHREYS, LAUD, *Tearoom Trade*, Duckworth, 1970

HUTCHIN, K., *Looking Ahead: Health and Sex*, Longmans, 1969

JANEWAY, ELIZABETH, *Man's World, Woman's Place*, Michael Joseph, 1972

JELINCK, GUSTAV, "Venereal Diseases: Gonorrhoea", *British Journal of Hospital Medicine*, 1972, 7 (1), 15

KANOWITZ, LEO, *Women and the Law*, University of New Mexico Press, 1969

KARIM, S. M. M. (ed.), *Prostaglandins and Human Reproduction: Physiological Roles and Clinical Uses of Prostaglandins in Relation to Human Reproduction*, Oxford, 1971

KARMAN, H., "The Paramedic Abortionist", *Clinical Obstetrics and Gynaecology*, 1972, 15 (2), 379–87

KARMAN, H. and POTTS, D. M., "Very Early Abortion Using Syringe Vacuum Source", *Lancet*, 1972, 1051

KERSLAKE, C. and CASEY, D., "Abortion Induced by Means of the Uterine Aspirator", *Obstetrics and Gynaecology*, 1967, 30 (1), 35–45

KIND, R., "The Sexual Attitudes of Young People", *Family Planning*, 1969, 18 (1)

KINSEY, A. C., POMEROY, W. B. and MARTIN, C. E., *Sexual Behaviour in the Human Male*, Saunders, 1948

KINSEY, A. C., POMEROY, W. B., MARTIN, C. E. and GEBHARD, P. H., *Sexual Behaviour in the Human Female*, Saunders, 1953

KLAUSNER, SAMUEL, "Sex Life in Israel", in ELLIS, A. and ABARBANEL, A. (eds.), *The Encylopedia of Sexual Behaviour*, Hawthorn, New York, 1961

KOYAMA, I. and OATO, H., "Condom Use in Japan", in REDFORD, M. H., DUNCAN, C. W. and PRAGER, D. J. (eds.), *The Condom: Increasing Utilization in the United States*, San Francisco Press, 1974

KRELLIN, EILEEN, KELLMER-PRINGLE, MIA and WEST, PATRICK, *Born Illegitimate: Social and Educational Implications*, National Foundation for Educational Research, 1971

LACY, D. and PETTIT, A. J., "Sites of Hormone Production in the Mammalian Testis and their Significance in the Control of Male Fertility", *British Medical Bulletin*, 1970, 26, 87

LAING, W., "The Costs and Benefits of Family Planning to Public Authorities Responsible for the Health and Welfare Services", *P.E.P.*, 1972, Broadsheet 534

LAKEMAN, H., *Any Questions Please?*, Independent Press, 1958

LAMBERT, JOAN, "Survey of 3,000 Unwanted Pregnancies", *British Medical Journal*, 16 October 1971, 156

LEWIS, OSCAR, *The Children of Sanchez*, Secker and Warburg, 1962

LOGAN, W. P. D., "Marriage and Childbearing in Relation to Cancer of the Breast and Uterus", *Lancet*, 1953, 2, 1199

LORAINE, J. A., *Sex and the Population Crisis*, Heinemann, 1970

MALHOTRA, S. L., "A Study of Carcinova of Uterine Cervix", *British Journal of Cancer*, 1971, 25, 62–71

MALINOWSKI, BRONISLAV, *The Sexual Life of Savages in North-Western Melonesia*, Routledge, 1932

MARGOLIS, A. J. and GOLDSMITH, S., "Techniques for Early Abortion", in OSOFSKY, H. and OSOFSKY, J. (eds.), *The Abortion Experience*, Harper and Row, New York, 1973

MARTIN, CLYDE, "Marital and Coital Factors in Cervical Cancer", *American Journal of Public Health*, 1967, 57, 803

MASTERS, WILLIAM and JOHNSON, VIRGINIA, *Human Sexual Response*, Little Brown, Boston, 1966

——, *Human Sexual Inadequacy*, Churchill, 1970

MATSUMOTO, Y. S., KOIZUMA, A. and NOHARA, T., "Condom Use in Japan", *Studies in Family Planning*, 1972, 3 (10), 251–5

MAYHEW, H., *London Labour and the London Poor*, Griffin Bohn, 1862

MEAD, MARGARET, *Male and Female: A Study of the Sexes in a Changing World*, Gollancz, 1949

——, "Deprivation of Material Care: A Reassessment of its Effects", *WHO*, 1963

MEHTA, K. C. and RAMANI, M. S. R., "A Simple Technique for Reanastomosis After Vasectomy", *British Journal of Urology*, 1970, 42, 815

MONEY, J., HAMPSON, J. G. and HAMPSON, J. I., "An Examination of Some Basic Sexual Concepts: The Evidence of Human Hermaphroditism", *Bulletin, John Hopkins Hospital*, 1955, 97, 301–10

MORAES, DOM, *A Matter of People*, Deutch, 1974

MORTON, R. S., *Sexual Freedom and Venereal Disease*, Owen, 1971

MORTON-WILLIAMS, J. and HINDELL, K., "Abortion and Contraception: A Study of Patient's Attitudes", *P.E.P.*, 1972, Broadsheet 536.

MURDOCK, GEORGE, P., *Social Structure*, Macmillan, 1949

NATHANSON, B. N., "Drugs for the Production of Abortion: A Review", *Obstetrics and Gynaecological Survey*, 1970, 25, 727

NEILL, A. S., *Summerhill: A Radical Approach to Education*, Gollancz, 1962

NERCIAT, ANDREA, *Les Aphrodites*, 1793

O'NEIL, WILLIAM, *Divorce in the Progressive Era*, Yale University Press, 1967

PANDYA, G. N. and SCOMMEGNA, A., "Intrauterine Progesterone Releasing Devices: A Clinical Trial", *Advances in Planned Parenthood*, 1972, 7, 103

PARE, C. M. B. and RAVEN, H., "Follow-Up of Patients Referred for Termination of Pregnancy", *Lancet*, 28 March 1970, 635

PERRY, PAULINE, *Your Guide to the Opposite Sex*, Pitman, 1969

PERUTZ, KATHRIN, *The Marriage Fallacy*, Hodder and Stoughton, 1972

PONTING, L. I., "The Social Aspects of Venereal Disease Among Young People in Leeds and London", *British Journal of Venereal Disease*, 1963, 39, 273–7

POTTS, L., "Counselling Women With Unwanted Pregnancies", in *Family Planning: Readings and Case Materials*, Council on Social Work Education, 1971

POTTS, MALCOLM, "The Glorious Japanese Condom", *World Medicine*, 1973, 27–30

——, "Abortion: The Modern Experience", *New Humanist*, October 1973, 89 (6)

RIGBY, ANDREW, *Alternative Realities: A Study of Communes and their Members*, Routledge and Kegan Paul, 1974

ROBERTSON, GEOFF, "The Abominable Crime", *New Statesman*, 1 November 1974

RODKIN, D., "Adolescent Coitus and Cancer of the Cervix", *Cancer Research*, 1967, 27, 603

——, "A Comparison Review of Key Epidemiological Studies of Cervical Cancer Related to Current Searches for Transmissible Agents", *Cancer Research*, 1973, 33, 1353

ROGERS, REX (ed.), *Sex Education: Rationale and Reaction*, Cambridge, 1974

ROLPH, C. H. (ed.), *Women of the Streets*, Secker and Warburg, 1955

——, *Does Pornography Matter?* Routledge and Kegan Paul, 1961

ROSCOE, J., "The Bakitaro of Banyoro", in *Report of the*

Mackie Ethnological Expedition to Central Africa, Cambridge, 1923

ROSEBURY, THEODOR, *Microbes and Morals*, The Viking Press, New York, 1971

RUSSELL, BERTRAND, *Education and the Social Order*, Allen & Unwin, 1956

SADE, MARQUIS, DE, *Le Philosophe dans le Boudoir*, Collected Works, 1909

SCHOFIELD, MICHAEL, *Sociological Aspects of Homosexuality*, Longmans, 1965

——, *The Sexual Behaviour of Young People*, Penguin, 1968

——, *The Strange Case of Pot*, Penguin, 1971

——, *The Sexual Behaviour of Young Adults*, Allen Lane, 1973

——, "VD and the Young", *New Society*, 1973, 26, 135

SCLARE, A. B. and GERAGHTY, B. P., "Therapeutic Abortion : A Follow-Up Study", *Scottish Medical Journal*, 1971, 16, 438

SINGER, ALBERT, "Cancer of the Cervix", *Lancet*, 1974, 2, 41

SINGER, IRVING, *The Goals of Human Sexuality*, Wildwood House, 1973

SMITH, MICHAEL and KANE, PENNY, *The Pill off Prescription*, The Birth Control Trust, 1975

SPECK, ROSS, *et al.*, *The New Families*, Tavistock, 1972

STOPES, MARIE, *Married Love*, Hogarth Press, 1918

TERMAN, L. M., *Psychological Factors in Married Happiness*, McGraw-Hill, New York, 1938

TERRIS, M. and OALMANN, M. C., "Carcinova of the Cervix : Epidemiologic Studies", *Journal of the American Medical Association*, 1960, 174, 1847

THOMPSON, B. and ILLSLEY, R., "Family Growth in Aberdeen", *Journal of Biosocial Science*, 1969, 1, 23–39

TODD, N. A., "Psychiatric Experience of the Abortion Act", *British Journal of Psychiatry*, 1971, 119

TOWNE, J., "Carcinova of the Cervix in Nulliparous and Celibate Women", *American Journal of Obstetrics and Gynaecology*, 1955, 69, 606

TRAILL, H. D. and MANN, J. S., "Social England", 1893

UDRY, J. R., CLARK, L. T., CHASE, C. L. and LEVY, M., "Can Mass-media Advertising Increase Contraceptive Use?", *Family Planning Perspectives*, 1972, 4 (3)

ULLERSTAM, LARS, *The Erotic Minorities*, Calder and Boyars, 1967

VAN DE VELDE, T. H., *Ideal Marriage*, Covici Friede, New York, 1926

WARD, AUDREY, "General Practitioners and Family Planning in Sheffield", *Journal of Biosocial Science*, 1969, 1, 15

WATT, A. W., *Nature, Man and Woman*, Wildwood House, 1973

WATTS, G. O. and WILSON, R. A., "A Study of Personality Factors Among Venereal Disease Patients", *Canadian Medical Association*, 1945, 53, 119

WEST, D. J., *The Young Offender*, Penguin, 1967

WESTWOOD, GORDON, *A Minority*, Longmans, 1960

WITTKOWER, E. D. and COWAN, J., "Some Psychological Aspects of Sexual Promiscuity", *Psychosomatic Medicine*, 1944, 6, 287

WOODWARD, JOAN, "A Follow-Up Study of 100 Clients", Birmingham Brook Advisory Centre, 1970.

WYNDER, E., CORNFIELD, J., SHROFF, P. and DORAISWAMI, K., "A Study of Environment Factors in Carcinova of the Cervix", *American Journal of Obstetrics and Gynaecology*, 1954, 68, 1016

YOUNG, WAYLAND, *Eros Denied*, Weidenfeld and Nicolson, 1965

ZIPPER, J., TATUM, H. J., MEDEL, M., PASTENE, L. and RIVERA, M., "Metallic Copper as an Intrauterine Contraceptive Adjunct to the 'T' Device", *American Journal of Obstetrics and Gynaecology*, 1969, 105, 1274

The Report on the Committee on Homosexual Offences and Prostitution (The Wolfenden Report), HMSO, 1957

Report of the Committee on the Working of the Abortion Act (The Lane Report), HMSO, 1974

INDEX